Authentic Victorian Dressmaking Techniques

Edited by
Kristina Harris

Dover Publications, Inc.,
Mineola, New York

Bibliographical Note

This Dover edition, first published in 1999, is an unabridged republication of the work originally published in 1905 by the Butterick Publishing Company, Limited, New York, under the title *Dressmaking, Up to Date.* It contains a new Introduction written especially for the Dover edition.

Library of Congress Cataloging-in-Publication Data

Dressmaking up to date
  Authentic Victorian dressmaking techniques / [edited by] Kristina Harris.
    p.   cm.
  Originally published: Dressmaking up to date. New York : Butterick Pub. Co., c1905.
  ISBN 0-486-40485-4 (pbk.)
  1. Dressmaking. 2. Costume—United States—History—19th century.
3. Costume—United States—History—20th century. I. Harris, Kristina.
II. Title.
TT518.D74   1999
646.4—dc21
                                                                98-51587
                                                                CIP

Manufactured in the United States of America
Dover Publications, Inc., 31 East 2nd Street, Mineola, N.Y. 11501

INTRODUCTION

Sewing and Dressmaking in Victorian America

Butterick's *Dressmaking, Up To Date* (the original title of this work), dates from 1905, and was the first modern American sewing book. The book is so rare that even Butterick's extensive archives do not contain a copy of it. Nevertheless, this volume, which sold in its day for a mere 25¢ postpaid, was a milestone in the history of American fashion.

When we think of Victorian women today, we often visualize them lavishly dressed—and by their own hands. However, this is not altogether accurate. By the early 1900s, for example, many American women cast off the extravagantly frilled and lace-trimmed dresses styled in the mode of their European counterparts, in favor of tailored shirtwaists and rather plain skirts. Also, American women were not likely to sew all—or even most—of their clothing; they hired seamstresses and dressmakers to do most of their sewing.

"It is estimated that there are eight thousand dressmakers in the City of New York, exclusively engaged in making ladies' and children's dresses," Mrs. M.L. Rayne wrote in the 1893 edition of *What Can A Woman Do*, a book whose avowed purpose was to help turn-of-the-century women find work in a male-dominated society. The author was quick to point out, however, that not even the trade of dressmaking belonged exclusively to women, the figure cited above including "more than three hundred men dressmakers." Wages varied according to skill, class of society served, and (undoubtedly) sex; according to Rayne, $40–$60 per week was typical in New York.

Arthur's Magazine offered less optimistic figures. Although the editors quoted a newspaper article which reported that "a good dressmaker receives from one dollar and a half to three dollars per day," they suggested that few seamstresses actually earned that much. Furthermore, seamstresses working in factories or sewing in their own cramped tenements were likely to develop poor eyesight in addition to the general health problems associated with their lot. (However, the circumstances American seamstresses found themselves in were an improvement over those in England, where women who plied the trade were frequently little more than prostitutes who sewed for extra money.) Nonetheless, *Arthur's* noted that "a competent dressmaker, who goes from house to house, can always command good wages, nearly, if not quite, equal to those of a man."

But whether a woman wished to make dressmaking her trade (for, as *Arthur's Magazine* pointed out in 1870, there were "three, and only three, branches of labor to which women may turn with perfect 'propriety'—teaching, sewing, and housekeeping"), or simply wished to take on a certain amount of sewing at home, there was no formal system of education in place for women who wished to learn dressmaking skills.

Although young girls were supposed to learn sewing at home, the evidence suggests that most American women didn't possess sufficient skills to teach their daughters how to sew properly. If a girl decided to become a professional dressmaker or seamstress, she typically served as an apprentice for about six months with a dressmaker, often beginning, one fashion magazine of the time proclaimed, "in comparative ignorance of the plainest of sewing, so that much of her time is lost in mastering the rudiments, which ought to have been familiar to her before she entered the workroom. At the end of six months, she has learned how to sew a straight seam, can put a dress body together if it is properly cut out and basted, and, if she be quick and ready with eye and needle, can, when the pattern is plainly indicated, put on a fold or a ruffle." This was in sharp contrast to male apprenticeships, which, for almost any trade, lasted for years rather than months.

However, probably the most important reason American women were lacking in sewing skills pertained to class conventions. Many middle- and upper-class American women were raised to believe they would always be taken care of by men. Yes, they might learn to sew fancy ornamental stitches, but why should they bother to learn the rudimentary skills? Not infrequently, these "cultivated" women became "reduced in life," and although they seldom knew anything about dressmaking, it might be the only occupation open to them: "She has been forced into [sewing] by circumstances not because she understands or has any taste for the use of the needle, but because she knows nothing about anything else, and is a victim of the popular fallacy that all women can sew, whether they have ever tried or not," *Arthur's* commented.

Rayne also noted that, in general, American sewing skills left much to be desired. "How many women are there who can make a beautiful button-hole?" she asked. "How many who can do fine and elegant needle work, as it used to be done before the era of sewing machines? . . . The average seamstress makes everything on a crazy machine that runs off the track persistently, and what she finishes with the needle is an awful alternative. . . . Hand sewing is still considered superior to machine work, and the goods sold in the Ladies' Exchange, and in some of the best stores in the large cities, are of fine needle work. There are several stores in New York devoted to the sale of ready-made underwear, all of which is done by hand, and the prices are proportionally high."

The Modern Sewing Book is Born

A woman who did not sew for a living, but needed to sew some items for herself and her family, had even fewer resources to call upon in order to learn to sew. She might pick up hints here and there from family or friends, and she might read some of the rather complex yet scant directions offered in fashion magazines like *Godey's Lady's Book* or Butterick's own *Delineator*. The only books that taught dressmaking were often mathematically mind-boggling and written for professional dressmakers—not for women who sewed at home.

In the early 1800s, *The Workwoman's Guide* was a staple how-to book for amateurs; later, *The Ladies Hand-book of Plain Needlework* (1842), *The Ladies' Self Instructor* (1853), Butterick's *Needle-Craft: Artistic & Practical* (1889), and *The Art of Garment Cutting, Fitting & Making* (advertised in 1895) were popular. These differed markedly, however, from the current volume. Most manuals contained scaled patterns, or instructions on how to draft crude, home-made sewing patterns, unlike this book, which relied on the fact that turn-of-the-century women had ready access to superior, professionally drafted, commercial sewing patterns. The old manuals also focused on fancy work (like embroidery), household furnishings and accessories, and gave hints at making only very basic clothes meant to be given away to charity.

In their 1905 advertisement for the just-released *Dressmaking, Up to Date* (of which this book is the reprint), Butterick announced: "In response to repeated requests for a book explaining the intricacies and difficulties of dressmaking we have issued with lucid explanations and wide scope of subject matter the best book on dressmaking ever published." Unlike any of its predecessors, it gave thorough coverage to skills required for dressmaking: How to alter a commercial pattern for fit, make an elegantly bound edge, sew an eyelet, whip and gather a ruffle, create stunning ruches, and much more. Also, unlike any other sewing manual before it, the book was fully illustrated with photographs. "These are not theories," Butterick stressed in their ad, "but are practical results, being the issue of numberless tests and experiments, covering a period of many years. In cases where several methods are equally applicable, all are given. . . . *Dressmaking, Up To Date*, as a book of instruction, takes its place as the best assistant to the family seamstress and the general dressmaker ever published." As it turned out, this was not just idle an idle boast.

Butterick followed up the success of this volume with *The Dressmaker* (1911) and *The Art of Dressmaking* (1927); and since the 1920s, similar how-to books for home sewers —especially those produced by pattern companies—have become standard. Even today, pattern companies like Vogue and McCall's continue to issue books for home sewers that are remarkably similar in style to this one. What distinguishes this reprint from modern manuals is, of course, technique.

Perhaps you want to learn about the kind of details that can help you date and identify clothing of the early 1900s. Perhaps you want to create an antique-style garment, or an authentic-looking costume. Perhaps you want to learn the art of making skirt sweepers, or boning a bodice perfectly, or creating bust enhancers, fully interlined skirts, and perfectly concealed hooks and eyes. Or perhaps you want to apply these lovely, old-fashioned techniques to a modern wedding gown, or even to some items in your everyday wardrobe. This book puts all those possibilities at your fingertips.

Finally, perhaps this volume, which so changed the art of sewing and improved the skills of American sewers at the dawn of the 20th century, will inspire you to the point where you'll find yourself feeling just a bit like the average turn-of-the-century American woman, who—according to period fashion magazines—felt that her sewing would never be done. Rayne recounted an anecdote about just such a woman and her little boy, "who had heard his mother wish a great many times that her sewing was done." One day, when the boy was out walking with her, he "suddenly exclaimed: 'Look, look, mamma! there is one woman who has all her sewing done.' He had discovered a sign which said, 'Sewing done here.'" Indeed, Butterick made sure the Victorian woman's sewing was done—*and* done well.

CONTENTS

Frontispiece—The Sewing Circle   2

Hand-Sewing Stitches   3

Important Points and Aids in Dressmaking   13

The Correct Method of Altering Patterns   21

Shirt-Blouses   33

Draped Waists   44

Skirts   51

Novel, Artistic Seams   70

Wedding and Evening Gowns   73

The Tailor-Made Gown   80

Coats and Jackets   84

Practical and Ornamental Stitches   93

Bias Bands and Folds—Turning Corners   98

An Empire Tea-Gown   101

Desirable Garments for Maternity Wear   104

Making and Finishing Underwear   105

The Bath-Robe   111

Children's Clothes   112

Boys' Suits   122

The Sewing Circle

Dressmaking, Up to Date

SIMPLE SEWING STITCHES

MAKING A KNOT.—Holding the threaded needle in the right hand, twist the end of the thread once and a half, around the forefinger of the left hand; press, roll downward on the ball of the thumb, twisting once or twice; slip off and draw down with the middle finger of the left hand.

BASTING.—There are two kinds of basting; even and uneven. In even basting the stitches and spaces are the same length; in uneven basting, as its name implies, the stitches are so formed that they are not of equal length.

EVEN BASTING STITCH.—Start with a knot in basting and always have it on the right side; it is more easily removed. Pass

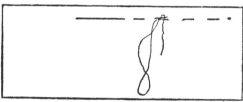

No. 1.—Even Basting

the needle over and under the material, making the stitches and the spaces the same size. To fasten the thread, take a stitch twice over the last stitch. (No. 1.)

No. 2.—Uneven Basting

UNEVEN BASTING.—In uneven basting the stitch and space are not of equal length. The same directions are followed as for even basting, except that the stitch which is taken up on the needle is about one-third shorter than the space covered by the thread, as seen at No. 2.

RUNNING.—In running, the stitches are shorter than in basting and spaces and stitches are the same length. It is used on seams that need not be very strong.

BACK-STITCH.—In back-stitch, a short stitch is taken on the upper and a longer one on the under side, bringing the needle out a stitch in advance. Insert the needle to meet the last stitch, passing it under the material and out

No. 3.—Back-Stitch

No. 4.—Combination Stitch

again a stitch in advance of the one last taken. (No. 3.) This is used on seams requiring strength, to sew raw edges together, and also in stitching sleeves in a garment. Fasten by carefully taking two stitches over the last ones which were made.

HALF-BACK STITCH.—This is the same as back-stitch, with the exception that the stitch is taken half-way back instead of all the way, leaving a small space between each stitch.

COMBINATION STITCH.—This consists of one back-stitch and two small running stitches, as shown at No. 4, and is used on seams not requiring very great strength. It is fastened like back-stitch.

FRENCH SEAM.—This is made by joining a narrow seam on the right side and trimming evenly, close to the stitching; turn the seam on the wrong side, crease the edge and take off another seam a quarter of an inch deep. This must fully cover the edges of the previous seam; consequently the first seam must be trimmed off evenly and the second seam be of sufficient depth to cover this, else instead of a smooth finished seam the raw edges will protrude on the right side. The method is shown at No. 5.

FLAT FELL SEAM.—A fell is a seam hemmed down to protect the raw edge. Place the edges together, baste a three-eighths of an inch seam and sew with combination stitch. If the goods is bias, stitch so that the needle follows the thread of the goods and prevents ravelling. Remove the bastings; trim off the edge which is toward you close to the line of sewing, turn the other edge down flat to cover the line of sewing, press hard with the thumb nail, then baste and hem. (No. 6.)

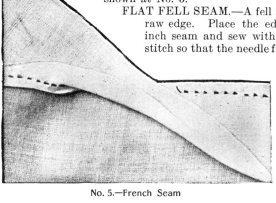

No. 5.—French Seam

OVERCASTING.—Overcasting is a slanting stitch, used to keep raw edges from ravelling. In taking the stitch the needle should always point toward the left shoulder. Hold the material loosely in the left hand. Do not use a knot, but turn the end of the thread to the left and take the first two stitches over to fasten. Make the stitches about one-eighth of an inch apart and one-eighth of an inch deep. Keep the spaces between the stitches even, as shown at No. 7.

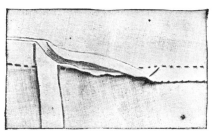

No. 6.—Flat Fell Seam

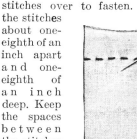

No. 7.—Overcasting

OVERHANDING.—Selvages in muslin and certain other materials are best joined by overhanding. Baste the muslin with the two selvages together and overhand with close stitches over and over the edge, taking up as few threads of the material as possible, as shown at No. 8, so that when finished the edge will be smooth and flat and not form a cord.

CAT-STITCHING.—Cat-stitching, or, as it is sometimes called, catch-stitching, is a small stitch used to hold the edges of flannel and various edges in dressmaking. In the former, place the pieces of flannel together and run a seam, taking an occasional

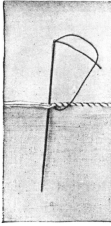

No. 8.—Overhanding

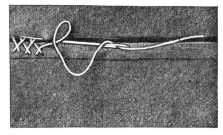

No. 9.—Method of Cat-Stitching

back-stitch. Trim off one edge and press the other edge flat to cover the seam, holding the material as shown at No. 9. Insert the needle under the flat seam at the upper left-hand corner; cross the edge and take a small stitch a few threads to the right through all thicknesses; cross again and insert the needle as pictured, taking a similar stitch, always pointing the needle to the left and encasing the raw edges. Finish the seam, the effect being shown at No. 10.

Seams in flannel are also pressed open and cat-stitched, working the stitches over the raw edge of each side of the seam, thus holding both down well, as shown at No. 11. Cat-stitching is referred to frequently in the following chapters for holding down the edges of

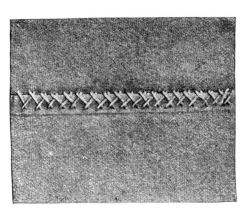

No. 10.—Finished Cat-Stitching

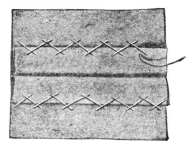

No. 11.—Cat-Stitch on Open Seam

collars, sleeves, etc., and in other places where it is necessary to hold an edge firmly. In these instances it may be made by taking a small stitch at the upper side, then another across the edge and below, but making a plain stitch instead of a cross-stitch. This style of cat-stitch is worked from right to left.

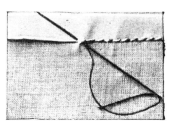

No. 12.—Hemming

HEMMING.—A hem is a fold of goods turned down and folded over to protect a raw edge. The first turn of a hem is the most important; if even, the second turn will be even also. Always turn a hem toward you. The hemming stitch is a slanting stitch, the needle pointing directly across the middle of the left thumb.

In turning a hem, crease the edge over one-quarter of an inch exactly, creasing with the thumb and forefinger. Mark a card for the width of the hem, place the end of the card at the turned edge and mark the desired width, making a perforation with a pin. Move the line to the left and make another perforation; continue across the material. Fold the hem on the perforation. Baste with even basting.

In hemming do not use a knot. Pointing the needle toward you (to the right), insert it under the fold, close to the right hand. Draw the needle through, leaving a little of the thread to be tucked under and then sewed down, point the needle toward the middle of the left thumb and take up one or two threads of the cloth and the same of the fold (No. 12).

Hold the hem across the end of the fore-

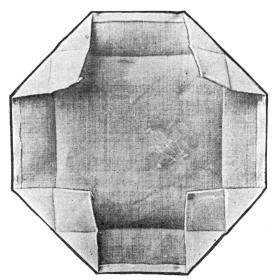

No. 13.—Folding for Mitred Corners

finger of the left hand, but not too tight. Continue hemming in this manner. It is important to have all the stitches slant in the same direction and of uniform size.

MITRED CORNERS.—A mitred corner is the joining of two edges to form a right angle. Make quarter-inch turnings on the edges to be hemmed, then turn over the desired hem width. Open the material, turn one corner toward the centre and crease exactly where the lines of the hem cross, as seen at No. 13. A quarter of an inch below (or toward the point) fold and cut the corner on the crease last made. Arrange the remaining corners the same. Turn the edge of the diagonal cut in on the crease, as shown at No. 14, fold the hem down all around, bringing the mitred corners together and hem the sides. Hem the mitred corners but do not catch through the under material.

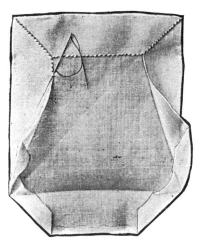

No. 14.—Hemming Mitred Corners

No. 15.—Cutting Square Corners

SQUARE COR-NER.—Fold the turned hem down, and where the hems cross in the corner fold back and crease hard. Open the material and cut an oblong a quarter of an inch from the last crease made (cutting toward the corner) and a quarter of an inch from the crease made for the hem. This is shown in the upper left hand corner of No. 15. Fold the square corners down as seen at No. 16, hemming the turned over edge to the side hem, but through the latter only and not through to the right side. Finish the hems on all sides in the same manner if the material is square.

When a handkerchief is to be hemstitched the corners are not cut away but are folded one over the other and the hemstitching continued across. A corner may be finished with a plain hem in this way also.

TO MAKE A DAMASK OR FRENCH HEM.—Make a narrow turn on one edge of the material, then a second; in the illustration this turn is very narrow. Fold the hem *back* on the right side and overhand the edge formed. Do not try to take too deep a stitch. Open the hem and crease with the thumb. If the article is square turn the opposite side the same. Hem the remaining sides, overhanding the corners before folding back on the right side. The method is shown at No. 17.

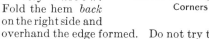

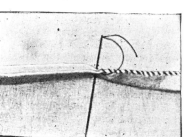

No. 17.—Damask Hem

No. 16.—Hemming Square Corners

No. 18.—Stroking Gathers

GATHERING AND STROKING OR LAYING GATHERS.—A gathering stitch is an uneven running stitch. Always begin by inserting the needle on the wrong side to conceal the knot. Take up two threads and pass over four. Never use a double thread for gathering. Gather on the right side a quarter of an inch from the edge. It is always better to slip the stitches along on the needle and not remove it from the material. When the edge is gathered remove the needle and draw the gathers up tight. Place a pin in vertically close to the last stitch and wind the thread around several times in the form of a figure 8, as seen at No. 18. This holds the gathers well together and facilitates the stroking.

Use a coarser needle for stroking. Hold the work between the thumb and fingers of the left hand, with the thumb below the gathering thread. Put the point of the needle under the gathering thread and press the little plait under the thumb, drawing the needle down. Care must be taken not to scratch the material. Continue entirely across the gathers, putting the needle under each stitch, and holding the plait firmly with the thumb. Stroke the upper edge of the gathers as well.

INSERTING RUFFLE IN HEM.—To insert this gathered ruffle, cut the hem open at the lower edge. Divide the ruffle in quarters, then divide the hem in quarters and mark these places with colored thread. Pin the hem and ruffle together after quartering. Place the right side of the ruffle to the right side of the hem and join in a quarter of an inch seam with combination stitch. Turn the seam up on the hem as pictured at No. 19; this also discloses the hem turned back. Turn over one-quarter of an inch of the remaining edge of the hem and hem down to cover the sewing line. The finished effect of this, showing the turned edge of the hem with the stitching above, is pictured at No. 20.

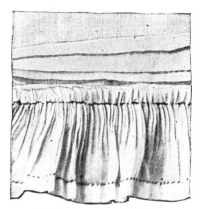

No. 19.—Inserting Ruffle in Hem

No. 20.—Finished Effect of Inserted Ruffle

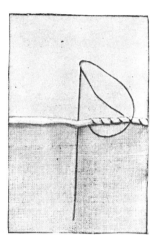

No. 21.—Rolling and Whipping

Although directions are here given for hand sewing, machine sewing may be accomplished in the same manner for seams, hems, etc., as explained here for hand-work.

ROLLING AND WHIPPING.—Holding the wrong side of the cambric toward you and beginning at the right-hand end, roll the edges between the thumb and forefinger of the left hand for about an inch. Take a needle and thread to correspond with the material, make a small knot, insert the needle at the corner of the roll and fasten. Hold the roll firmly with the right thumb and forefinger, and with the left hand roll one inch. Overcast with the thread as far as the cloth is rolled, taking care to take the stitch below the roll, and not through it. (No 21.) Continue to roll and whip (or overcast) across the length of material.

WHIPPING AND SEWING ON LACE. —The lace may be gathered by pulling the thread which will usually be found at the top of the lace, or it may be whipped over and over with needle and thread. Roll an inch or two of the material and place the lace with the right side against the right side of the material, then whip both together (No. 22),

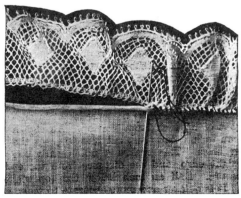

No. 22.—Whipping and Sewing on Lace

as directed before. The lace need not be gathered unless so preferred, but, instead, may be whipped on plain; although it is always advisable to hold the lace at least "easy."

WHIPPING AND GATHERING.—Divide the hem on the bottom of the garment into halves and quarters, marking each division with a cross-stitch. Divide the ruffle in the same manner and mark. Trim off all ravellings. Now whip the edge as explained for No. 21,

No. 23. Whipping and Gathering

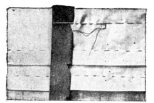

No. 24.—Notched Measure for Tucks

but after every inch whipped draw up the thread. (No. 23.) Place the right side of the ruffle to the right side of the hem, end to end, centre to centre, matching the cross-stitches. Adjust the gathers evenly and pin. Overhand the ruffle to the edge of the hem, taking a stitch in every whipping stitch of the ruffle. For whipping make the ruffle twice as full as the garment to be trimmed. The lower edge of the ruffle may be trimmed with lace whipped on, as shown at No. 22, or hemmed.

TUCKING.—When making a tuck, it is always best to use a measure or gage so that the tuck will be the same width from beginning to end. The size of the gage must be regulated by the size of the tuck since a deep tuck requires a longer and broader gage than a fine tuck. The method of basting the tuck by the aid of the notched measure is seen at No. 24. When one desires to mark

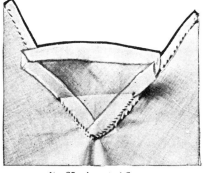

No. 25.—Inserted Gusset

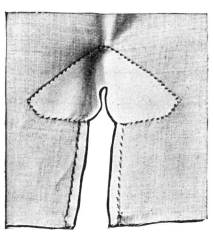

No. 26.—Hemmed Gusset on Wrong Side

a number of tucks where they are not indicated in a pattern, as, for instance, in tucking a straight piece of material from which to cut a yoke, a second notch may be cut by which to measure from the fold of one tuck to the next. This also is shown in the illustration.

Cut the measure from a piece of card or stiff paper. When the tucks are one-eighth of an inch deep and the space between an eighth of an inch, the measure is cut in one-eighth of an inch from the top. An eighth of an inch below this, cut bias to meet the first slash. This makes a notch with one straight edge, and the distance from the end of the card to this straight edge will form the measure. Half an inch below the top make another cut and below this the bias slash.

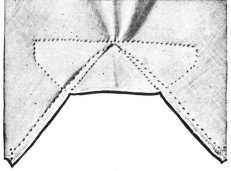

No. 27.—Finished Gusset

It is quicker and more accurate to make a measure of this sort whenever short spaces, as hems, tucks and the spaces between, are to be measured, than to use the tape measure, as sometimes the eye becomes confused at the eighth marks on the tape, and mistakes may occur that will prove quite serious, particularly when a number of tucks and uneven spaces are to be made.

SETTING IN A GUSSET.—A gusset is a triangle of cloth set into a garment to enlarge and strengthen an opening.

Fold diagonally a piece of muslin two inches and one-quarter square and cut it on the fold. Take one of the triangles and fold it down a quarter of an inch all around, folding straight lines first. Holding it with the wrong side toward you, right angle down, fold the point at the bottom up to meet the folded bias edge. This crease is shown at No. 25. Fold the ends together and cut the projecting points at the sides, cutting straight with the grain of the goods. If the gusset is not at the end of a seam slash the material the desired depth, cutting by a thread. Make a narrow hem all around, tapering at the corner so it will be little more than a roll.

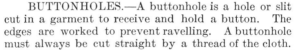

Pin the corner of the gusset to the corner of the opening, right side to right side. (No. 25.) Beginning at the centre, overhand to the edge of the hem as far as the crease. Overhand the other side the same. Fold the gusset over on the crease and pin at the centre, also at each corner. Take care that the warp and woof threads at each side run parallel with the warp and woof threads of the garment. Baste and hem all around, as shown at No. 26. The lower edge of the gusset will have to be stretched to fit. The finished effect is pictured at No. 27.

BUTTONHOLES.—A buttonhole is a hole or slit cut in a garment to receive and hold a button. The edges are worked to prevent ravelling. A buttonhole must always be cut straight by a thread of the cloth.

No. 29.—Overcast Buttonhole

No. 28.—Barred Buttonhole

At No. 28 will be seen the several processes for working a buttonhole. This model is made by simply barring the edges with the thread or twist used for the buttonhole. Put the needle in from the wrong side at the lower right-hand side of the slit, which is the farthest edge from the fold of the material; this is shown at the lowest figure in the illustration. Carry the thread to the end and form a bar by taking two stitches as shown in this, and finished in the second figure; then carry the thread across the opposite side.

Begin to work the buttonhole close to the corner or starting point. Insert the needle and, while it is pointing toward you, bring the double thread as it hangs from the eye of the needle around to the left (third figure) under the needle, draw the needle through the loop formed, and draw the thread up tight, letting the purl come exactly to the edge of the slit. Skip two threads of material and repeat the stitch.

When the end is reached take the stitches around in a curve and continue working on the other side. Bar the end for finishing; insert the needle to the wrong side and work several stitches over the bar stitches on the wrong side. The finished buttonhole is shown in the upper figure.

Another method of working a button-hole is shown at No. 29. In this, the edges

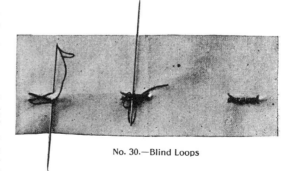

No. 30.—Blind Loops

are overcast and both ends are barred. This is more generally employed when the button-hole is in the centre of a fold or box-plait, and is cut in a vertical instead of a horizontal position. Holding the fold edge toward you begin at the lower right-hand corner as explained for the previous buttonhole and bring the needle up through the material three or four threads from the edge of the slit, leaving a short end of the thread.

Skip four or five threads of the material and take a slanting or overcasting stitch, catching in the short end of the thread; skip an equal space and take another stitch. At the end take two stitches straight across, the depth of the buttonhole, forming a bar. Pass the needle underneath the slit and bring it up through to the other side and overcast the same, as seen at the upper figure, making the straight stitches or bars across the end.

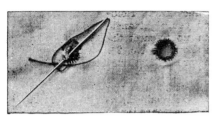

No. 31.—Eyelets

Now work the buttonhole stitches on the first side. At the end turn the work around, so that the bar end is toward you, slip the needle under the bars and buttonhole them, taking one stitch into the cloth to hold it. Work the other end of the buttonhole and the second bar. Sometimes the bars are simply worked with an over-and-over stitch instead of buttonholing; this is according to the worker's preference.

BLIND LOOPS.—A blind loop is used on a garment to take the place of an eye. Having marked the position of the loop opposite the hook, knot the thread and bring the needle up through the material. Make a bar of three stitches one over the other, one-quarter of an inch long. This may be made in the form of a cross-stitch, as shown in the first figure of No. 30. After these are laid, hold the thread down with the left thumb and insert the needle, eye foremost, under the bars and over the thread (second figure). This method of putting the eye first facilitates the work. Draw the thread up letting the purl come to the lower edge of the loop; fasten on the wrong side. The third figure shows the finished loop.

Sometimes the bars are laid straight across and not in the form of a cross-stitch as pictured; the former method being considered by some as the stronger. In either event the buttonhole-stitch is worked in the manner described.

EYELETS.—An eyelet is a hole made and worked in a garment to hold a cord or button. Pierce the eye-let-hole with a stiletto or bodkin. Place running stitches around the circle, hold the hole over the forefinger of the left hand and buttonhole the edge, covering the running stitches. Work from right to left as seen in the first figure at No. 31. The second figure shows the finished eyelet.

No. 32.—Position of Pin on Button

No. 33.—Rows of Shirring

SEWING ON BUTTONS.—In sewing on buttons always use a coarse thread, never a double one. Make a knot in the thread, put the needle through from the right side that the knot may be on the right side directly under the button; bring it up and through a hole in the button. Draw it down in place. Place a pin across the button as shown at No. 32, and pass the thread over it and down through the opposite hole. Take several stitches across the pin without removing it. Turn the pin and sew across into the other holes. Remove the pin, draw the button away from the band as far as possible, wind the thread around several times with the thread in the needle. Pass the needle through to the wrong side and fasten.

SHIRRINGS.—Shirrings are of different and varied styles, the more simple being the straight plain shirring, while for more elaborate requirements the tucked shirring and the corded shirring will be found more effective.

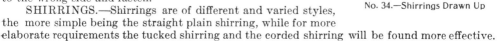

No. 34.—Shirrings Drawn Up

No. 33 gives the most simple method of shirring, and one particularly easy of execution. It is a plain straight shirring with the top shirr turned in to form the finish. This is left raw edge on the under side. A good plan in marking is to make faint dots with a lead pencil (white pencils may also be procured for the black and dark materials), but, should the material be too thin to allow this, mark with blue cotton, removing the thread after the shirr thread has been arranged in proper place. Do not attempt to erase lead pencil marks. The thread or silk used should not be too fine, for there is nothing more discouraging than to find the thread broken at the end of a long shirring. Knots should be made very large, so that they will not pull through, thus making a hole in the material. Threads should be left long, about the length of the material. No. 34 shows successive rows of shirring with the threads drawn up.

No. 35 shows a bias pin-tuck shirring. This is made by taking the material perfectly straight and folding the corner over to form a perfect bias, marking the line thus acquired. The shirring is run through the material double, taking as small an amount as possible. This forms the tuck.

Successive rows of tucks a trifle larger than the former are shown at No. 36. This pictures the arrangement of shirred tucks over the shoulder of a waist. Each row is evenly spaced and drawn up to an even size;

No. 36.—Tucked Shirrings Shaped to Fit

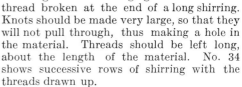

No. 35.—Pin-Tuck Shirrings

however, tucked shirrings of this character will readily accommodate themselves to almost any shaping the pattern may demand, and, if need be, the thread of the first tuck may be considerably shorter than the last, if a curve is being formed.

No. 37 shows the mode of shirring in cluster tucks. This style is perhaps a trifle more difficult to accomplish, but by carefully following the directions and keeping the tucks and spaces even, no trouble should be experienced with the work.

No. 37.—Tucked Shirrings in Clusters

First turn over the top to form a tuck as pictured. This is run straight, like a plain tuck, but the thread is left at the end for drawing and spacing. Make all of these very even. It is sometimes found necessary to fasten these shirrings on a band or stay at the back. This is particularly essential when the lines of shirrings are shaped or curved after the shirrings are arranged in the desired place. Take either binding tape, if this is found wide enough, or, if not, strips of lawn cut straight; or if necessary, cut a lining to fit the required outline and sew securely with long stitches on the wrong side and short stitches on the right side. This forms a solid back for the shirrings. However, when possible, this lining should·

be omitted, as it invariably will show, especially if the material be quite sheer.   The shirring may be basted on tissue paper cut to the required shaping and a row of machine-stitching made through material and paper at each row of shirring.   The stitching will hold the shirrings firmly in place.   The paper may afterward be easily pulled away from the back.

When adjusting a quantity of material to a comparatively small space, as is sometimes fashionable at the backs of skirts, the shirrings are not accomplished by even stitches, but by what are called French gathers.   These are made by taking a succession of small stitches through the material, with longer threads on top, to the following stitches.   This places the stitches rather far apart, as seen at No. 38; always remember that the stitches and spaces in the following rows must continue the same size as when begun, in order to insure evenness.   This method is particularly desirable for heavy cloths and several rows are generally made. In French gathers the stitches in each successive row must come one below the other to draw up properly.

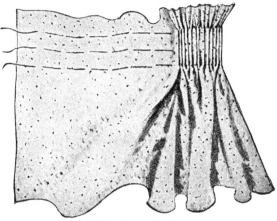

No. 38.—French Gathers

CORDING. — Rows of plain cording are made by folding over the material at the desired point, putting the cord in po-

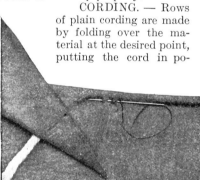

No. 39.—Inserted Cord

No. 40.—Cording for Facing

sition and sewing along with fine running stitches as pictured at No. 39.   As many rows as desired may be run in at regular intervals, whether for the bottom of a skirt or other cording.

No. 40 shows a cording inserted in a bias strip with one side of the material narrower than the other.   This is made exactly as explained for the previous cording and is used for an edge which needs to be faced.   After joining the cording to the garment the broad edge is turned over one-quarter of an inch and hemmed down.

For shirred cording a cord of the desired size is selected and this is put under the material at the line of marking; the stitching is run along the same as for a tucked shirr, the cord filling in the tuck. The desired number should all be run in, then the threads drawn up together, care being exercised that

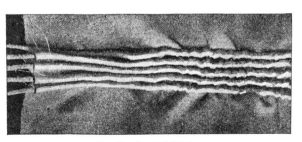

No. 41.—Shirred Cording

the cord is drawn evenly at the same time.   This detail is shown at No. 41.   The method of securing the curved shirrs on a bodice is accomplished in the same manner and adjusted by fastening them to an underlining.   The material is held rather firmly over the cord, but not so tight as to draw.

IMPORTANT POINTS AND AIDS IN DRESSMAKING

IT IS imperative when expecting to accomplish good work in dressmaking to begin by supplying oneself with the proper and necessary tools. Very fine sewing can never be accomplished with coarse needles and thread, nor can material be properly cut without a pair of sharp scissors; in all other instances it is equally expedient to provide the proper requisites. Basting threads, several sizes of needles, shears and a pair of small scissors for ripping are all quite important and are never neglected where good work would be accomplished.

Provide a *tracing-wheel*, or *tailors' chalk* and *colored thread*, for tracing on materials where it is not wise to mark with the wheel or on which the marks would not show—woolens, for instance. On taffeta and other materials which hold the marks use as few pins as possible.

The *table* or surface upon which the material is laid preparatory to cutting is another matter of importance. It should be smooth and hard and of sufficient dimensions to permit the largest pattern to be fully spread out upon it. There are exceptional cases to which this suggestion may not apply; as, for instance, where a kilted skirt is to be cut by a pattern, or when there is no long surface convenient, in which case the worker must exercise her ingenuity and judgment and do the best she can with those surfaces which are at hand. In the ordinary household the dining-table, usually of the extension style, will provide all the surface necessary for cutting out.

When the material is smoothly spread out upon the cutting surface, ready for the patterns or linings to be laid upon it, it should be held smoothly in place by *weights*, the worker being careful not to draw the goods. The pattern should also be properly secured to the material.

No. 1.—Pattern Marked at Different Outline Perforations

When checked, plaid or figured goods are cut, the corresponding checks, plaids or figures must be evenly laid together, then pinned, thrusting only the points through the fabric.

Cut all edges evenly, and for this a pair of sharp *shears* are necessary; those of medium size are best. If an edge is cut unevenly, the eye is apt to be involuntarily influenced by this unevenness when basting or sewing the seam. This is, to a certain extent, the influence of a good beginning, which should never in any way be slighted by anyone fully cognizant of the best practical methods for all parts of dressmaking, such as we intend to describe in this book.

In cutting garments that are to have *linings*, it is generally well to cut, baste and try on the lining before the outside is cut; then, if any mistake occurs, it can be inexpensively rectified;

and, besides, should much alteration be necessary, it will be an economy of the outside fabric to make the change needed in the lining first.

A proper lining is necessary to the perfect fit of a close-fitting waist, although, if it is not properly cut and added, even the best lining will not attain the result desired.   Percalines, soft silesias, sateens and the substitutes for silk are the approved fabrics for both waist and skirt linings when silk is not to be used.

In *laying out* the pattern on the lining, arrange so that two thicknesses may be cut at one time; if percaline, silesia or other double-fold material is used it may be laid out folded as when bought; but if silk, which is much narrower, is employed, double it at one-half the length, bringing the two cut ends together.   Lay the lining out on a large table and dispose the several pieces of the pattern on it to the best advantage.   Cut out through the two thicknesses, carefully making all notches.

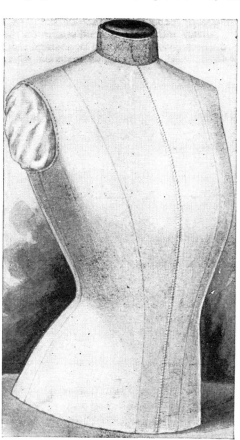

No. 2.—Padded Lining on Waist Form

At the large perforations, which indicate the darts and the under-arm and shoulder seams, mark with a *tracing-wheel* through the centre of each perforation a continuous line, which will be the sewing line.   Remember that unless specified in the label an allowance of three-eighths of an inch is made for all seams not marked by perforations.

To cut any of the *different lengths* marked on the pattern, pin the paper pattern together at all the seams as if it were cloth.   Lay the pinned pattern flat on a table and note the continuous line at each row of perforations which indicates the several lengths, then mark with a pencil through all these lengths or simply the length selected.   Having decided upon the length, when laying out the pattern on the lining, trace with the wheel through the mark that outlines that length, and cut three-eighths of an inch below it.   Although a waist is used for illustration at No. 1, the instruction applies equally well to skirts. This plan should always be followed in cutting from a pattern that provides more than one length, as frequently quite a quantity of material may be saved.

It is a good plan, too, to lay a ruler or yardstick on each piece of the pattern and draw a continuous line through the small perforations, which show how the pattern is to lie on the grain of the goods.   The pencil mark can be seen more readily than the perforations, and will prevent mistakes.

After the lining has been fitted but not yet stitched, a good plan is to rip one side, separate the pieces on which any alterations have been made and lay these pieces on the original pattern; make the same alterations in the pattern and keep this corrected pattern for future occasions. In using the pattern of another gown the new waist or skirt lining may be marked by the corrected pattern, and it will save much time and trouble.

A PADDED BUST FORM

One great difficulty in making one's own gowns is that as the work progresses it becomes necessary to try on again and again, and it is not always easy to see whether the desired effect has been reached.   One of the most important aids in dressmaking—in fact, the most important when one is making her own waists—is the waist or bust form. It is almost impossible to fit oneself without it and those who have one realize its very great value. One which is the exact proportions of one's figure, so that a waist may be correctly fitted over it, is to be had at very slight expense if the worker will follow the directions given here. A form covered with a fitted lining and padded out to correct proportions is shown at No. 2.

Ordinary bust forms, made of papier mâché covered with stockinet, etc., may be purchased at any department store. It is advisable to get a form one or two sizes smaller than the bust measure to be used.

Cut from heavy unbleached muslin or from cotton duck the lining parts of a waist pattern and transfer all the marks, notches and large perforations that the pattern contains. Cut the collar from two thicknesses of canvas and stitch them together with a wave line of stitching. Observe the small perforations which show how the pieces should lie on the grain of the goods.

Join the seams according to the notches and observe all the directions contained in the label of the pattern. The closing should be in the front in making the form cover, as the worker will find it easier to manage it fitting herself. Fold a line from one notch on the front to the other, keeping the hem the same width, and run a colored basting along the edge of this fold. The basting or tracing will indicate the meeting line of the waist if it is to close without a lap; this will be indicated on the label of the pattern. On some waist linings a hem is not provided, but the fronts are to be faced. Three-eighths of an inch seam allowance is made at the front (or back) closing in this case.

Try on the waist, pin the two traced edges together closely; be sure to have the two fronts even at the top and bottom and fit the waist carefully. If it is possible to have assistance in doing this, it will save trouble; but even without it, patience will enable one to make the lining a perfect fit. Draw the lining up well on the shoulders, but not enough to pull it up from the waist-line. Many figures depart from the normal measurement in some particular, hence a certain amount of fitting is usually necessary; but if very much alteration is required, alter the pattern first as directed in the chapter "The Correct Method of Altering Patterns." After basting the alterations at the seams, try the lining on again.

Place a tape around the waist at the natural waist-line, mark on the lining at the lower edge of the tape with a pencil or chalk, and after taking off the lining, trace through this mark with a colored thread. Stitch, bone and press the seams as if for a lining; but it is not necessary to bind or overcast them. Fold under and stitch the front edges. Run a strong basting around the armholes and the neck to prevent them from stretching out of shape. Baste the canvas collar to the neck.

Place the lining on the waist form, draw it well on and pin the fronts together for two or three inches up from the bottom and from

No. 3.—Padded Sleeve Lining

the neck down one or two inches, just enough to hold it well on the figure but open at the bust-line; with tissue-paper, rags or wadding pad in between the form and the lining wherever necessary to make the lining fit smoothly and evenly and look just as it should when worn. As the padding progresses sew the two edges of the front together with an overhand stitch and continue to pad till the figure is quite firm and will not dent in handling. Especial attention is needed at the shoulders and neck. Some care will be needed for this work, but it is worth the trouble because it will simplify all the work in the future and save many fittings. It is for this reason that this method is employed in many dressmaking establishments, as the extra labor required is more than made up for by the greater amount of work that can be done in the workroom, avoiding the necessity of subjecting the customer to long and tiresome fittings. Shirt-waists can be basted, fitted on the form and finished without once trying on, since every fault can be seen and corrected.

Certain patterns are issued having extra length below the waist-line and any of these are desirable patterns for the form cover, on account of length. The patterns are quite long enough to reach to the bottom of the waist form, but for ordinary waist linings four shorter lengths are indicated by perforations, and the waist may terminate at the waist-line, in dip length, in a point at front and back or in short round length.

A sleeve is not used in these form covers, but sometimes the sleeve lining is made and fitted quite tight, then padded out to represent the arm in order to try sleeves on it, but the sleeve is not sewed into the armhole, as it would be in the way. This padded arm figure is shown at No. 3. In draping fancy sleeves, arranging lace or insertion, and, in fact, trimming sleeves generally, the sleeve form will be found of great value.

SPONGING MATERIAL

Upon purchasing the material inquire if it has been sponged; if not, this must be attended to before cutting, or every spot of water will leave a disfiguring mark, and if caught in a shower the dress will be not only all spotted, but the skirt may shrink one or more inches, causing the lower edge to turn up, exposing the velveteen or facing.

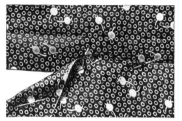

No. 4.—Matching the Design in Figured Silk

In the stores of large cities sponging will be done at a slight extra cost per yard, and as it takes some time and necessitates great care we advise those who can to leave the cloth with the merchant for shrinking. For those who reside in small towns and cannot have the work done for them, or for those who prefer doing it themselves, the following directions, if carried out, will accomplish excellent results:

The articles used in sponging goods are a large-sized table that will not be impaired by water, and a sponging-sheet, which may be a strip of heavy unbleached muslin or drilling one yard wide and one or two yards long. Clip the selvages before sponging light-weight goods, but in heavy cloths and cloakings they are best torn off.

Place a large-sized ironing blanket very smoothly upon a table. It is imperative that there should be no uneven places or humps, as these cause a gloss on the material when the iron is passed over them. Lay the goods, if single fold, right side down upon the blanket and cover with a wet sponge-cloth well wrung out; pass the iron over this several times, steaming well. Remove the cloth and press the material almost dry. Shrink only a small portion at a time, moving the material on the ironing blanket until the full length has been sponged and pressed. Allow double-width materials to remain folded with the right side turned in. If the material is very heavy and the steaming does not seem to go through the second fold, the process may be repeated on the other side.

It is not advisable, however, to sponge some of the thinner fancy weaves of woollen goods as the steam makes them shrivel up. When doubtful, experiment with a small piece of the material, and if it is found that water may not be used, press it well with a moderately warm—not hot—iron before cutting. One should always bear in mind the fact that it is quite as important that washable materials such as linen, piqué, duck and other linen and cotton fabrics be shrunk and pressed before

No. 5.—Slip-Stitching the Breadths Together

cutting as cloth and woollens, for after these are laundered they frequently shrink considerably.

Plain white or a solid color that may spot if sprinkled should be wet thoroughly by dipping in water and hanging up to dry. For colored fabrics a handful of salt or enough vinegar to make the water slightly acid to the taste may be added. Care is necessary in pressing material after it has been dampened not to stretch or draw either side, but keep the grain of the material straight in both the length and the width. Canvas or haircloth used for interlining should always be shrunk before applying to the garment.

Colored wash fabrics may be sprinkled by dipping a clean whisk broom in water, then shaking, and rolling its entire length. If figured, it will be wise to lay a plain white material over the goods when rolling; this will prevent the cloth from touching and perhaps marking.

THE NAP OF DIFFERENT FABRICS

In all woollen cloths having a smooth, close nap (or pile) the latter should invariably run toward the bottom of the garment; and this general result is obtained if the cutting line of perforations in the patterns and the directions for their use are properly observed. In waists and skirts that are cut bias of the goods the lines and directions are also so arranged that the proper result will certainly follow their observance.

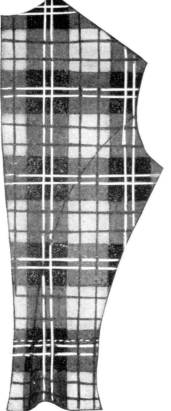

When a garment is made of velvet or plush, the pile should run *upward* just as the pile of the fur does in a garment of seal-skin. When in these fabrics the pile runs *upward* its tendency is to fall outward, thus bringing out and enhancing its depth of color. When it runs downward, however, it is more liable to flatten, just as fur will when stroked, so that its richness and intensity of color are rendered less apparent and, therefore, less effective.

Great care should be taken to have the nap or pile of adjoining sections run in the same direction; otherwise, by different reflections of light caused by the varying directions of the nap, a garment may appear to be made of two shades of goods

MATCHING FIGURES AND PLAIDS

The effort to match figured, striped, checked or plaided goods in cutting and fitting a garment is often attended by very unsatisfactory results at the hands of the amateur, and not infrequently of the professional; yet it is a comparatively easy matter, especially if a few simple points, such as are here given, are borne well in mind.

Figures and flowers must perforce be perfectly matched, and unless one line of flowers is up and the next down, as occurs occasionally, one position will have to be selected for the top, and this generally with the stems of the flowers in a downward direction. When cutting a garment where several breadths of silk must be joined (a circular skirt, for instance), it is important that the pattern or figures on the material should be matched, and often this cannot be done when the breadths are simply joined at the selvages. Cut the front breadth first by folding the silk lengthwise through

No. 6.—Back and Side-Back
Matched

the centre (if the circular skirt has no seam at the front) and laying the front edge of the pattern even with the fold. If there is a decided figure in the silk, fold this front breadth so the figures may balance and not make the skirt look one-sided when it is worn. Lay the paper pattern out on a table; lay the front breadth on it and match the figures of the silk at the edge of the second breadth to those at or near the edge of the first. It will sometimes be necessary to lap the second breadth some little way over the first, as shown at No. 4 in order to find the corresponding figures. Turn under the edge of the second breadth and pin it to the first. The breadth may then be cut according to the paper pattern. Proceed in the same way to join the breadths for both sides of the skirt. Slip-stitch the breadths together, from the outside, by slipping the needle along inside the fold edge of the applied breadth and then taking a stitch in the under breadth, as seen at No. 5. When the skirt is turned wrong side out, it will be found that the slip-stitching from the right side forms the basting of the seam.

In purchasing plaid, striped or figured goods, an extra quantity will always be required beyond that needed for a gown of the same design, but of plain material. With very few exceptions ordinary plaids have no up and down, and unless finished with a nap the position for the top is at the option of the worker; usually, however, plaids are arranged that the darkest strips run across the bottom with the lighter tones up, as the shading in this direction is better.

If there is a nap, always have this run down; that is, in such a manner that the cloth will run smooth toward the bottom of the garment. With stripes the lines are frequently shaded, or they may have a right and left side, particularly if the stripe is composed of a double or treble line.

It must aways be borne in mind throughout the cutting that all portions of the pattern or lining must be placed with the upper part in the direction selected for the top of the material. Before cutting, study the plaid well and do not be in too great a hurry to use the scissors.

The most satisfactory results are obtained by folding the material and pinning through both thicknesses as for a seam, then turning over on the right side and noting the effect; in this way it may be easily ascertained which strip, plaid or figure it will be best to use for the centres of the front and back respectively. Be careful in replacing goods not to lose the original position.

In cutting the skirt for a plaid costume place the chosen plaid exactly in the centre of the front gore, or if the skirt is circular, directly down the centre of the front. After the front is cut, the uncut material is laid on the table and the cut front placed near the edge, the crosswise as well as the lengthwise stripes matching exactly.

Place the pattern of the side gore on the material, matching the front, and if the position is correct, cut; otherwise move the front gore to the next block or plaid on the material. This may necessitate some waste, but there is no alternative. Frequently in plaid or figured materials the pattern will have to be moved half a yard or more to a corresponding figure or flower before the correct position will be found. Cut each gore after the manner directed and baste and stitch carefully.

In cutting a skirt bias the same rules must be observed and each stripe matched exactly. When a skirt is cut with a seam down the centre of the front, whether of stripe or plaid, cut the front on the bias directed on the particular label, instead of a lengthwise fold, as usual. Place the cut half on the material with every block and line matching, and cut the corresponding half from this.

With the present style of stretching the back of the draped waist little difficulty is experienced in the making. Having

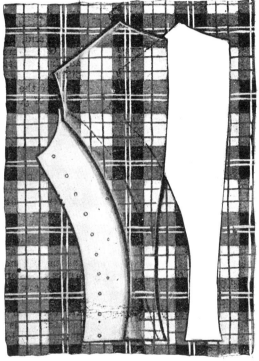

No. 7.—Position of Back When Cutting Side-Back

chosen the stripe which is most suitable for the centre of the back, select also for the crosswise stripe a position which will give the best contour to the figure. For the front, arrange the plaid so that when the waist is closed the centre will form a succession of perfect blocks. Other ideas may be considered for the front closing; this is simply a matter of choice, since most of the draped waists have a vest or fancy front trimming. In shirt-waists, however, the lines across the front must match, and, in any event, the crosswise plaids of the front must be on a line with those of the back, so that when the under-arm seam is joined the crosswise stripe of both will match perfectly.

In making a waist or bodice which is not stretched, but has each seam stitched in with the lining, or the lining added later, as explained in the chapter "The Tailor-Made Gown," greater care must be exercised, as more difficulties are likely to be encountered in consequence of the curves and the number and shape of the seams.

Having selected the plaid for the centre of the back, lay the pattern on the material with the line of perforations in a position as directed on the label; this will give a very effective back, as may be seen at No. 6, which also shows the side-back joined to the back. The side-back is cut by placing the back on the uncut material in such a position that all the plaids match, both the lengthwise and crosswise stripes being in exactly the same position directly underneath. By this is not meant that the back is to be placed as far in or out on the material as one pleases, but to be disposed so that the material will cut as economically as possible For this reason the back must be placed only as far away from the cut-out space as is consistent with good cutting, allowing for seams and perfect matching.

In a plaid of the design shown it would be impossible to place the pattern of the side-back nearer the cut edge, as the blocks would not match. In a plaid of a different character it might be possible to save at least a seam or, perhaps, move it nearer the top and save a little there but these are problems which must be worked up by the cutter, using her judgment according to the different designs and patterns used.

No. 7 indicates the space from which the back has been cut out, with the cut back laid on the material after it has been shifted around and the correct position found for the side-back.

No. 8.—Plaid Material After Cutting

As will be observed by the faint outline, the back is not placed entirely beyond the cut-out space, but only as far as is essential to cut a perfect side-back, the pattern of which is placed in position on the material with the dotted lines showing the back of this form under the material back. Accuracy in this is gained chiefly by experience. No. 8 shows exactly how the material looks after the back and side-back are both cut and the least possible quantity of material wasted.

With patience matching is easily done, and the trials necessitated by this apparently bewildering work are repaid by the workmanlike finish.

STITCHING, PRESSING AND FINISHING SEAMS

Bastings should be just *inside* or *outside* the line on which the stitching is to be made, thus avoiding the possibility of catching the bastings in with the stitching. If, however, the bastings have been put in along the centre of the perforations, make the stitching just a trifle outside the bastings, bearing in mind that the sewing of the seams has a tightening tendency. In sewing side-back seams always have the back next the "feed" of the machine and the side-back next the "presser-foot," and hold the parts well up at each end of the " presser-foot"; otherwise the side-back seam is liable to pucker or full when being sewed. In making seams in which one portion is fulled on to another, place the full portion next the "feed" or underneath, because if it is placed next the "presser-foot," the latter is liable to shove the fulness out of place and into wrinkles. All outside stitching should be carefully and evenly stitched. It is advisable to put a strip of thin crinoline, taffeta or percaline between the folds, as it improves the stitching. At No. 9 is shown the effect of rows of stitching on the bottom of a skirt.

Careful pressing is quite as important as any other part of dressmaking, perhaps more, for darts and seams that have been properly sewed are often stretched and pulled out of shape by careless pressing. Special boards may be bought from dressmakers' supply houses, but home-made substitutes answer the purpose quite as well.

Skirts, coats and long garments require a large, flat surface for pressing and either the family ironing board or a table will be found best.   For sleeves, a small sleeve board, made of hard wood smoothly planed is generally used.   It is usually made from two to three feet long, and tapering from five to six inches wide at one end to three inches wide at the other, and both ends, as well as all edges, are rounded.   An ordinary rolling-pin, covered with a piece of old blanket sewed firmly in place and then with smooth cotton cloth, makes a satisfactory sleeve board and also answers well for pressing other seams.

To obtain the best result in opening seams, the board should be covered with one thickness of firm, smooth woollen cloth which in character is similar to broadcloth.   The texture of a pressing cloth upon which goods are to be sponged or pressed should be fine and soft and several thicknesses are advisable—as a coarse fabric will leave the imprint of its texture and weave. A hard surface must be provided for seams that require thorough pressing to keep them permanently open.   A large cushion, tightly padded, is very useful in pressing darts or other curved seams.

No. 9.—Rows of Stitching on Skirt

A narrow iron is considered better for pressing seams than a wide one.   In the average household, however, the ordinary flat-iron will be mostly used.   While it is a very general custom to press a seam open with the *point* of the pressing iron, a far better result is obtained by reversing the iron and using the *square end*, as the edges of the seam are thus stretched or spread out evenly at the same time that the seam is pressed.

In pressing the seams of cloth garments, the seam edges should be dampened with a wet sponge or cloth; but soft fabrics, such as cashmeres and suitings, and also silks, do not require dampening. Silk should not be pressed at all in the ordinary way of pressing, as the heat of the iron takes out the dressing and leaves the silk soft and old looking.   When it is necessary to press seams in silk, this should be done the same as for velvet; do not press on a table or board, but hold one end of the seam in the left hand and let someone else hold the other end; then with the right hand run the iron along the seam, pressing it open or closed, as desired; in this way the iron touches only the seam. If no assistant is at hand, lay the iron on its side and use both hands to draw the seam across the *edge* of the iron. The hem of a silk skirt may be pressed in the usual way on the table or board, but do not have the iron hot, and press only the hem.

The finish most commonly employed for seams is overcasting, generally working from left to right; but unless one is quite expert, the ravellings and short threads will escape as the stitches are made, producing a very undesirable roughness. Dressmakers usually finish each edge of every seam with a narrow ribbon binding, placing the binding over the edge in such a manner that a single row of "running" will sew it at both edges at the same time.

In heavy garments, such as jackets and cloaks, where the seams are to be bound with satin, silk or farmer satin, the binding is sometimes put on before the seam is stitched and is cut bias, wide enough to extend just a trifle beyond the basting of the seam.   It is applied to the right side, turned over the edge, and the seam stitched through the binding as well as the fabric. Seams finished in this way are not

No. 10.—Bias Binding on Seam

pressed, of course, until the binding has been added and sewed in.   A safer way is to baste the binding on the right side after the seams are pressed; turn over on the seam edge and fell down on the under side. (No. 10.)   Arrange this, so that one row of machine-stitching will catch through upper and under side.   Another style of finish consists in folding the edges of the lining and outside fabric at each side of every seam, and then running or "overhanding" them together.   It is well, as far as possible, to press all seams before binding them, since their edges will then be in shape to receive the proper amount of the binding material. Seams in waists should be notched and the binding follow the curves and points.

For armholes, make the ordinary three-eighths-inch seam, but at the same time sew in a narrow bias binding-strip of the goods. When the seam is made, trim it down closely, turn the binding over it, turn under the loose edge of the strip and fell it down along the seam stitching.

CORRECT METHOD OF ALTERING PATTERNS

A KNOWLEDGE of the proportionate measurements used in cutting Butterick patterns is very necessary for the dressmaker, whether professional or amateur. If one makes only her own clothes she decides upon the size that fits her, and always calls for that; but when making for others whose measurements vary, it is of great service to know just what are the corresponding waist, hip and bust measures in any particular pattern. A table of corresponding measures is printed in the Catalogue of Metropolitan Fashions, and is usually to be found in the back pages of THE DELINEATOR. Tables of the proportionate measurements by which Butterick patterns are cut for girls and boys also are found in these places. The table of ladies' measures is reproduced on this page, and reference to it will assist materially in deciding what pattern may come nearest to the figure to be fitted. It should be borne in mind always that the number designated as "bust measure" is not taken at the fullest part of the figure, but close up under the arms and across the chest, as seen at No. 1. Remember, too, that the bust measure printed at the top of the label is *that* measure taken by the tape and that the pattern is *always* larger, varying from two inches in a tight-fitting waist lining to six or eight inches for a loose blouse or waist.

TABLE OF PROPORTIONATE BUST, WAIST AND HIP MEASUREMENTS IN INCHES.		
BUST	WAIST	HIP
30	20	37
32	22	39
34	24	41
36	26	43½
38	28	46½
40	30	49½
42	32	52½
44	34	55½
46	36	58½
48	38	61½

No. 1.—Position for Taking Bust Measure

Many of our patrons have learned that Butterick patterns are so accurately adjusted that it is unnecessary to change them in order to secure a perfect fit; at the same time ladies whose figures vary from the average standards in waist lengths, sleeve lengths, bust size, waist size, or in any other way, can, with full confidence, change the patterns to suit their individual peculiarities by following the instructions given.

It is easy to lengthen or shorten a waist or sleeve without in any way detracting from the symmetry of the original lines, if the work is done at the right time and in the proper manner. Nevertheless, ladies sometimes work a long time endeavoring to fit a bodice cut the normal length to a long-waisted person, and they are not quite satisfied with the effect when completed, because the lines of the seams and the proportionate length of the bodice are not just what they were designed to be, a very slight change sometimes destroying the effect of the whole garment. Fitting a waist pattern cut the average length to a short-waisted person is also sometimes trying to the fitter, as she cannot make all the seams run just as they were intended to do. The dressmaker may easily obviate these little trials by carefully studying the illustrations here presented and following the methods and principles elaborated in the description accompanying them.

A very necessary point to bear in mind when ordering a waist pattern is that the required size be determined by correct measurement. The bust-line is variable. When the low-bust corset was worn, the line of greatest bust fulness was only about four inches above the natural waist-line; a high-bust corset brings that line from two to four inches higher. These facts readily show that the measurement over the bust fulness is not sufficiently exact to use as a standard on which to base the proportionate measures of the other parts—the waist, neck, armhole, etc. A measurement less liable to variation—therefore, a surer guarantee of correctness—is the measure that is taken around the chest as shown at No. 1. The tape is brought across the back and around close up under the arms, slanting upward at the front and meeting well up on the chest. The measure is taken closely, but should not be drawn tight, and it is this number of inches that should be given in ordering a waist pattern.

No. 2 shows how the tape measure should cross the back, well up on the shoulder blades, when this measure is taken. The reason for taking the measure over this portion of the figure rather than at the fullest point of the bust is this:

The measurement around the fullest line of the bust will be several inches larger than the measure taken as shown, and it will be seen that if a waist pattern is ordered by the size of the bust-line measurement, when the pattern designers and makers base their cutting and proportionment on the higher line, the pattern

No. 2.—Position at Back, for Bust Measure

will prove too large. When the proper chest measurement is given, the pattern will be found large enough at the bust-line for the correctly proportioned figure.

The exaggerated waist-line "dip" is seldom seen now, but it should never be considered in taking the waist measure. This should always be taken as shown at No. 3, and the tape should be drawn quite snug. The hip measure should be taken as seen at No. 4, holding the tape evenly around the figure at about five inches below the waist-line. It is not necessary to take the sleeve measure unless one is ordering a separate sleeve pattern; in that case it is taken, as shown at No. 5, around the fullest part of the

No. 3.—Taking the Waist Measure

arm, about one inch below the armhole. If the measures are not taken in the manner illustrated, which corresponds with the measurements employed in making the patterns, it is quite evident that one cannot expect the garment to fit. The point to be emphasized is that the number designated on the pattern label as "bust measure" is not taken at the fullest part of the figure, but close up under the arms and across the chest, as seen at No. 1.

ADAPTING PATTERNS TO TALL AND SHORT FIGURES

In the matter of selecting a model or arranging a pattern to fit a very short or an unusually tall person, a thorough knowledge of the figure is the first requirement; just what proportion the different measurements bear to each other, and whether one is long or short waisted in proportion to the skirt length.

Before cutting the material the figure should be measured from the back of the neck to the waist-line and from the under-arm to the waist-line. Measure the waist and take the hip measure five inches below the waist-line. Measure the length of the skirt in the centre front from the natural waist-line to the floor. If the dip waist-line is liked, that must be arranged after the skirt is fitted; it should be cut and have its first fitting with the natural waist-line.

Make a note of all the measures as they are taken, then compare with the corresponding measures on the pattern.

The back of the waist lining may be shortened in the upper or the lower part or in

No 4. —Taking the Hip Measure

No. 5.—Position for Sleeve Measure

both. Some figures are long-waisted from the under-arm to the waist-line, but short from the middle of the back to the neck. Draw a pencil line through the small perforations, and at right angles to this line draw another three-eighths of an inch (a seam's width) below the lowest curve of the arm-holes. This divides the back into upper and lower portions. If the lower part is too long (this is determined by the length of the under-arm measure), lay a plait or tuck the necessary size across at right angles to the line of small perforations and two and one-half inches above the waist-line. If the back is too long in the upper portion, fold a plait across half way between the under-arm line and the back of the neck. (No. 6.) The back may be lengthened by cutting across at either or both of these points and separating the amount required to make it the desired length.

No. 7 depicts the manner of shortening the front. To shorten the length below the under-arm, it is necessary to cut the dart through the centre between the perforations. The plait is made by measuring two and one-half inches from the waist-line upward at the seam edge of the dart and at the under-arm seam and folding the plait straight across between these two

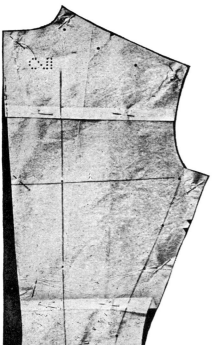

No. 6.—The Back Made Shorter

points. The size of the plait is determined by the difference between the measure from under-arm to waist-line of the pattern and of the figure to be fitted. The illustration shows also the way to lay a plait in the upper part of the lining front and how to even the perforations and seam edges after the plaits are folded in place. Whatever alteration is made in the length of the lining, a corresponding alteration must be made in the outside drapery of the waist; take out the same amounts and at the same places. When the bust is larger than the proportionate size the value of the outlet or allowance seams is proven, for the pattern may be enlarged quite three inches across the bust by making the sewing line of the under-arm seams three-quarters of an inch *outside* of the large perforations. This allowance will add three-quarters of an inch to both the front and the back portions (equal to an inch and one-half at each seam), or three inches altogether. It is hardly likely that an addition so great as this will be necessary, but what-

ever it is divide by four and make the sewing line one-quarter of the whole amount required *outside* of the line of large perforations. For instance, if an inch and one-half more breadth is required, the sewing line should be made three-eighths of an inch—which is one-quarter of an inch and a half —beyond the large perforations.

When double under-arm forms are provided in a pattern the extra allowance should be made so that it is equally divided and the forms increased in proportion, otherwise an increase at a single seam will spoil the symmetry of the waist. When it is necessary to make much allowance at the under-arm seam, the armhole should not be cut quite so large as when the seam may be sewed at the line of the large perforations. The material should be allowed to extend beyond the armhole line of the pattern the same distance that has been allowed beyond the perforated line at the under-arm seam. (No. 8.)

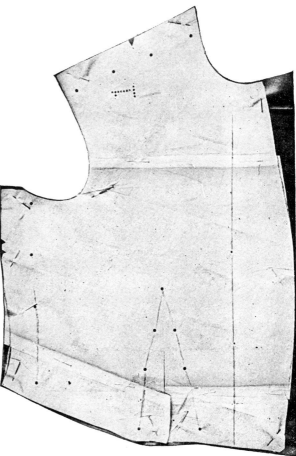

No. 7.—To Shorten the Lining Front

TO FIT PATTERNS TO FIGURES WITH EXTRA SMALL OR LARGE BUST

The styles of patterns with which it is sometimes found difficult to avoid wrinkles in fitting garments to ladies of disproportionate busts, are those having large or moderately large second bust darts. The directions found in the labels of all patterns are of themselves sufficient—in fact, it may be said that the cases are infrequent when these suggestions will become necessary at all. In a word, they will be found useful chiefly where a "glove fit" at the bust is desired for a lady of marked irregularity of development at that point. It should also be remarked that the suggestions here submitted are not to be understood as affecting the adjustment of garments to ladies who, although slender or stout, are yet proportionately developed. For them no modification, other than such as the patterns may direct, is in any case necessary.

No. 9 shows the pattern for the front lapped and ad-

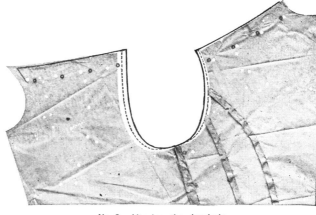

No. 8.—Altering the Armhole

justed to fit a lady whose bust is disproportionately small at the fullest part. This illustration represents an extreme case, where the bust is very small, although the measure taken about the chest is the same as for a well-proportioned lady. Where the bust at the fullest part is not so small—that is to say, but slightly undersized—such extreme laps are unnecessary. For such a figure, therefore, the fold should only be lapped slightly, but in the same way as shown in the illustration. The principle is the same in each instance, and the method of procedure, in the light of our explanation, will, we believe, be found so easy as to prove a great convenience.

No. 10 shows the pattern for the front slashed and adjusted to fit a lady having an extra large bust. Our readers will understand that what is here meant by an "extra large bust" is a bust that is extra large only at the fullest part in the front, which is below the point where the bust measure is usually taken. In this illustration the edges of the three slashes are *separated* instead of being *lapped*, thus giving more room across the bust proper and from a point near the bottom of the armhole to the waist-line of the second bust dart.

The modification herein suggested being, as explained, for a lady of extreme fulness at the bust, it will, of course, not be necessary to depart so far from the standard shape for ladies more nearly approaching the normal proportions,

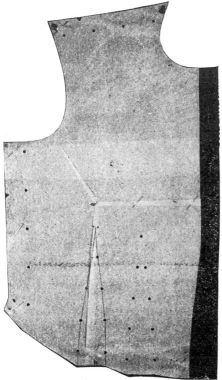

No. 9.—Decreasing the Bust Size

It makes no difference whether the front edge of the front in the pattern is straight or curved; satisfactory results can be secured with either style of front. The same treatment may be employed to increase or diminish the bust size when only one dart is employed, as in blouse and shirt-waist linings.

No. 11 represents the easy curve commonly followed in terminating darts in waist patterns. The picture shows the effect when the goods is folded, with the corresponding dart perforations together, as directed in the label of the pattern. The point to be emphasized here is that the line of the dart seam should follow the reversed curve toward the point, running into the folded edge almost in a line with the fold. When this curve is followed, the "pouting" effect, as it is called by professionals, often seen at the top of darts, is avoided.

No. 12 shows the line of the dart seam running straight from the third perforation from the point of the dart to this point. This is the cause of a "pouting" effect, which, as explained in the preceding description, is easily avoided. Careless seamstresses sometimes create an even worse effect by following the original rounding curve to the end of the dart, instead of changing the direction of the seam to follow the reversed curve shown at No. 11.

Although the darts in skirts are reversed this caution should be observed, as the points should be finished perfectly, avoiding the pouting effect referred to in the waist darts.

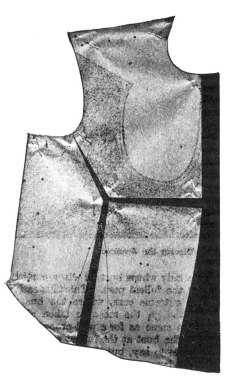

No. 10.—Increasing the Bust Size

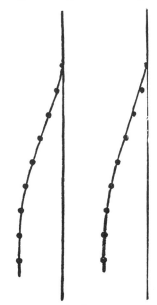

Nos. 11 and 12.—Terminating Darts

TO FIT PATTERNS TO ROUND-SHOULDERED AND STOOPING FIGURES

The reader will appreciate the fact that to fit garments without wrinkling to persons who are of abnormal proportions is a very desirable accomplishment; but we must endeavor to do even more than that, for it is possible, by making a slight change in the run of a seam here or there, to cause a person to appear much less out of proportion than she really is. At the same time, however, if we change a pattern in the wrong direction, we might make the effect appear much greater than it is; thus, if we hollow the front edges of the back and side-back too much, and narrow the back at the arm's-eye edge, because the person is broad in the back and we would have her appear narrower, we will surely be disappointed in the result, and will, perhaps, wonder why the more we try to fit the garments so as to make the defect appear less, the more noticeable that defect becomes.

We should not try to fit a person who is disproportionately large in any part with a garment cut comparatively small at a corresponding part, in the hope that it may make the person appear less out of natural proportion; for almost invariably the misfit will attract attention to the part and give even a casual observer the impression that the figure is of bad shape, when in reality it is not sufficiently out of proportion to be noticed at all if fitted fairly, without being too tight, and without any effort to make it look very different from what it really is.

In fitting garments we sometimes find one shoulder of the person being fitted higher than the other, or one shoulder-blade considerably more prominent than the other; and frequently the whole of one shoulder is more fully developed than the corresponding one, which occasionally causes doubt in the mind of the fitter regarding what she should do to make the disproportion appear slight as possible. In any case the utmost care should be exercised in placing the seams to the best possible advantage. Always bear in mind that when changes must be made to allow for disproportion several slight alterations in different places will do much more toward preserving the symmetrical lines of the pattern than can be achieved by making the entire alteration at any one place, even though the garment should fit, without wrinkling, if changed at one seam only.

No. 13.—Slashed for Stooping Shoulders

When thick goods are being made up it is sometimes desirable to leave the outside a little loose when fitting the smaller side of a person who is not alike at both sides, building up a shoulder that is low, or filling out a shoulder-blade that is much smaller than the corresponding one, with wadding. Great care should be exercised in such cases not to use too much wadding; a safe guide will be to use only a small quantity in any doubtful case, as it is more objectionable to have the garment show that it is wadded than to have one side of a person appear larger than the other. Always thin the wadding out on the ends.

No. 14.—Lapped for Over-Erect Figure

Sometimes it is not easy altogether to remove the wrinkles in a hollow shoulder, but the front can generally be made nearly smooth by stretching the shoulder edge of the front and the upper part of the neck edge a trifle, and by holding the back quite full on the front when basting the shoulder seam, cutting the back from a quarter to a half inch wider than the front at the shoulder edge. Be assured that almost invariably those little wrinkles, so troublesome to many, are not the result of a misfit in the front, where they are seen, but are caused by the back shoulder being cut a little too short to cover easily the shoulder-blade.

No. 13 represents a back and side-back gore, which have been slashed across and separated to fit a lady who is more or less round-shouldered and stooping. If the person to be fitted stoops very much, a second cut should be made nearly all the way across the back, commencing it at a point about one-third the distance from the neck edge to the broken line and terminating it near the armhole edge just below the outlet line of the perforations, separating the edges made by the slash more or less according as the person stoops—generally from an eighth to half an inch. In cutting out the side back, preserve a nice even curve all along the edge. The under-arm gore very seldom needs any change for disproportion such as is considered under this heading.

No. 14 illustrates the same back and side back as are shown in the preceding illustrations;

but in this case we find the back and side back adjusted to fit a person who is comparatively flat at the shoulder-blades and over-erect. The edges of the back and side back made by slashing along the broken lines in the previous illustration are overlapped, as shown at No. 14, and the back is trimmed off a trifle as pictured by the line near the armhole and side-back seam edges. In cutting out the side back be careful to cut on a graceful, even curve when shaping the upper part of the back edge where the edges are lapped.

It is impossible to state exactly how much to change the parts for the different figures, but the maker will meet with very little difficulty in deciding that point; an inch at the shoulder-seam edge at the armhole is sufficient change to cause a pattern to fit a person of extreme disproportion, and the change should be smaller according as the disproportion is less noticeable.

In changing a pattern which has been correctly fitted to a person of normal proportions so as to make it fit a person whose shoulders are disproportionately high and square, or, in fact, any alterations which may be puzzling to the amateur it is always advisable to cut the pattern in cambric after making the alterations, and fit the cambric to the figure so that any little deficiency may be adjusted before the material is cut out. This cambric pattern should be preserved for future uses.

We have used illustrations of ladies' patterns, but the same alterations are equally appropriate for the same class of disproportion in all sizes or ages.

ALTERING SLEEVES

Before altering a sleeve pattern the arm should be measured from the arm socket to the bend of the elbow and thence to the wrist. These two measurements are necessary that the elbow of the sleeve may be in correct position on the arm, as the upper and lower arm may vary in proportionate length. If all the alterations be made at the top or the bottom of the sleeve, the elbow will be drawn out of place.

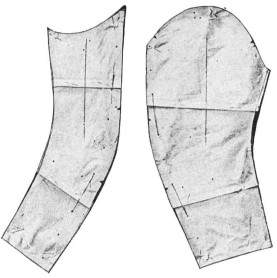

Nos. 15 and 16.—Sleeve Pattern Shortened Above and Below the Elbow

To shorten the sleeves, make the alteration first in the under-arm piece. If the arm, from the socket to the bend of the elbow, measures one inch less than the corresponding part of the pattern, fold a half-inch-wide tuck or plait straight across the pattern half way between the elbow and the top of the sleeve; make the tuck straight across and see that the line marking the small perforations is kept straight. Fold the tuck over flat and pin it through to the pattern. If it is necessary to shorten the lower arm portion, make a tuck half as wide as the amount to be taken out, lay it across the lower part of the sleeve pattern about three inches below the elbow and parallel with the wrist edge of the sleeve. The plaits across the upper sleeve piece should be made to correspond in size and position with those on the under piece. The sleeve portions with the tucks pinned in them are shown at Nos. 15 and 16.

When the tucks or plaits are folded over, the perforations and the edges of the pattern are made uneven; to correct this, lay the altered pattern on a large piece of paper and mark a new outline running across the edge of the folded part. If the arm is very full, the space between the elbow and the greater width at the top of the sleeve should be filled out as shown in black in the illustration, but if the arm is not large the surplus width may be trimmed off to make a symmetrical outline from the elbow to the top of the sleeve. Whatever alteration is made at the edge of the seam, a corresponding alteration must be made in the large perforations.

If the sleeve needs lengthening, make the alteration at the same places by cutting across the pattern instead of making the plaits. Lay the pattern on another piece of paper and separate the pieces far enough to make the required length. Correct the outlines in the same way as when the sleeve is shortened. Alter the outside sleeve to correspond with the lining.

ALTERING SKIRTS

In ordering a skirt pattern it is of greatest importance that one should know the hip measure as well as the waist measure of the figure to be fitted, and the table of measurements should be referred to in order to ascertain if the figure's proportions correspond to those of the pattern. If they do not, it will be better to order by the hip measure, as alterations may be easily made at the waist when the hip measure is correct.

To shorten a gored skirt, lay a plait across each breadth about six inches below the hip. The hip-line in No. 17 is traced across the pattern five inches below the waist-line or five and three-eighth inches below the upper edge of the pattern, the three-eighths of an inch being the seam allowance at the waist. If the figure is full, the slope of the gore at the bias side should be filled out, as shown in the illustration, from the folded plait to the hip-curve above; but if the figure is slight, this little extension may be taken off. First mark with pencil a cutting line along the yardstick from the plait to the edge of the seam near the bottom of the skirt.

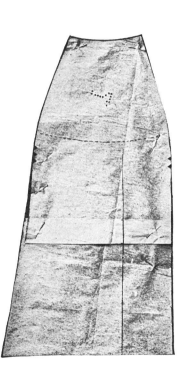
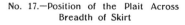

The way of lengthening a gored skirt is represented at No. 18 The hip is marked across in the same way as already described and about six inches below. Measure at the straight edge if the gores are cut with one straight edge, or if both sides of the gores are bias, measure along the line of perforations that indicate a lengthwise thread of the goods. Cut the breadth straight across.

No. 17.—Position of the Plait Across Breadth of Skirt

No. 18.—Breadth Cut Across and Separated to Lengthen

The two pieces are then laid on a large piece of paper, the space desired to lengthen the skirt is measured accurately between the two pieces. They are pinned in place, the straight edges exactly even, and the yardstick is used to draw a line from the upper piece to a point near the bottom of the lower piece where it will gradually and naturally join. Continue to lengthen or shorten each breadth of the skirt in the same way, taking out or adding the same amount on every breadth.

If the hip measure is large in proportion to the waist, the alteration of a gored skirt is quite simple, and can be made in fitting the skirt, after the gores are basted together, by making each seam a little wider from the hip toward the waist. If, however, the opposite result is desired, to make the waist larger, proportionately, than the hip, this must be calculated and planned for before the skirt is cut. We may find, for instance, a figure with 30-inch waist and hips that measure 44. Referring to the "table" we find that the nearest hip measure is 43½ inches and that the waist measure of the pattern that has this hip size is 26 inches—four inches less than the waist we are required to fit. The first consideration will be the number of gores in which the skirt is cut, as this governs the number of seams at which allowance may be provided in cutting, and the amount that may be added at each seam.   Another and very important consideration is the shape of the figure to be fitted.   The same number of inches may result from the measurement of figures that differ entirely in shape.   The hip measure of the nicely rounded "model" figure, with perfectly proportioned bust and waist measures, may be the same as that of another that is perfectly flat at front and back with abnormal development at the sides only, or of still another that has unusual abdominal prominence with extreme flatness at the back.   It will be readily seen that the allowance at the seams must be so distributed

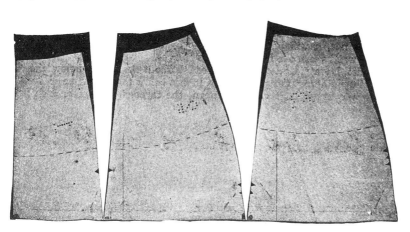

No. 19.—Increasing Waist Size, with Extension for Prominent Abdomen

that the greater amount will come where the figure has fullest development.   Under ordinary circumstances, it is preferable to make no alteration on either the front or the back gores, but this rule cannot be followed when the figure is unusually full at the front.

In the measurements cited, 30 inches waist and 44 inches hip, it becomes necessary to add 4 inches to the pattern at the waistline or 2 inches at each side; No. 19 shows how this amount may be added to a seven-gored skirt. Pin the pattern to the material and be careful that the line of small perforations near the front edge of each of the side breadths lies over a straight lengthwise thread of the material. The first step in using a pattern should be to read the label carefully, then open the pattern and, referring to the label, identify each piece by its number or description.   It will be found an aid to correct cutting if a ruler or yardstick be laid on each piece of the pattern, its edge touching each of the small perforations that indicate the way the pattern should lie on the goods, and a heavy pencil mark made along the line formed by the ruler.   In order to produce the correct flare or ripple, it is important in some cases that the front edge of the side gores be cut slightly bias, and the pencilled line on the pattern enables one to be certain that the

No. 20.—Increasing Waist Size of Circular Skirt

pattern is properly placed. Measure from each end of the line to the straight edge or selvage of the goods and move the pattern until both ends of the line are the same number of inches from the edge.

The hip measure, as said before, is taken about five inches below the waist-line, and as three-eighths of an inch is the seam allowance at the top of the skirt, measure five and three-eighths from the upper edge of the pattern, and make a line across each breadth at this measure, following the same outline as the top edge of the breadth. Mark on the material with tailors' chalk the outline of the front edge, from top to bottom, of each breadth. If the hips of the figure to be fitted measure 44 inches (one-half inch more than the pattern), the one-quarter-inch increase needed at each side can be made now by moving each of the two side breadths back one-eighth of an inch and pinning the pattern on the goods again with the chalk outline of the front edge one-eighth of an inch nearer the selvage than the pattern edge. No alteration need be made at the back edge of the gore. If the hip measure of the pattern is the correct size, this chalk outline of the full length of the front edge of the breadth will not be necessary, but any alteration made at the hip to make it either larger or smaller must be carried to the bottom of the skirt.

When only the waist size is to be increased, lay the pattern correctly on the material and allow a sufficient amount at each seam to make up the extra amount required. Mark with chalk the outline of the pattern from hip to waist, then measure the necessary allowance at the waist outside of the outline, and draw a chalk-line touching the pattern outline at the hip and gradually widening to the allowed amount at the waist. An allowance of three-eighths of an inch at both sides of a seam, as at the top of the front gore, and of the first side gore, will equal three-quarters of an inch when the seam is made. The same allowance (three-eighths of an inch) at the waist-line of each of the next two gores will give another three-quarters of an inch, and one-half inch at the waist-line of the back edge of the second side gore will complete the required amount of two inches.

At No. 19 may be seen, also, the allowance that should be made at the top of the front and side gores when the abdomen is prominent. In this case it is not enough to allow extra width only, but each gore must be extended an inch or more at the top, gradually decreasing until it meets the edge of the second gore at its back edge. This extra length at the top of the skirt will prevent it from drawing up in the front and standing out at the bottom in a point, or "poking out," as is sometimes said. All garments, whether dresses, petticoats or drawers, should have this allowance left at the top of the front when cutting if the figure is full at the front. Always mark the outline of the pattern as a guide in fitting, but leave enough material above it to raise the waist-line sufficiently to make the garment hang in a straight line at the front, from the fullest point of the abdomen to the lower edge.

When the waist size of a circular skirt is to be changed, it is advisable, if much alteration is required, to cut one-half of the skirt in cheap lining cambric and fit this before cutting the material. If the waist is to be made very much smaller, it may be necessary to make

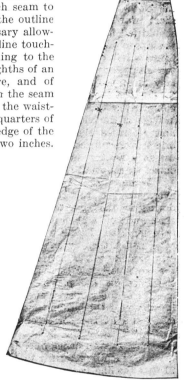

No. 21.—Alteration on a Breadth of a Plaited Skirt

one or two small darts, but if only a small reduction is necessary, it may often be "shrunk in." In this case it will not be necessary to make the cambric pattern, but when the skirt is fitted, mark on the waist-line where the reduction is necessary, and gather this portion, on a strong thread, to the required size. Dampen the material or place the wet sponge cloth over it and press it over a round cushion, repeating this until the cloth has shrunk in to the correct size. This needs to be done very carefully in order not to leave any "bubbles" in the cloth, but when properly done, it is most satisfactory.

When the waist size is to be made much larger the cambric pattern will be necessary Mark on it the hip-line five and three-eighth inches from the upper edge, as directed for the gored skirt. Pin the half-skirt to the figure and be careful to keep the front edge straight and exactly at the centre. Slash the top of the skirt from the waist to the hip-line in as many .places as necessary to make the waist the correct size and to make it hang correctly from the hips toward the lower edge. Try to make these slashes come at about the places the seams would be in a gored skirt. Pin a tape to the skirt at the waist-line, and be careful that it holds these slashes open in the proper way. Remove the skirt and pin or baste pieces of cambric under the V-shaped slashes; then try on the skirt again to be sure the alteration from the waist to hip is correct. Lay the half-skirt on a table and smooth out the upper part where the alteration has been made until it lies perfectly flat. This will throw an excess of fulness into the lower part of the skirt and will form ripples or "flutes" that will begin at the lower point of each of the slashes. Lay these ripples in flat plaits, pinning them in place so the half-skirt will lie perfectly flat and may be used as a pattern by which the cloth skirt may be cut. A short ripple or circular skirt should fall in straight lines from the hips to the lower edge. If the figure is full over the abdomen, the alteration at the waist-line may throw too much fulness into the front of the skirt, and it may be necessary to lay another plait in front of the one formed by the first V-shaped slash. The cambric half-skirt fitted and ready to use as a pattern in cutting the outside is shown at No. 20.

When a *plaited* skirt is too long, measure the same space down from the hip as in the gored skirt and fold a plait across, the necessary size. Equalize the seam edge, and it then becomes necessary to make a new line through the large perforations that show the lines for the plaits. Place one end of the yardstick at a perforation near the hip-line and the other end at the corresponding perforation near the bottom of the skirt. Draw a pencil line, and it will be seen by referring to No. 21 that the line passes a little inside of the perforation just below

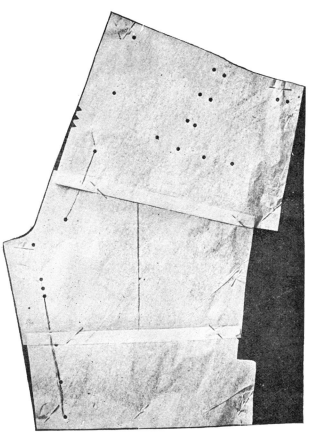

No. 22.—Back Portion of Boys' Knickerbockers

where the tuck was folded. A new perforation should be made on each line where necessary. The breadth is then marked and traced for the side or box plaits, as the case may be.

BOYS' PATTERNS.—It happens sometimes that a boy of five or six years will have the breast and waist measure of a nine-year-old size, though not the height. In such a case it is better to get a seven-year-old pattern—to divide the difference between the two extremes —and let out the under-arm, waist and shoulder allowance. It then becomes necessary to shorten the coat, the sleeves and trousers. The coat and sleeves are shortened in practically the same way as already shown in the woman's waist. Considerable care is needed in determining just where to shorten the trousers. The length of the under-waist to which they fasten has a great deal to do with their length when worn. It is well to measure an old pair of trousers on the child, taking the measure from the waist to the crotch and thence to just below the knee, allowing for the extra fulness to fall over the knee if knickerbockers are to be made. Any alteration in length above the crotch should be made across below the allowed extension for the pocket opening, changing the seam edges as little as possible. In the lower leg part, fold the plait across above the extension piece at the lower part of the leg. (No. 20.)

SHIRT-BLOUSES

THE title "shirt-blouse" or "shirt-waist" covers a large field, embracing the perfectly plain waist of linen, madras or flannel with a single narrow box-plait at the front and modelled on the style of a man's shirt, and advancing through varying degrees of elaboration to the shirred and draped models of silk, chiffon and lace. Though a shirt-waist needs careful fitting, not so much skill is required in the process, and it is quite possible to fit oneself. The neck requires care; it should not be trimmed out too much, and the neck-band should fit closely, though not tightly, to the neck, or the adjustment of a fancy collar or stock will be difficult. After the neck is satisfactorily fitted, the correct waist-line and the adjustment of the fulness at the front and centre back can be readily done by drawing a piece of tape around the waist and pinning it in proper places. Shirt-waists are usually made unlined, though in many patterns a lining is provided, its use being optional and much depending upon the material of which the waist is made. If this is transparent or a thin, soft silk, a lining is advisable; but for the ordinary waists of linen, the numerous fancy weaves of cotton and flannel, a well-fitted corset-cover answers about the same purpose as a lining. In the majority of instances sleeves are made to accord with the design of the shirt-waist. Plain shirt-waists have plain sleeves finished with shirt sleeve or band cuffs. More elaborate waists have the sleeves either tucked or box-plaited, completed with deep gauntlets or cuffs of fancy design.

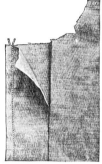

No. 1.—Making Simulated Box-Plait at Front

In making a plain shirt-waist the seams are joined in what is known as a French seam. A description and detail of the way to make a French seam is given in the chapter entitled "Hand Sewing Stitches."

The shoulder seams are never stitched until later, but are basted, and when the waist is tried on, any little adjustment may be made or fulness disposed without having to rip a finished seam.

A favorite model is a plain, seamless back with slight fulness at the waist. This may or may not be reinforced by a yoke portion, as the wearer prefers.

The front closing is finished on the right side by turning under the front edge at the indicating notches and simulating a box-plait—by making a backward-turning plait or tuck according to the perforations in the pattern. Place a row of stitching three-sixteenths of an inch, or whatever space may be directed in the pattern label, from each edge of the box-plait, being careful to catch in the front raw edge which has previously been turned under. Turn under the left edge of the front as directed on the pattern; this is usually an inch, and again a designated amount for a hem. The description may be readily understood by referring to No. 1, where the wrong side of the simulated plait is shown. Buttonholes are worked at the centre of the simulated box-plait, and buttons are sewed to the left side.

No. 2.—Gathers at Back of Waist

According to the perforations, the back is gathered at the waist-line, two or three rows being sufficient. These are stayed at the back with a strip of the material about half an inch wide and stitched all around, as shown at No. 2; or, if a tape is used to tie around the waist, this is adjusted in the same manner at the back, confining the fulness in place.

The fronts are also gathered, the fulness properly disposed so that the waist sets perfectly smooth under the arms, and the gathers reinforced on the wrong side by a stay of the same width as that at the back and long enough to extend just beyond the shirrings. Some shirt-waists are not gathered at the waist-line in front, but allowed to fall free from the neck and shoulders. In this event the belt or tape is applied to the outside at the back, over the gathers, and tied in front each time the garment is put on, adjusting the fulness to the liking of the wearer. Many prefer this plan, since some trouble in the making and laundering is obviated, and the same shirt-waist may be adjusted differently; that is, it may be drawn down tight, allowed to fall slightly pouched, or to be bouffant.

Where the waist is made very full in front or of heavy material, the front portion is frequently cut up to the waist-line at a point where the gathers commence, and the fulness gathered into a band. This band is an inch and a quarter deep when finished and is cut a trifle bias in front, as seen in No. 3. With this band the waist may be drawn down or allowed to pouch in front; it has also the added advantage that it does away completely with the quantity of material below the waist-line, which is so detrimental to the fit of a snugly adjusted skirt. The bottom of the remainder of the waist is finished with a quarter-inch hem. With waists developed in lace, embroidery or any of the more costly textiles a circular peplum is frequently added; this is made of the plain material, joined to the bodice at the bottom of the waist, extends below and holds the shirt-waist well in position. For waists with seamless backs and having no fulness the peplum-extension is employed to give the proper spring below the waist-line.

Shirt-waists opened in the front are usually made with adjustable collars, simply a collar band completing the neck of the garment. In making the collar band cut two sections

No. 4.—Neck-Band showing Protection Finish

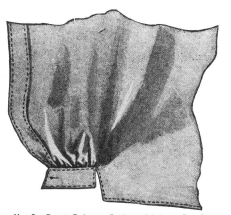

No. 3.—Front Fulness Gathered into a Band

like the pattern. Only one-quarter inch is allowed for seams on the neck-band and neck edges.

Place them together with the right sides facing. Stitch an even one-quarter-inch seam off the top and ends, turn the band right side out and crease and baste the edges. Sew the band to the neck of the waist through the inside section, having the seam on the right side; turn the seams up, turn in the remaining edge of the band and stitch the outside, fully covering the seam; continue this stitching all around the band.

Some of the waists show at the back of the neck-band the protection for the collar-button. This is formed in the following manner:

After the layers of the band have been stitched together and turned over, face the outside of the band at the centre of the back, by joining a strip of the material three inches long and the width of the band to the lower edge; turn over, crease the seam on the right side and stitch the desired length for slipping in the finger; allow the remaining edge to touch the top of the band without turning over. Sew the band to the neck, and face the back part by covering with a strip of material the same size (three inches long), stitching on the outside at the bottom and allowing it to touch the top of the band. This will afterward be caught in the upper ·stitching. When stitching the lower edge of the band, discontinue at the beginning of the protection stitching, and begin again at an equal distance on the opposite side. Draw the threads through and tie. At No. 4 is shown this band finished. The finger has just been slipped in and the illustration shows the band distended, ready for the button.

The buttonholes may now be worked, those in the collar band on the cross and those on the front box-plait preferably in a vertical position. Buttons are placed in corresponding position on the underlap; or if studs are to be worn, buttonholes are worked in both under and over lap. These are preferably made lengthwise and are finished at the ends with bar-tacks. The finished effect of both collar-band and box-plait with the positions of the buttonholes is shown at No. 5.

The removable standing collar is made with a double interlining. Place the outside and inside of the collar together with the right sides touching, and place a layer of interlining on each; join by seaming at the top and ends. Turn the right side out, crease the seam, turn in the lower edges and stitch all around; but if the collar is to be permanent, sew the latter edges to the neck. If a turn-down collar is to be made, the directions are practically the same, but a band section is placed on each side of the collar at the lower edge, with an interlining on one side; join, turn the band over, crease and finish the remaining edge by stitching.

No. 5.—Adjustment of Neck-Band

The buttonholes are worked crosswise, one in the centre of the back and one at each side of the front.

According to the edict of fashion the sleeve openings of shirt-waists vary their positions. Sometimes the opening may be made at the seam

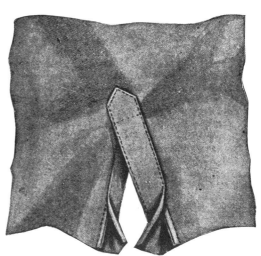

No. 6.—Over and Underlap for Shirt Cuff

at the inside of the arm, at the back of the sleeve or at the underside.

For a shirt cuff the sleeves are slashed at the wrist to the depth indicated, and an underlap is sewed to the back of the slash with the seam on the right side; crease the seam over on the lap, turn in

the top and remaining edge and stitch down, entirely covering the joining. The overlap is joined to the front of the slash on the right side, folded over on the perforations and all edges turned in except the lower one. Adjust the overlap so as to conceal entirely the underlap and baste in position. When this is properly arranged, stitch all around the overlap, keeping the point a good shape, and at the finish of the opening the stitching should cross the lap and catch through the underlap, holding the opening in correct position, as seen at No. 6.

The cuff is usually made with an interlining and sewed to the sleeve after it has been gathered, although some of these sleeves admit of very slight fulness. If a stud cuff-button is to be worn, the cuff is sewed across the underlap. If preferred,

No. 7.—Sleeve with Lapped Cuff, Opening at the Underside

buttons and buttonholes may be used instead on this plain lapped cuff, as shown at No. 7. If for links, the edges of the cuff must simply meet. If the lower portion of the cuff is shaped with a tab extension piece, that is stitched to the underlap on the sleeve. If the cuff has not this tab extension, it should not be joined to the underlap but should finish at the seam that joins the underlap to the sleeve. A button and buttonhole should be placed in the under and overlap close to the cuff. The finish for link cuff-buttons is shown at No. 8. The interlining for cuffs and collars should be of white linen or muslin.

SHIRT-WAISTS WITH TUCKS

When making tucked or plaited shirt-waists it will sometimes be found that the fronts, by reason of the number of tucks, are too wide to cut from one width of the goods; in this case it is necessary to piece the material, making the seam come where it will not show. At No. 9 the right front of a shirt-waist is shown with this seam made, the method of piecing being easily seen. The pattern should be laid on the material, and if this is not wide enough, the best place to make the joining must be considered, this depending on the width of the goods and the style of shirt-waist to be cut. In some cases it may be made at the stitching of the last tuck, but in others this tuck is not stitched to the waist, but terminates at yoke depth; consequently the seam would not be hidden. In the model illustrated the best place proved to be at the stitching of the first turned-back tuck on the right front. According to the instructions one inch *back* of the indicated fold edge of the tuck will be the stitching line, as the tucks are to be one inch wide. Mark this stitching line with chalk and, allowing three-eighths of an

No. 8.—Sleeve with Link-Button Cuff, Opening at Back

inch beyond it toward the front edge for seaming, cut off the rest of the material.

A piece wide enough to complete the front must now be joined at the stitching line, and when the tuck is made, both raw edges of this seam should be turned to one side and included in the tuck so that the seam is completely hidden on both the outside and the inside of the waist. It is quite likely that the left front may not need any piecing, since the manner of lapping the waist requires the right front to be much wider, the hem of the right front forming the first turned-back tuck on the left front; but if it should, the method is the same. The joining seam

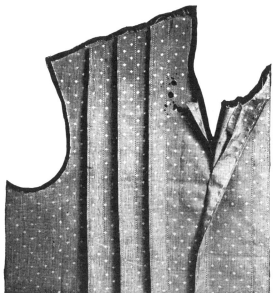

No. 9.—Right Front Pieced under Tuck

should always be made *under* the tuck and on the side toward which the tuck laps, never on the top. When one has a scant amount of material, as in remodelling, the joining may be made at the fold of the tuck, but this is not desirable if it can be avoided. A piece sufficiently wide to piece out the front may sometimes be cut from one side of the width from which the back is cut. The left front of the waist is to be cut off according to the directions on the label, and hemmed. Always open the pattern, identify each piece and get a clear idea of the construction by reading the label carefully before beginning to cut. This care at the beginning will make the work easier and save mistakes and consequent waste of material.

The closing of a waist of this description is best made with a narrow fly in which button-holes are worked. Usually this fly may be made from the piece that was cut off the left front. It should be made double, folded lengthwise through the centre, a seam turned in at each edge and the fold edges basted together; the fly when finished should be about one- eighth of an inch narrower than the hem of the right front (which in this case is one inch wide), and should be basted under the hem so the one row of stitching will make the hem and hold the fly. Buttonholes should be worked about two inches apart in the fly. To determine where to place the buttons, measure the space on the right front from the edge of the first turned-back tuck to the one just back of it, then measure the same space on the left front and place a colored thread at the line where the edge of the hem of the right front should reach. Bring the right front over to this line, and, using the buttonholes in the fly as a guide, mark on the left front the position for the buttons. Before sewing them on, baste a piece of tape to the inside of the waist at the line of the buttons to act as a stay-piece through which the stitches may be taken. The placing of the fly and the buttons is seen at No. 10. Reference to this illustration will also show the neck-band properly applied to the neck. It will be seen that the wide lap from right to left requires that the neck-band be longer on the right side than on the left, measuring from the centre back. If the neck-band supplied with the pattern is not the right size of one's neck, alteration should be made at the centre back, cutting the pattern straight across and pasting a piece of paper in the space to make it larger or lapping it at the centre to make it smaller. Any necessary alterations in the shirt-waist should be made at the shoulder and under-arm seams, never at the front. The

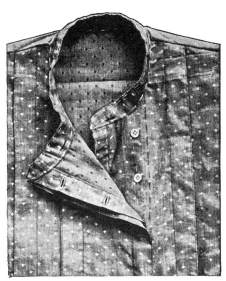

No. 10.—Fly, Buttons and Neck-Band

buttonholes, which may be worked in the front of the neck-band to accommodate the wearing of a linen collar, are indicated in the illustration by black threads. Work one at the back also.

No. 11.—Tucks Cut Away Below Waist

After the neck-band has been basted to the neck the shirt-waist should be tried on and arranged at the waist-line. If the figure corresponds exactly to the pattern measurements and no alterations are found necessary, the waist may be gathered across according to the per-forations in the pattern, but some persons, as previously stated, prefer to have a tape fastened at the back and leave the front and sides loose, adjusting the fulness each time the waist is worn by tying or buckling the tape at the front.

A neat and very satisfactory finish, espe-cially desirable for a stout figure, is made by slashing the material as shown at No. 11. When there is much fulness in the front of the waist it will be found a good plan to draw the sides of the waist toward the front (be careful not to disarrange the correct line of the seam joining the front to the back). The material will be slightly bias under the arm, and this should be drawn smoothly toward the front as far as it will reach and pinned at the waist; the tucks may then be lapped over each other, and the waist may be drawn down or bloused, as is most becoming. The plain portion that was drawn toward the front will lie under the lapped tucks and will dispose of a great deal of fulness in somewhat the same manner as a dart. The tape should be pinned around, carefully following the waist-line. When the waist is taken off, baste the tape in place; then take either a strong twilled tape or a narrow strip of the material with the edges turned in and baste along its *upper* edge to the inside of the waist, exactly following the line of the tape on the outside; then remove the outside tape and stitch the upper edge of the basted strip to the waist, after disposing of the fulness at the back by making two rows of gathers the width of the tape apart.

The lapped tucks at the front form too much thickness below the waist to be left in place, so this must be cut across just above the lower edge of the strip that is stitched to the inside. The cut must extend only as far as necessary to open out flat the piece so cut off, as seen at No. 11. The uneven upper edge of this piece may be trimmed and turned in and hemmed down to the part from which it was cut, providing sufficient length to hold the waist down but avoiding the excess of material. The piece joined to the waist is seen at No. 12. A row of stitching should be placed at the lower edge of the inside band, and this band will cover the

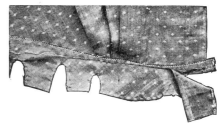

No. 12.—Extension Joined to Waist

raw edges of the cut portion at the front. The extension below the waist at the sides may need to be slashed several times in order that it may not draw over the hips. The lower edge is to be hemmed, and the hem may be carried around the slashes, or, if one prefers, small V-shaped pieces may be stitched into each of the slashes to provide the necessary amount of flare.

There are many patent appliances on the market for the purpose of holding the skirt and waist together at the back, but a simple and effective arrangement is to sew two, three or five button-holed rings to the back of the waist, as seen at No. 13. If two are used, each ring is an inch and one-eighth from the centre back, or they are placed one in the centre of the back with the others two inches apart. Hooks are sewed with the same spacing to the inside of the skirt belt. Do not use hooks any larger than are necessary to fit into the rings.

No. 13.—Covered Rings at Back of Waist

The bishop sleeve accompanying this shirt-waist has only a short slash at the cuff opening, and this is finished by sewing a straight strip of the material continuously along both edges of the slashed opening, the strip of material being the same width all its length. The other side is turned over and hemmed by hand or machine-stitched, to cover the seam first made. This applied band is seen at No. 14, and when the edge of the sleeve is gathered, this little band is turned under at the upper or overlapping edge of the slashed opening and extends on the underside to form an underlap. Two pieces are cut for each cuff, and an interlining of coarse muslin or crinoline, that will hold the starch when the waist is laundered, may be basted to the wrong side of one cuff piece; the second piece is then basted to the first, the right sides of the material facing each other. A seam is stitched along both ends and the side on which there is no notch, which will be the lower edge of the cuff. Trim off the seam at the corners and turn the cuff—baste around the seamed edge. Sew the cuff portion to which the stiffening was basted to the edge of the sleeve, making the seam toward the outside; turn under the edge of the outer cuff piece and baste it to the sleeve, covering the seam just made.

No. 14.—Straight Band Hemmed to Opening in Bishop Sleeve

No. 15.—Cuff Basted to Sleeve

The inner cuff piece is really the cuff lining and may be made of lining material if necessary, though the waist material is preferable. The cuff basted to the sleeve is seen at No. 15. One or two rows of machine-stitching should be made from the outside entirely around the cuff, and it may be more conveniently handled in stitching if the sleeve is turned wrong side out. In sleeves where the cuff opening comes at the seam, the cuff may be put on the sleeve before this seam is joined, when it may be more easily managed. If the cuff is intended for wear with link buttons it should finish at the edge of the slashed opening, and the underlap should be turned in at the top and left free from the cuff that the two ends may just meet and not lap.

Generally when the closing for the cuff is made at the seam, no lap or facing is used; the seam is left open a short distance and its edges are hemmed. A buttonholed bar finishes the opening and prevents the seam from ripping. A lap cuff must be used with this sleeve opening, and the fancy cuff shown at No. 16 is novel and pretty. The illustration shows the way to apply it to the sleeve. The cuff and its lining are first seamed together, leaving the upper edge open from the plain end to the notch. It is then turned and the cuff is basted to the sleeve (which has been gathered), according to directions on the pattern, and stitched all around with two or more rows of stitching. Buttons and buttonholes provide the closing; the cuff may be interlined if desired.

No. 16.—Sleeve Opening at Seam, with Fancy Cuff

The top of the sleeve should be gathered between the notches, and if it is very full, a second row of gathers three-eighths of an inch below the first gives a good effect at the armhole. A narrow, bias strip of cambric should be stitched in the same seam that stitches the sleeve into the armhole, and this strip is afterward turned over and stitched around to form a binding to the armhole as seen at No. 17. Or if the top of the sleeve is not too full, it may be sewed in with a French seam—first on the right and then on the wrong side. Directions for which are given in the chapter "Hand Sewing Stitches."

LINED SHIRT-WAISTS

Although shirt-waists are generally made unlined, a lining is provided in some patterns; and this lining differs from the lining used for a closely fitted tailored or draped waist. It reaches only to the waist-line and has but one dart, and is not in so many pieces, as the curved shaping at the waist and hips is not required. For the same reason a much simpler method of boning may be employed than that described for the fitted waists. A silk waist would, perhaps, be better lined, especially if for wear in cool weather, both for warmth and because the lining will protect the silk from strain and make it wear longer. No. 18 shows the front of a lining in state of preparation. The lining should be basted and fitted, any necessary alterations made and the under-arm seams stitched. A hem is usually allowed on the fronts, but even if only a seam three-eighths of an inch wide is allowed, this front line should be traced. In fitting, bring the fronts together and pin them on this tracing, forming a seam toward the outside. Alteration may be made on this front seam also if necessary, and it should be marked to form a corrected front line, then turned over for a hem. If it is to be faced, the edge is trimmed to leave only a seam beyond this line. Cut a straight piece of the lining two inches wide, and a trifle longer than the front edge of the lining, to serve as a facing for each side of the front.

No. 17.—Binding the Armhole

Place a piece on the outside of the lining with one edge even with the edge of the front, and stitch a seam three-eighths of an inch back from the edge; turn the facing over, making the fold come just at the seam, place a row of stitching one-eighth of an inch back of the edge and make a second row three-eighths of an inch back of the first. Make a second row of stitching three-eighths of an inch beyond the first row at each of the seams, notch the edges that extend beyond the stitching, and into each of the casings thus formed run a piece of whale or feather bone and tack it in place, as seen in the dart seam at No. 19.

Place a bone in the casing made at each of the front edges, allowing it to reach to about the same height as the bone in the dart seam. Spread the back part of each hook and sew them on, alternating a hook and an eye as seen in No. 18. Place the hooks well inside the edge and sew through the two rings at the back and also around the hook end, sewing this to the row of stitching near the edge. Sew completely through, allowing the stitches to show on the outside of the lining. Be sure to place the bone in the front before sewing the hooks and eyes on the lower part of the fronts. Observe care in sewing the hooks and eyes on the second side of the front that they shall be in exactly corresponding positions to those sewed to the first side. Turn under a seam at the edge of the facing piece and hem it over to the first row of stitching, covering the sewed parts of the hooks and eyes as seen at No. 19.

No. 19.—Hem or Facing Covering Hooks and Eyes

The under-arm seam of the outside may be basted separately from the lining, although it is frequently joined in the same seam. The shoulder seams are usually included in the same seam with those of the lining. If any alterations have been made at these seams in fitting the lining, corresponding alterations must be made in the seams of the outer waist.

At No. 20 is shown the way to close the outer waist parts when the lining is used. The method is always practically the same in waists of this description. The outside is placed on the lining with the centre front of the outside (which in this case is the centre of the middle box-plait) at the edge of the lining. The outer waist is basted to the lining at the neck and the armholes only. The left outer front is placed on the left lining front in such a way that the tucks or plaits on both front portions shall correspond when the waist is fastened. This must be ascertained by hooking the lining at the front and bringing the lap on the right outside part over the left until the parts correspond; the left outer front is then pinned to the lining in this position and is basted to it at the neck and armholes, as was the right side. Small hooks should be sewed to the right front and button-holed loops to correspond worked on the left front; or a fly with buttonholes may be attached to the right front, as previously described, and buttons sewed to the left.

No. 18.—Dart in Lining Stitched for the Bone

It is generally preferable to finish the neck with a neck-band and make the collar detachable, that different collars and stocks may be worn with the same waist. The sleeves should be basted into the waist in an ordinary seam; try on the waist to see that the sleeves are properly arranged and note if any slight adjustment needs to be made at any part of the waist; this is best attended to now before the waist is considered finished. When stitching the sleeves in the armhole include in the seam the bias strip for binding the edge, as previously explained. Turn this over and hem by hand, fully covering all raw edges.

LINGERIE WAISTS WITH INSETS OF LACE

The shirt-waists buttoned in the back, although great favorites, apparently divide the honors with those buttoned in front. Among the simple models, the variety lies not so much in the multiplicity of designs as in the different adjustment of trimming. Insertions of various widths are arranged full length, front and back, or simply the front is decorated; again, the arrangement is in yoke outline between clusters of tucks. Others, which are plain in effect, have the front and back laid in box-plaits, with the sleeves either plain or plaited to match the waist.

Although many varieties of lace insertions and edgings are used, Valenciennes seems to be the favorite; principally, perhaps, because it adapts itself so readily to shaping into curves, medallions and designs, under which the material may be cut away. There is a thread woven in each edge of the insertion

No. 20.—Material Waist over the Lining

and at the straight side of the edging lace by which it may be drawn up as on a gathering thread. It is often combined with other kinds of lace; one sees medallions of Irish crochet or other heavy lace as the central figure from which radiate lines and loops of Valenciennes, the whole forming a design that almost covers the original material. The waist at No. 21 is a happy combination of two favorites—eyelet embroidery and Valenciennes insertion. The embroidery is of the all-over variety, to be bought by the yard; a pattern with well-separated figures was secured. The lace is basted to the waist in long lines, and the curves are so arranged that it will run between the figures. The same arrangement of lace would be effective on a waist of plain lawn or batiste.

Ordinarily the lace would be machine-stitched in place, but when time and patience may be depended upon, the lace may be held to the waist by using the imitation hemstitching or fagoting stitch. This is done with a very coarse needle and a very fine cotton, and looks like hemstitching, although it requires no threads to be drawn; the stitch is called Bermuda Fagoting, and is fully illustrated and explained in our book entitled, "Embroideries and Their Stitches"; price 25 cents. The lace should be

No. 21.—All-over Embroidery with Lace

pinned on the waist in the desired design, then basted with small stitches very close to each edge. Cut away the material that lies under the lace, leaving only one-eighth of an inch inside the bastings at each side; turn back this edge and work the fagoting stitch through the foundation material and this turned-back edge together, and across the edge of the lace. The open-work stitch adds to the beauty of the lace and produces an excellent finish.

Simple designs, as suggestions, are seen at Nos. 22 and 23. The lace in these cases is machine-stitched in place, the material is cut away underneath, and the edges rolled back and overcast. No. 24 shows a yoke where hand-embroidery is combined with the lace insertion, the lace radiating from the neck forming panels with the embroidery between.

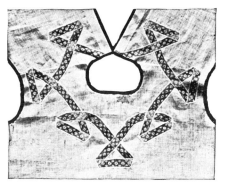

No. 22.—Valenciennes Insertion in a Lawn Waist

No. 23.—Valenciennes Insertion

Valenciennes edging is applied to the waist front seen at No. 25, but in the same way as described for applying the insertion. A round dot is worked in satin stitch, with embroidery cotton to fill the centre of each of the lace wheels.

It is quite important that the plain lower part of a lingerie sleeve shall follow the shape of the forearm and fit nicely, though not tightly, at the wrist. To accomplish this it is advisable to leave the seam at the inner or thumb side of the arm open from one to two inches. For an unlined sleeve of thin material French seams are best, and when preparing the sleeve for fitting,

No. 24.—Lace and Embroidery

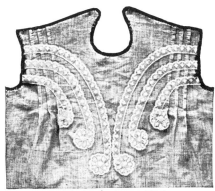

No. 25.—Valenciennes Edging

baste it with the seams toward the outside. Fit them in as closely as required and baste the alterations. Stitch the seams one-quarter of an inch *outside* of the basting and cut the extra seam away one-eighth of an inch beyond the stitching. Remove the bastings, turn the sleeve and baste it again in the same place, but from the *inside*, and stitch it, making a quarter-inch seam. This completes the French seam. While the sleeve is still basted the inner seam should be ripped up as far as necessary to allow the hand to pass easily through the wrist opening. Both sides of the opening should be finished with a narrow hem, and small lace buttons sewed to one side of the opening and buttonholed loops made at the other. This wrist finish is seen at No. 26, with a tiny lace frill falling over the hand.

The long sleeve that extends an inch or more over the hand is usually graceful and becoming. It is prepared and fitted in the way already described, though this style sleeve requires two sleeve seams as seen in a sleeve lining, to fit it properly. After the sleeve is fitted, and before stitching, open the inner seam at the narrowest part of the wrist to allow width for the hand to slip through, but not to extend the opening to the end of the sleeve. Hem the opening and close with buttons and loops as shown at No. 27. When the material is very thin and soft the sleeve need not be fitted in so closely at the wrist but may be left large enough for the hand to slip through, then drawn in at the wrist by buttons and buttonholed loops placed at each side of the seam as seen at No. 28. The buttons employed for this purpose should be inconspicuous and match the waist in color. Lace buttons are best for a white lingerie waist, but for a color that may be difficult to match, the small brass

No. 26.—Fitted Sleeve Opened at the Wrist

rings, used in many instances instead of the eye that accompanies a hook, may be used. Cover them by buttonholing with twist of the gown color, then cross the thread from side to side, twisting it and making the threads meet in the centre, at which point they may be sewed on like buttons. Buttonholed loops of the same twist will fasten over them. A ring button is shown at No. 29.

The plain lower portion of a puff sleeve which is unlined is joined to the puff part in a French seam and a piece of tape should be sewed at the inside to this seam, and again to the seam of the puff part to hold it to the proper length and allow the puff to droop over the lower or gauntlet portion.

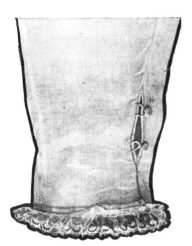

No. 27.—Sleeve Fitted Over the Hand

Fashion dictates whether the sleeve shall be open at the front, back or under portion, but whether at one point or another it is necessary in a good-looking shirt-blouse, to have the wrist quite snug-fitting and not permit it to remain large enough that the hand may be conveniently slipped through. To this end the several methods of finishing with buttons and buttonholes are given. Sometimes, in the deep gauntlet cuffs, buttons and buttonholes are arranged at the back seam reaching from the elbow to the wrist, and while on some occasions the upper part of the gauntlet may be closed, with the opening only at the wrist, it is in better taste to open the cuff to the elbow and have the buttonholes worked the entire length.

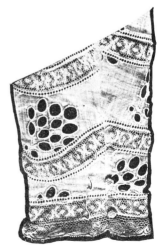

No. 29.—A Ring Button

No. 28.—Buttons and Loops at Wrist

The stock collar is joined to the waist permanently and is usually composed of rows of the lace insertion with perhaps beading between. A frill of lace or ruching finishes the upper edge. Uprights of collar featherbone should be placed on a slanting line each side of the centre front and one on the left side of the centre back on a line with the buttons. Worked loops are placed here to correspond with the eyes on the right side of the collar.

DRAPED WAISTS

THE construction of a waist requires the most minute attention to every detail, but if extreme care be observed all through the work and sufficient perseverance exercised, one can be reasonably sure of a good effect. For a draped bodice the lining is made separately; it is fitted, and the seams are pressed open and boned before the outer material is adjusted. The seams must be slashed at the proper points and enough to allow the lining to fit in snugly. The boning must be of the correct height for the figure that is being fitted, and the "spring" of the bones must be just right. On all such small items depends the effect of the finished waist, and accounts for the home-made look so often deplored.

When cutting the lining, observe the perforations indicating the grain of the goods. If the directions in this respect are not followed exactly, the waist-line of each section of the pattern will not come on the correct grain, and a lining that will stretch out of shape will be the result. The fronts or backs are reinforced and this sufficiently strengthens the place of closing.

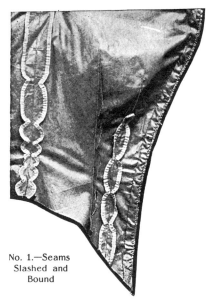

No. 1.—Seams Slashed and Bound

Some dressmakers advocate cutting cotton linings across the grain of the material, but it does not cut to such good advantage in this way. The argument is that the completed lining will not stretch and that it is not so likely to split. A correctly fitted and boned lining will stretch very little, if any, and the lining may be strengthened by making it double at the points where the greatest strain will come.

To accomplish this do not cut out the darts, but before basting the dart seams, baste an extra piece of lining from the front of the waist to the second or back dart and reaching from the top of the dart to the bottom of the lining. Now cut up the centre of each dart between the rows of perforations, then bring the tracings of these perforations together and beginning at the top, baste the darts and include the stay pieces in the seams. This is particularly desirable for a stout figure. A waist fastening at the back has the back forms reinforced to corresponding height. Directions for finishing a draped waist which is closed at the back are given in the chapter "Wedding and Evening Gowns."

At the seams of the under-arms, the shoulders, and the darts, mark the sewing line by running the tracing-wheel along the line formed by the large perforations. Do this when cutting the lining and while it is doubled, that both sides may be marked exactly alike. Read carefully the instructions contained in the label of the pattern. Mark with a colored thread the small perforations that indicate the waist-line and also those marking the elbow in the large sleeve portion, and where the front seam of the sleeve should be placed in sewing the sleeve into the armhole of the waist. Baste the seams of the lining portions, first pinning them along and matching the notches.

Dressmakers usually baste the under-arm and shoulder seams toward the outside for the first fitting, for it is at these seams that the alterations, if any, are to be made, and this can be more easily done if the seams are toward the outside. It will be better for the amateur to baste them with moderately small stitches than to depend on pins. When the waist is first put on, draw it toward the front and, bringing the two raw edges together, pin them as in a seam, taking the first pin at the marks indicating the waist-line. Smooth the pattern over the figure at both front and back, and be careful that the indicated waist-line of the pattern is at the waist-line of the person being fitted. Make alterations at the under-arm seam and, if necessary, at the front edge.   Draw the lining up well at the shoulder seams, but not enough to draw it from the correct waist-line; it may be fitted here a little more snugly at the final fitting.

If the armholes feel too tight be very careful not to gouge them out under the arms or around the front; this done too hastily often results in ruining the waist.   The best plan is to snip the armholes for about three-eighths of an inch; this will be found to give sufficient spring and the sleeve will be stitched in just beyond the end of the snippings.   If, however, this does not give sufficient ease to the armhole, pare the seams off a little and snip the seams a trifle deeper.   The same caution applies to the neck.

Pin the alterations carefully, and remove the lining.   Mark the alterations by running the tracing-wheel along the seam, and be careful that it marks through both sides of the altered seam; then remove the pins and mark the tracing marks on each piece with a colored thread, as the tracing marks are apt to fade.   Mark the alterations on the other side of the waist by using the corrected side as a pattern.   Baste the seams again, this time with the seams toward the inside.   Now stitch all seams except the shoulder seams; these are left open until after the material has been draped.   Stitch the seams just outside the basting so as not to make the waist any tighter.   This also allows the bastings to be drawn easily.   If the seam is stitched directly on top of the basting, both rows will be so interwoven that it will be almost impossible to pull out the bastings, and besides, the waist is likely to be too tight after it is boned.   Notch the seams at the waist-line and two or three times above and below—enough to allow them to lie flat when pressed.   Bind the seams neatly with taffeta seam binding, run on loosely, and press the seams open.   Some dressmakers prefer to overcast the seams, and most of the imported French dresses are finished in this way, but it does not present as neat a finish and occupies a great deal of time, as the overcasting must be done closely and very neatly. No. 1 shows a seam bound and another notched and ready to bind.   It also shows the notching necessary to make the side seam lie flat when it is pressed open.   When no hem is allowed at the front edge of the lining, it is necessary to face it.   Cut two pieces of the lining material in the same outline as the front and two inches wide.   Baste one on the outside of each front, stitch a seam at the edge, and turn the facing over toward the inside.   Place a row of stitching one-eighth of an inch inside the edge and another far enough inside the first to allow a whalebone or featherbone to be slipped in.   If a hem is allowed at the closing edge turn it over toward the inside of the lining and make the two rows of machine-stitching to form a casing for the bone.

Whalebone may be bought in strips one-yard long, about three yards being required to bone a waist.   Get a medium-weight quality and let the whalebone soak in warm water to soften, so the needle can be passed through it.

No. 2—Whalebone
Properly Sprung

A bone is slipped into the casing just formed at each side of the closing, allowing it to reach to within an inch of the top of the first dart, and sewed through the lining and the bone near the top to hold it in place.   Round the ends of the bones and shave them for half an inch to make the bone thinner there, using a dull knife or blade of the scissors.

Sew the hooks and eyes down the place of closing after the bone is in place.   Alternate a hook and an eye, an inch and one-quarter apart, down one side; then measure the other side against this, having them even at the top and bottom, and mark with pins the places on that side.   Be sure that a hook and an eye come opposite each other.   They should be sewed firmly and entirely through the lining.

Hem back over the hooks and eyes, the silk or percaline of the allowed hem or facing, bringing it close up under the turned-over part of hook and covering the sewing, (No. 1.)

The seams should now be boned.   For whalebone or the uncovered featherbone that is now made to slip into a bone-casing and used in the same manner as whalebone, mark on each seam the point where the bone is to start.   Five inches above the waist-line is the rule, the bone to finish half an inch above the lower edge of the waist.   Procure a piece of single bone-casing, or Prussian binding, as it is called.   This may be had in several colors but black or white is preferable; do not cut it in lengths before sewing on.   Double over one inch and over-hand the edges together to make a little pocket.   Do not sew this pocket fast to the seam but begin three-quarters of an inch down from its folded-over end to sew the casing on with a running stitch.   Sew both edges, holding the casing somewhat full and keeping it over the middle of the seam.   Run the bone into the pocket at the top of each casing and fasten it there by sewing through both bone and casing.   Sew through again three inches above the waist-line.   Then push the bone very tight, so it will stretch out the seam and give the curve

No. 3.—Hook and Eye on Ends of Belt Tape

or spring at the waist.   Sew through bone and casing again one inch from the bottom.   (No. 2.)   Do not spring the bones in the front so much as at the sides and back.   The greatest curve is required at the side seams, and less at the front and back.

For covered featherbone, the method is somewhat different, since it is adjusted to position on the machine, without an applied casing.   A machine attachment for this purpose is convenient, but not absolutely necessary.   The seams of the waist are pressed, bound and marked as for whaleboning.   The covering is ripped about half an inch on one end of the featherbone, the bone is cut away, then the covering is turned over the end, making a neat finish.   This finished end is placed over the seam at

the mark, and, keeping the centre of the bone over the centre of the seam—stitched to the lining seam.   Care must be taken to push the bone up and draw the lining down while stitching, as otherwise the lining is likely to be held in on the bone, which causes it to wrinkle. Its adaptability, inexpensiveness and convenience in applying have made featherbone very popular.

The bone is cut off a trifle shorter than the mark for the length of the waist, a bias strip of crinoline is basted to the inside of the lower edge and both lining and crinoline are turned in and basted.

Cut a belt of the webbing, which is sold for the purpose.   Make it three inches longer than the waist meas-

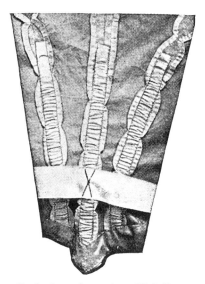

No. 4.—Bones Sprung in and Belt Tape Tacked to Back Seam

ure; turn back one inch and one-half at each end, sew a hook on one end and an eye on the other, and hem the raw edges over them, as shown at No. 3.   Mark the centre of this belt and sew it to the centre-front seam if the waist opens in the back—or the centre-back, if it is made to open in the front—and to the next seam on each side of it.   Place the lower edge of the belt one-half inch above the waist-line; sew firmly across the width of the belt with a long cross-stitch to the inside of the seam. (No. 4.)

No. 5.—Frills, as Padding, at Armhofe

If the figure is flat over the bust, arrange the taffeta bust ruffles as directed for the evening waist.   For a figure which is hollow around the armholes, similar ruffles may be placed as shown in No. 5.   Then arrange the lining on the bust form.

The waist is now ready to be draped, the process being greatly facilitated by the use of the bust form. Cut the material for the outside of the waist by the pattern for that part and attach it to the lining according to the corresponding perforations and notches, as described in the label of the pattern. In the draped waists, which are generally worn now, the outside material is usually not caught in with the lining at any seam except the shoulder seam. However, there are occasions when the material is caught in the under-arm seams as well; these are not stitched when the other seams of the waist are, but are left basted until the entire waist is draped. When the seams of the lining are all stitched and boned the outside is adjusted in this manner:

The material for the back of the waist, after being prepared according to the directions accompanying the pattern, should be pinned to the lining straight down the centre of the back, being drawn well down, then across toward the sides; pin it at the shoulder, the armhole and down the under-arm seam, stretching it down that it may lie smooth and flat, and placing the pins near enough together to hold it well in place. The front is then draped on the lining according to the indicating perforations and notches at the neck and shoulder, but when the draped portion of the waist is reached a very elastic material may require to be stretched or drawn a little more tightly than one of firmer texture, and allowance must be made for this fact in matching the perforations that indicate where the outer material is to be tacked to the lining. When the front drapery is arranged from the shoulder to the bust-line, pin carefully about the armhole, then arrange the drapery below the bust; make the rounded part of the bust that lies at the second dart of the lining a central point from which to work the drapery in both directions. Draw the front drapery toward the under-arm seam, turn under the raw edge and fit it in a straight, well-shaped line to cover the raw edge of the back drapery. Pin this in place to be sure the line is good.

No. 6.—The Front Waist-Drapery Lapped Across the Back at the Under-Arm

After the other side has been draped and pinned in the same manner (making the same changes on both sides), remove the waist from the form and sew the front and back together by hand, slip-stitching with close stitches from top to bottom of the seam holding all firmly together.

Another method of finishing this seam under the arm is to drape it on the form as directed, but after pinning the drapery and being sure that the line is good, baste this folded edge through the front drapery only; remove the pins and place a row of machine-stitching, using silk the same color as the material, close to the edge. Pin the stitched edge in place again, stretching it down well. This seam is pictured at No. 6. Pin the other side in the same manner, remove the waist from the form and stitch by hand, taking the stitches through the row of machine-stitching made in the front portion. Try on the waist after draping and, if it is correct, stitch the shoulders. Then press them open and finish like the other seams, because it often happens that boning pushes the waist up so that it needs taking up a little more on the shoulders.

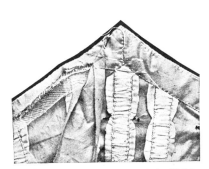

No. 7.—Facing the Bottom of the Waist

If the material is heavy or there is any likelihood of the lower edge of the waist being bulky, this portion is finished as directed in the chapter "Wedding and Evening Gowns," that is, facing the bottom before the material is draped on the outside. If the material is thin and it is desirable to turn up the outside portion and the lining together, turn the outer material over the turned-over lower edge of the lining. Both outer material and lining may then be cat-stitched to the crinoline. A narrow bias facing of lining silk is hemmed to the turned-over edge and the upper edge of this facing is hemmed to the lining. The bottom facing is shown at No. 7. Mitre the point at the back as shown.

A desirable way to finish waists that are to be worn without a belt is to cord the edge. Cut strips of the material an inch and three-quarters wide, baste in a medium-size cable cord one-half an inch from one edge. Sew the cord to the lower edge of the waist. The wide side of the bias strip may have its edge turned under and be hemmed to the lining to form the facing. The method of applying this cord facing is shown at No. 8.

No. 8.—Inside View of Cord Finish and Facing in One

For a waist made to hook over on the left side these directions may be followed with very few exceptions, but before stitching the lining fronts the left side is faced with the material. This is more easily applied when the lining is flat and should continue across the shoulders, around the armhole and down the side, as depicted in No. 9, being at least two inches wide at all points. It is best cut from the piece without seams, but if this is impossible on account of the material being inadequate, joinings may be made, forming mitres at the upper and lower points of the armhole. These seams should be pressed flat so that the joinings are as inconspicuous as possible.

The seams of the lining are joined and boned, and the hooks and eyes applied to the front as previously directed. Although the material is in one piece across both fronts, the lining is hooked down the centre. If desired, the hooks and eyes may alternate for the entire length.

Hook the lining together on the bust form and

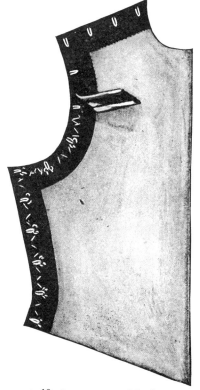

No. 10.—Arrangement of Hooks at Left Side

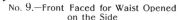

No. 9.—Front Faced for Waist Opened on the Side

drape the material according to the design selected. Before removing from the form, mark the left side through the material alone, at the shoulder line, the line for sewing in the sleeve and the under-arm seam. Remove from the form. After these are basted fit a piece of crinoline around the above-mentioned places as pictured in No. 10. Turn over the edge and cat-stitch; sew the hooks at equal distances apart and in the positions shown in the illustration. Buttonholed loops are worked on the opposite side in corresponding positions.

After the sleeves are inserted the correct position for these loops is indicated by pinning the outer front over the lining of the left side and marking directly opposite each hook. These buttonholed loops are worked on the facing and directly on the seams and are made in the manner explained in the chapter "Hand Sewing Stitches." They should be made firm and strong so that they will stand the strain placed upon them. Face the shoulder and under-arm, covering the sewing of the hooks with a piece of bias silk, but shape the piece to be used for the armhole.

It is always advisable to close the collar at the back, whether the waist closes at the front, the back or even the side. If a collar of the dress material is used it should be interlined with

No. 11.—Collar Applied to Neck

crinoline, then turned over on all its edges. If the waist is closed at the back the collar is simply slip-stitched all around to the neck. If closed at the left side the entire collar, except a small portion at the back, is stitched firmly to the neck, and the left lining neck, which is free, is bound with ribbon. For a waist with front closing bind the left side of the neck with seam binding, pin the collar around the right side, with the centre of the collar at the front edge of the right front and the right end of the collar one-quarter of an inch to the left side of the centre-back seam. Sew the collar to the neck, being careful not to catch the stitches through the outside material. Sew three hooks on the left end of the collar (on the inner side) and one to its lower edge about half-way of the left side. Cut the facing (preferably of silk) the same shape as the collar. Turn in the edges of the facing and hem it to the collar and to the neck of the right side of the waist. Work three buttonholed

No. 12.—Fulness at Elbow
of Sleeve Lining

loops at the right end of the collar and one in the left side of the waist at the neck, to catch the hook sewed at the lower edge of the collar and prevent it from riding up from the waist. The collar and facing are seen at No. 11.

If the collar is made of transparent material the crinoline should not be used, but the collar may be held up by strips of collar bone as explained for transparent collars in the chapter "Wedding and Evening Gowns."

MAKING THE SLEEVES

The making of sleeves is considered by the amateur, and many dressmakers, as the most difficult part of the costume. There being two to be made exactly alike, greater caution is necessary from the time the sleeves are cut until they are inserted and sewed in the armhole. If not cut and basted correctly, one sleeve may be larger than the other; and if not stitched in the armhole exactly alike, one may twist and the other hang without a wrinkle.

The first step before cutting is to study the instructions on the label of the pattern. Read these carefully, as each label is different irrespective of the fact that certain sleeves look very much alike. Measure for the sleeve as instructed in the chapter "The Correct Method of Altering Patterns" and make the necessary changes.

Next, the sleeve must be accurately cut and carefully basted. Much depends upon correct basting and the exact location of the elbow, since a very ill-fitting sleeve may result through carelessness in either direction.

To be very accurate, the pattern may have the three-eighths inch seam marked off; this is traced through the pattern to the lining with a tracing wheel, the back seam being traced through the line of perforations.

In joining waist and sleeve seams short basting stitches are employed, as pictured at No. 12. Never place machine-stitching directly on top of a basting; if the seam is stitched just outside the basting there will be no difficulty in removing the latter. Enough cannot be said of careful basting, as, next to cutting, it is the groundwork of dressmaking. If it is poorly done, it is the source of many future difficulties.

No. 13.—Correct Location of Front Seam

If a fancy sleeve is to be made, the lining must be fitted first and the material draped or arranged later. In basting the lining, place the under piece of the sleeve upon the upper with the notches of the front seam together and pin in position; then baste this seam with small running stitches. Pin the back seam through the outlet perforations from the top to the upper notch, and again from the lower notch to the bottom. The surplice material of the upper sleeve portion is gathered into the space between the notches to form the elbow, and the seam is basted full length. The sleeve should always be basted through the tracings, since in doing so the same width of the seam will be taken off both upper and under and the outlet basted correctly on the line of perforations.

Adjust the sleeve in the proper position, draw it up well on the arm, so that the elbow is in the correct location, and pin the sleeve in the armhole, with the front seam to the indicating mark as directed in the label. It may be perfectly correct in a great many instances, but if the sleeve does not set correctly, move the front seam either above or below the mark as the case demands.

In a sleeve which sets properly after basting, it will be noticed that the front seam instead of continuing along the edge, when laid flat on the table, will roll somewhat toward the under of the sleeve from the centre of the seam to the wrist, as shown at No. 13. This is quite important, as many workers imagine that the sleeve should set perfectly flat the length of this seam, with the seam directly on the edge.

No. 14.—Wrist of Sleeve Prepared for Facing

Drape the material sleeve on the lining, remove the bastings and press the seams flat. Clip the front seam, then overcast or bind with a narrow silk binding ribbon. An interlining of plain crinoline is placed in the bottom, one to two inches deep. With the sleeve right side out, roll the crinoline until it can be slipped into the wrist. Place the hand inside and move the fingers about until the crinoline fits the shape without either drawing or falling in folds; then baste. The work is now done from the wrong side. Turn the sleeve inside out and turn up the bottom three-eighths of an inch. (No. 14.) Cat-stitch this to hold it down, then press. Face the wrist with a bias piece of silk, and slip-stitch or hem at the upper and lower edges. Any embellishment or trimming· is added and the sleeve fully finished before it is basted in the armhole.

The sleeve now fits the arm correctly and comfortably, and it remains for the worker to insert it accurately in the armhole that it may be equally comfortable when sewed in the waist.

If the armhole feels too tight, do not hurry to trim it out. The waist may feel a little tight when first tried on, but it must be remembered that a three-eighths-inch seam must be taken off when the sleeve is sewed in, and this will make the armhole about one inch larger. Of course, if it feels very snug it may be trimmed a little or clipped at intervals as explained for fitting the armholes. After the sleeve has been sewed in the armhole the seam is overcast.

SKIRTS

T HE styles of skirts are diverse and varied, and as it is necessary to know just how to proceed when finishing any particular mode, we have selected a number which require different finishing, so that when these are understood it will hardly be possible for the worker to encounter any difficulties in other styles that may be put forth, which she cannot master. However, due consideration should be given the label on each pattern.

The lengths of skirts vary according to circumstances. The instep skirt and short round skirt are solely for walking purposes. The round skirt, which touches the floor, runs the gamut of the dancing skirt, the walking skirt and the house skirt; it is available for all conditions. The medium sweep and the long sweep skirts are usually admired for the more ceremonious occasions, the carriage, the theatre, the festival, etc.

Comparatively few of the skirts at present are lined, or, if a lining is used, it is in the form of a foundation petticoat and is often made entirely separate from the outer skirt, having its own waistband and placket closing. In neutral colors or black, one lining skirt may be worn with different outside skirts, though, unless the material of the gown is transparent, the lining skirt is often omitted entirely, one of the colored petticoats of silk or its imitations, now so generally worn, taking its place. The flat-lined skirt, as it is called when skirt and lining are made in one, is scarcely ever seen; its return has been rumored, but it seems hardly likely to find much favor, as a skirt of this sort is always heavy. It is true that so much cloth and so much lining have probably the same actual weight whether made together or separately, but the unlined skirt worn over the foundation petticoat is apparently much lighter and certainly more graceful, and, when made of cloth, even the foundation skirt may be dispensed with. Taffeta is usually employed for the foundation skirt, but where the cost is a considera-

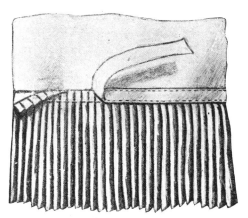

No. 1.—Plaiting Stitched on Foundation Skirt

tion, percaline, nearsilk or any like substitute may be used instead of silk.

If percaline or any double-width material is used and a skirt with wide gores is to be cut, fold the lining crosswise, allowing the cut ends to meet, and cut the largest piece first, placing the broadest end of the pattern at the cut end and the straight side to the selvage of the lining. The narrower gores may be inverted and cut from the remaining width. When cutting circular or other skirts which are to be bias at the centre front, the directions on the label should be followed implicitly. With the tracing-wheel trace through the pattern, keeping an even, true line for the seam. If necessary the front or any single gore may be cut last by folding the remaining lining lengthwise, being careful to measure before the previous gores have been cut, that the length will be sufficient.

The foundation skirt is usually finished with an accordion-plaited flounce, which may be any prescribed depth. If made with a plaiting, the length of the upper skirt must be calculated before cutting, since the deeper the plaiting the shorter the upper portion, besides, allowance must be made for the seam which joins these together, and the hem on the plaiting. This hem is one-quarter of an inch deep and stitched by machine. It is joined to the skirt in an ordinary seam, turned up on the skirt and covered with a ribbon binding, as shown at No. 1, or a narrow facing of silk may be sewed in the seam at the same time and all turned up and stitched to the upper portion.

Sometimes this plaiting is hemmed top and bottom and the upper portion is permitted to extend under the flounce several inches. The latter edge is pinked or finished with a tiny hem and the flounce is placed at the line indicating the length on the upper portion, and stitched to this skirt one-quarter of an inch below the upper hemmed edge, forming a heading.

After cutting, the lining is stitched and pressed and the seams overcast or bound, after which the plaiting is added. This foundation skirt may now be basted on the belt, and is ready to be tried on, but is not finished until the drop skirt is added.

The belt is made of silk and should be cut on the warp or selvage. It is usually two inches and a quarter longer than the size of the waist, the width varying from very narrow for a stout figure to two inches and a half unfinished, for a slim figure. Crease three-eighths of an inch off each side and the same at both ends, double the belt over forming half the width and baste near the fold edge; now mark off one inch and a half which will be left beyond the size of the waist for the lap; this must be basted plain to the belt.

No. 2.—Cord on Top of Skirt

Find the centre of the skirt, also the centre of the belt after the inch and a half has been deducted for the lap, and pin together by placing the right side of the belt to the lining of the skirt; pin on half-way round, fold the belt at the centre crease and mark with chalk or pins where the seams or darts of the other side of the skirt are to be placed. In this manner corresponding seams applied at these marks will be fitted to their proper positions on each side and the skirt will be accurately adjusted on the belt. Baste off the three-eighths of an inch seam with strong cotton.

If there is any doubt that the skirt may not fit correctly it is a better plan not to baste the belt to the skirt in the beginning, but to pin it securely around the waist and pin the skirt to the belt after the hips are fitted and the placket carefully adjusted. In this way the correct lines for the seams may be positively ascertained. When fitting, the length is adjusted by raising or lowering the plaiting on the upper skirt portion where necessary.

If a plaiting is not desired on the bottom of the skirt, the lining is cut full length and the bottom interlined with crinoline or haircloth from five to ten inches deep and this is faced to its full depth with the lining, as explained in the chapter "Wedding and Evening Gowns." The interlining, however, may be omitted if a number of small ruffles are to finish this skirt.

After the skirt has been prepared, the correct length is measured off. Sometimes a skirt will be too long at the sides and back and it seems impossible to obtain the correct effect by turning up at the bottom; in this case raise the skirt above the belt at the sides and back, adjusting around the hips. When a skirt is to be short (for golfing or other wear) a good plan for obtaining an even length all around is to measure on a card the desired length from the floor. Having the figure on a pedestal or table, rest the card on the floor and with tailors' chalk mark all around the skirt at the top of the card. This is perhaps the simplest and best method for short skirts.

Trains are any desired length, but for these a special pattern should be bought, as through any attempt at experiment in lengthening the back, the gown is likely to be ruined by the imperfect shaping.

Pin the corresponding seams together at the top and bottom of the skirt and with either chalk or pins mark for the length through the opposite side. Baste a true line around the bottom, turn up on this tracing and try on the skirt. Any little variation or modification may be made at the top around the belt, and, if necessary, alterations may be made at the bottom.

If the lining has been carefully fitted, there will be very little trouble later, and the skirt may be readily completed. Never finish a skirt around the bottom before the belt is basted on, because no matter how carefully measured it is likely to hang unevenly; the skirt may be short in places, and, if completed with velveteen or braid, there is no possible way of lengthening.

The material skirt is cut from the pattern and may be the same or an entirely different shape from the foundation skirt. After the seams are joined and pressed this skirt is fitted to the foundation skirt and sewed in the same belt unless the petticoat is desired separate. The lower edge is usually finished with a hem about one inch and a half deep, which must be allowed in cutting, as only a seam finish is generally allowed on patterns. The hem may be stitched in rows on the machine or blind-stitched, or tucks or other decorations may be added.

In a great many skirts where few gores are provided it is necessary to hold the material a little full on the belt, so that the shaping of the gores may not be distorted to fit over the hips which may be a trifle larger, or a waist a little smaller than the average. In perfectly plain skirts of wool this fulness may be pressed so that it is not at all discernible. In stiff silks the effect cannot be entirely obliterated, but it may be somewhat relieved by judicious pressing.

If necessary, the skirt may be tried on for the last time, to be certain that it is thoroughly correct, in which case the belt is ready for finishing.

FINISHING THE BELT

One edge of the belt has been sewed to the skirt; turn the remaining edge over the top of the skirt covering the seam and stitch down by hand or machine. Overhand the ends that have been turned in.

When sewing the hooks and eyes on, place a hook one-eighth of an inch back from the right-hand edge at the bottom of the belt; sew an eye with the point touching the seam that joins the fly to the skirt. Put another eye directly on the end of this side of the belt and a hook on the opposite side to correspond. Hook the skirt before marking for this latter.

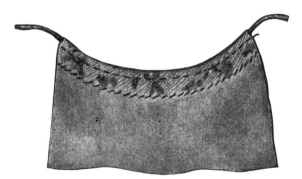

No. 3.—Finished Effect of Cord

Hangers four inches long are made of silk or cotton tape and sewed flat to the belt; one end fastened at the hook, drawing the tape its full length toward the front and sewing securely on the other end. Measure on the opposite side of the belt for the corresponding tape.

Work a herringbone or fancy stitch on the belt to indicate the centre of the skirt. This little mark is very useful inasmuch as it permits one to properly adjust the skirt on the figure, so that the centre of the front gore will always be directly below the centre of the front of the waist.

Skirts for stout figures are frequently finished with a cording, and this is accomplished in the following manner: After the skirt has been properly fitted, a bias strip of strong silk is cut one inch and a quarter wide. This must be a perfect bias, and an old-fashioned cording made by using a medium-sized cable cord. In basting, be very careful not to stretch either the top of the skirt or the cording. If the skirt is stretched, it will not cling properly to the figure, but stand out at the top in a very ungraceful manner. If the cording is stretched, it will not fit when turned over. Baste the skirt and cording together by placing the side having the narrow seam of silk against the right side of the skirt with the cording toward the bottom—No. 2—and having the line of running stitches three-eighths of an inch below the top of the skirt. Baste this carefully, after which sew it to the skirt by hand, using back-stitches directly on top of the previous row of stitches. Turn the skirt over on the line of stitching, so that the cording just forms the heading. None of the stitches should show here, and if the work is properly executed the cord will be snugly encased and the top of the skirt roll slightly. With the right side of the skirt toward the worker, baste along the top just below the cording. Turn on the wrong side, turn in the edge of the silk one-quarter of an inch and hem carefully to the lining. Stretch the bias silk slightly where necessary at the curves, and be careful not to take the stitches through to the outside. The finished effect is shown at No. 3.

Sew three or five hooks in an upright position on the back of the belt two inches apart to correspond with eyes or rings on the waist. This prevents any displacement or pulling away at the back and assures a feeling of security which is a relief to the wearer's mind. If the waist is to be worn outside the skirt, worked rings are placed on the belt and hooks on the waist. The method of finishing the skirt of a wedding or evening gown is described in the chapter "Wedding and Evening Gowns," and some of the points put forth may be adapted to other skirts, particularly those of a dressy sort. The placket may be finished as described in the chapter referred to, and either French patent hooks and eyes or patent fasteners used.

In finishing the lower edge of the material skirt a soft finish is usually desired, that is, the hem is simply turned over without interlining. When the material of which the skirt is made is soft and of light weight, albatross, voile and the like, and an interlining is preferred, it will be better to use strips of lining rather than crinoline inside the hem or facing, and when the skirt is of silk, light-weight cotton flannel is often used, as the idea is to give "body" and weight to the hem rather than

No. 5.—Hem Gathered at Top

No. 4.—Cambric Interlining in Hem

actual stiffness, and crinoline would quickly cut through the lighter materials. No. 4 shows the way of enclosing a bias strip of lining when the skirt is hemmed instead of faced. The lower edge is turned up and traced as previously described; the bias lining should be turned over a seam-width and the fold edge of this turn laid even with the tracing stitches. Stretch the lower edge of the bias lining to make it conform to the shaping of the lower edge of the skirt; baste the strip of lining in place, taking the basting stitches through its centre, then turn the lower edge

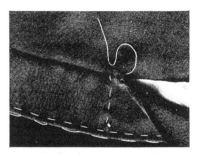

No. 6.—Slip-Stitching Hem to Skirt

of the skirt, that has been allowed for a hem over the lining (which now becomes an interlining when it is enclosed between the skirt and the hem), and baste along the fold edge, as shown at No. 5. The upper edge of the hem will be much fuller than the part of the skirt to which it is to be hemmed, and this fulness may be disposed of in gathers, as seen in the illustration. After the edge of the skirt is basted, measure on the hem straight up from the bottom of the skirt and mark the hem depth; this can be done with a card cut the required width; lay the edge of the card even with the bottom of the skirt and mark along the top with tailors' chalk. Turn over the top of the hem on a line with these chalk marks and gather through both thicknesses just below the fold edge. After the edge is gathered all the way around, baste it to the skirt. Be careful to keep the lines of fulness running straight up from the bottom of the skirt toward the gathered edge. Hem the skirt by hand or stitch it. No. 6 shows how the hand-hemming is done. In this case the turned-up hem portion was fitted to the skirt by laying small plaits where necessary, instead of gathering the edge. The same care should be observed to make these plaits run in straight lines, as only in this way can a smooth, flat-lying hem be formed. The plaits should be basted in place and then the overlapping part hemmed to the part under it, but not through into the interlining or the skirt. The upper edge of the hem is to be slip-stitched to the skirt, taking up only a thread or two in the skirt and slipping the needle along inside the fold edge of the hem; the stitches may be made about one-quarter of an inch apart. When the material is fairly thick, the stitch need not be taken entirely through it but can catch a thread of the wrong side of the cloth. In silk or thin woollen goods it is necessary to take the stitch through, but if only a couple of threads are picked up and the hemming thread is not drawn tight, these little stitches will scarcely show, especially after the hem is pressed when the skirt is finished.

An outside skirt which is cut circular and plaited is shown at No. 7. This is much easier to adjust at the waist-line than a plain circular skirt. The model illustrated has a seam at the centre front and is cut bias at both front and back, bringing the straighter part of the check on the sides. The small perforations in the pattern indicate how it should be placed on the material to cut the bias front edge, and the breadths should be matched and joined as though it were a plain circular skirt, but it is not necessary to fit a cambric pattern, as any necessary alteration at the waist-line may be made by lapping the plaits more or less, as may be required. Do not attempt to mark the position of the plaits until the breadths have been stitched together and the seams pressed open. A checked or small pattern is not so difficult to match at the seams as a large-figured pattern would be, but care should be observed to make

the checks match, else the line of joining will show irregularly when the skirt is finished. The bias seams at front and back should also be made to match accurately, and this is done by matching the *straight* lines of the check both horizontally and perpendicularly across the full width of both sides. It is only by such care that a skirt can be accurately and evenly made, with certainty that both sides shall be exactly alike. Place the pattern on the material and mark (with tailors' tacks) both the large and the small perforations from waist to hips. Separate the two parts by cutting the tacks and baste the fold of each plait one-eighth of an inch from the edge. As these plaits are all more or less bias, care must be observed not to stretch them. Stitch each basted edge, then lap the fold-edge to meet the line that represents the perforations that indicate where the plaits should reach. If the skirt is of thin material, the tailors' tacks in marking the perforations are liable to pull out in handling

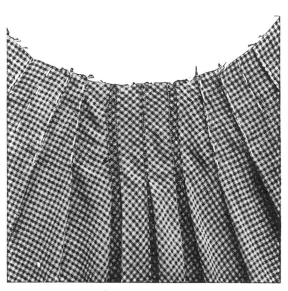

No. 7.—Skirt Ready for Foundation

the skirt, and it will be better to mark at each of these lines with a line of colored basting thread. Baste each plait from the hip to the waist, according to the indicated line, then try on the skirt. Make any required alterations at the waist-line, and slip-stitch each plait, by hand, to the skirt, making the stitches through the machine-stitching.

Tucks of various styles and sizes are fashionable at different periods and ornament drop skirts and full skirts of soft materials, which seem to demand something more than a plain hem for a finish. If the bottom of the skirt is straight or nearly so, this is not very difficult, but the increased fulness frequently requires the bottom of these skirts to be almost circular, and then to make the tucks lie flat is sometimes puzzling to the amateur. Since "nun" tucks are, perhaps, the most difficult to accomplish, the following will prove of great assistance to the worker.

"Nun" tucks are ordinary tucks, but on account of their depth require a little different treatment, because where the bottom of the skirt rounds at the sides and back the lower part is naturally fuller than the upper. The name "nun" tucks is given them because they are used as an edge finish on skirts worn by the members of certain religious orders. Bias folds are frequently used instead of these tucks, and directions for making these and folds of various kinds will be found in the chapter entitled "Bias Bands and Folds"

When making a skirt to be ornamented with "nun" tucks the lower edge should be turned under for a hem, baste this fold about half an inch from the edge with small basting stitches.

Measure to the required depth and turn under a seam; baste this, as it is turned under, separate from the skirt with small stitches and then draw up these stitches, thus shirring the edge until it is the same size as the part of the skirt it is to be stitched to and will lie flat against it. Then baste the hem as usual. Place a fine basting around the line of perforations which marks the under fold of the tuck; from this measure the width of the tuck and place another basting there; mark these through both sides at once, with either tailors' tacks or chalk. Bring these

No. 8.—Preparing "Nun" Tucks

two bastings together and pin through; baste the edges of the tuck thus formed in the same way as the edge of the hem was basted, then lay the skirt on a table or lap-board with the full side of the tuck upper-most, and draw the fulness so it will lie naturally, changing where it has been pinned, if necessary, and baste the tuck with small stitches. (No. 8.) After the hem and tuck have been stitched, press them well on the wrong side. The hem and tuck finished are shown at No. 9. Some-times the perforations will mark the fold line of the tuck, in which case follow the directions on the label.

If the tucks are not provided in the pattern they must be allowed for in cut-ting, and experiment in pinning them in place must determine their position, depth and the space between. Both sides of the skirt should be traced at once with tailors' tacks, as explained. After the stitches are cut and the two sides separated, fold each tuck along the line of the tracing thread and baste. Now measure from the tracing on the *under* side of the tuck, toward the bottom of the skirt, the allowed width of the tuck. Cut a measure or gage from a piece of card or stiff paper, as directed for ordinary tucks, making it three-quarters of an inch wide and several inches long, and cut it in straight, one-quarter of an inch at the measure the first tuck is to be, in this case an inch and one-half. Half an inch below this cut start a diagonal cut that shall reach the quarter-inch cut; this makes a notch with one straight edge, and the dis-tance from the end of the card to this straight edge will form the measure. Measure the width for the tucks at short intervals and make a chalk mark at each; then run a row of rather fine basting stitches along from one chalk mark to the next, forming a con-tinuous line, through only one thickness of the material. Lay the tuck at the folded and basted

No. 9.—Finished "Nun" Tucks

edge on a table or lap-board, and baste through at the line of fine bastings just made, draw-ing the fulness into little gathers when necessary and finishing the same as perforated tucks.

No. 10 shows the waist finish of a full skirt which would, in all probability, be finished with tucks above the hem. The skirt may be shirred in spaced rows around the hips, but this style is not becoming to every figure—and when used, the horizontal lines on which the shirring is done should be adapted to each individual; a line starting at the waist-line in the back and having a drop of from one and one-half to two and one-half inches will usually be found to give a satisfactory drop effect.

When waists have the long, pointed effect in the front, it is well to try on waist and skirt together and follow the line of the edge of the waist when marking for the shirrings. The skirt should be gathered into the belt for this trial, and the line for the shirring may then be marked around by the placing of pins, chalk marks or a piece of tape. These are afterward removed, the line so formed is straightened, and the shirrings are made. If three quarter-inch spacings are allowed in this shirring, the space between the top row and the belt at the front may be filled in with short rows, beginning at one side, running down to the centre of the front and up again toward the belt at the other side, finishing there at symmetrical distances. When the deep shirring composed of several rows is not desired it is advisable to place a second row of shirring one-quarter of an inch below the row over which the belt is placed, as shown in the illustration; this holds the gathers more closely in place.

The foundation skirt for light Summer fabrics is generally of lawn finished with a hem and trimmed with ruffles of lawn and lace as elaborately as one may desire. After the material skirt has been stitched and pressed it is trimmed, draped over the foundation skirt carefully, and the back properly adjusted; the belt is then turned over and finished.

FINISHING WALKING SKIRTS

In this day of repeated expressions of very great common sense in dress we are constantly being confronted and surprised at new methods and ideas which tend greatly to one's comfort, without in the least detracting from the beauty of a garment. Skirts which heretofore were a weight in themselves are now lightened to a greater or less degree, and where the material is heavy the weight is greatly decreased by the adoption of new methods of finish.

According to the most advanced and scientific ideas skirts of heavy cloth are tabooed entirely, but when insisted upon, they are made wholly devoid of lining. The seams are finished according to any of the methods illustrated in the chapter "Novel, Artistic Seams," and are

No. 10.—Skirt Ready for the Belt

overcast or bound, nothing but a facing being used for finishing the lower edge. This is usually decorated with several rows of machine-stitching, serving the double purpose of ornamentation and holding the facing in position.

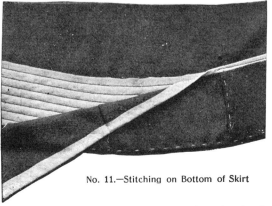

No. 11.—Stitching on Bottom of Skirt

Few goods are so tightly woven as to resist fraying, and in almost all cases where the seams are not finished according to the method for imitation strap seams, they are bound with a bias strip of farmer satin or sateen.

If the material is very heavy, only the outside edge of the double-welt seam is bound and the remaining edge cut from underneath, the latter edge being hidden after the second stitching is completed. The seam must be of sufficient width, however, that the work will not slip under the presser foot and thus make it impossible to stitch a perfectly correct line.

In exceedingly heavy cloths the seam may be joined and pressed and each edge bound, after which it is ornamented with one row of stitching directly each side of the seam and, again, three-eighths of an inch from these.

If the bottom of the skirt is to be ornamented with stitching, bias strips of flannel, light in weight, and cotton and wool mixture are basted to the cloth on the under side that the stitching may show with better effect. The length of the skirt should be marked with a tracing thread, and the edge of the flannel should reach just to the mark. The stitching except the top row is then made through the skirt and the flannel interlining (usually one-quarter of an inch apart), but the part to turn up for the hem, which has been allowed in cutting, is left separate. Be careful to have an easy tension on the machine, that the stitching may not draw. After the stitching is finished, turn up the hem and lay plaits in it wherever required to make it fit around the skirt. Baste these plaits in place, then with a bias strip of lining an inch and a quarter wide bind the top of this hem and baste into place. The top row of stitching should then be placed in the skirt and through this turned-up part of the hem also, to hold it in place. The plaits which have been basted in the under part of the hem should be slip-stitched with silk of the same color and the hem well pressed on the wrong side. This finish is shown at No. 11.

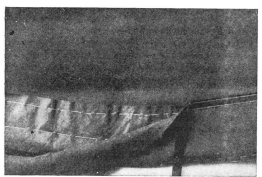

No. 12.—A Skirt with Hem as Bottom Finish

For a simple hem finish, when so much stitching is not desired, a bias strip of cambric or other lining should be basted in the bottom of the skirt in the same manner as the flannel. The hem is then turned up over it and basted in place and a piece of seam binding or bone casing should be basted flat over the raw edge and one or two rows of stitching placed through this and the skirt. This finish is shown at No. 12.

If only one or two rows of stitching are wanted they may be taken through both skirt and underhem. If no stitching is desired, if the material is of cloth weight, the top of the underhem should be bound and the hem basted in position, then, folding the cloth of the skirt just at the top of the hem, overhand the bound edge and skirt together, catching only partly through the cloth that the stitches may not show in the outside, and using fine thread or silk the color of the material. The method of working is shown at No. 13. If the material of the skirt is thin it will be more difficult to prevent the stitches from showing.

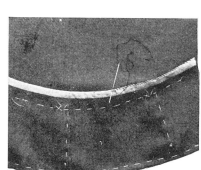

No. 13.—Bottom of Skirt Hand-Hemmed

The threads should be rather loose. The flannel or cambric which is placed inside the hem is intended more to give firmness and smoothness to the skirt and stitching than as stiffening.

PLACKETS APPROPRIATE FOR VARIOUS STYLES OF SKIRTS

The placket is one of the most important considerations in a well-made skirt, for it may either make or mar the general appearance of the entire gown and denotes at a glance the quality of the workmanship. Here, as elsewhere, untidiness is to be deplored, for the entire skirt may be thrown out of position and given a very careless and slipshod appearance simply because the placket hooks and eyes are absent, or because they are sewed on in such an indifferent manner as to be next to useless. The question of using either hooks and eyes or patent fasteners must be settled by each individual. Many prefer the latter, while others contend that these are no improvement over the former; in many cases, however, both have been used together with most satisfactory results, as will be explained later for the various methods of finishing.

One of the principal reasons why many plackets are gaping and ill-fitting is because the hooks and eyes are placed too far apart and insufficient protection is afforded against the strain at this point. Care should be exercised in sewing on fasteners, of whatever description. A few extra stitches when they are first sewed on, that they may be held firmly in place, will prove like the "stitch in time," and, perhaps, prevent the hook or eye from falling off entirely.

A placket may be at the back, front or side of a skirt, depending upon the design or con-

No. 14.—Finished Placket

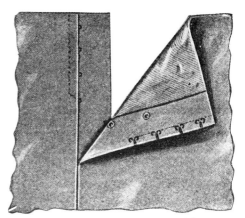

No. 15.—Placket Showing Hooks and Eyes

struction. There are many methods of finishing plackets or skirt openings, and after a few have been explained the worker will be able to judge upon which occasion each can be used most advantageously.

No. 14 pictures the style of skirt closing generally adopted, namely, an inverted box-plait at the back. If there is a seam at the centre of the back the placket may be finished here by adding an underlap as described for some of the later plackets; or, as shown at No. 15, the seam may be joined to the top of the skirt and after the plaits are properly laid, an opening cut at the crease of the under box-plait. This is bound on both edges with ribbon. The folded edge of each plait is stitched, that on the left-hand side through all thicknesses of the skirt, with the stitching on both edges tapering to a point; this is shown in the illustration.

The hooks and eyes are placed at even distances apart and in such a position that when the lower one is closed the stitching of the plaits will form a decided and perfect point. The placket, however, is opened below this point and should be held in position on the edge by either hooks or patent fasteners (the latter in this illustration). This also relieves the strain on the hooks.

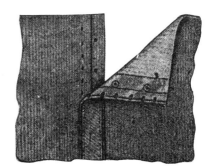

No. 16.—Placket Finish of Strapped Seam

Apropos of the length of plackets, the opening should be only as long as is necessary to carry the skirt easily over the hips without strain or tear. The shorter the placket the better, provided it is not too short to permit the skirt being put on and off easily; from ten to twelve inches, according to the hip measure, is the usual length.

The method of finishing the placket of a gored skirt having strapped seams and closed at the back is shown at No. 16, an underlap being applied to the left-hand side. The strap or fold is stitched to the back gore on the right-hand side, while the remaining edge is turned over and the hooks applied just back of the edge, so that they will not be visible from the outside. A silk facing is slipped under the hooks and an extra facing is added to the edge of the back gore; although one facing may suffice. The patent fasteners are now added. It will be observed that the hooks are very close together; this is essential since it is necessary to preserve the straight line of the strapping.   Loops are made of twist in corresponding positions.

An underlap is usually cut double and is one inch and a half wide when finished.   Join this to the skirt by machine, taking off an even seam and observing great care at the bottom that the skirt seam does not pucker.   Turn the seam over on the lap, turn in the remaining edge and hem or stitch over the joining seam.   It is a good plan to allow the underlap to extend an inch or an inch and a half below the placket opening.   Turn in the extension and the lower edge, and stitch; the latter may be continued on the fold of the lap if desired.   The effect of the reverse side is pictured at No. 17.

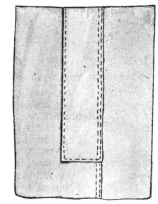

No. 17.—Reverse Side of Underlap

The habit-back skirt must be finished at the placket even more carefully than any of the other designs.   These closings must be made almost invisible, the seam being apparently continuous, and there should be no gap at the placket.   The most advisable method is as follows:

After the centre seam is joined and pressed, leaving the opening for the placket, lay a facing of canvas one inch wide from top to bottom of the placket on the right-hand side.   This gives the edge a firm body and admits of the hooks being sewed securely without catching through to the outside.   Turn the edge of the material over this the width of the seam and cat-stitch and press.   Now add the hooks even distances apart, at the same time close enough together to insure a perfect closing.   About one inch apart is safe.   Now face this, or turn in the edge of the lining, if there is one, and hem as pictured at No. 18.   Mark for the eyes on the underlap to correspond with the hooks.   Separate the rings of the eyes a trifle and slip them into position in the seam which joins the underlap to the skirt without breaking the machine-stitching. These may now be sewed firmly to the lap on the wrong side. The eyes may be prettily finished by buttonhole stitching all around the portion which is visible, and the raw edges of the seam may be bound together.

Sometimes the skirt is opened on the left-hand side of the front, in which case the seam is joined, allowing the depth of the placket at the top; this is regulated by the size of the hips.

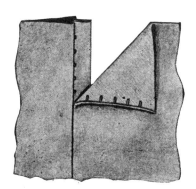

No. 18.—Placket for Habit-Back Skirt

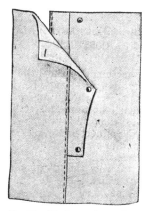

No. 19.—Placket at Front Gore of Skirt

If an extension lap is desired on the outside of a front closing, the underlap on the side gore is applied, as directed for that at No. 17.   The outside lap is cut the shape desired, either with straight lines or fanciful curves; if straight lines have been selected, a wide lap is cut and folded double; if curves—as seen at No. 19 —two laps are cut and joined around the outline, leaving the straight edge open to be sewed to the skirt.   This lap may be machine-stitched and finished complete even to the buttonholes before it is applied.   Join the straight edge of the lap to the front gore of the skirt on the line of the seam, fold the edges of the seam over on the lap, allowing the facing to cover the joining and hem down.   In the illustration the extension lap is turned down, showing the underlap.

Occasionally extensions are allowed on the front gore when cutting; these are lined and machine-stitched and rest upon the side gore, serving the same purpose as an applied lap and no underlap need be added, unless desired.

APPLYING VELVETEEN OR BRAID BINDING

The finishing of the bottom of a skirt is an important factor in dressmaking and one which necessitates the expenditure of as much care and skill as any other portion of the garment. Velveteen is much employed for binding, being regarded by many to be the most wear-resisting, although the different varieties of plain and brush braid are used by a large proportion. By a trial of each a person will soon be able to make a selection. Many consider the velveteen more suitable for silk and house dresses, preferring the braids and corduroy for wool and

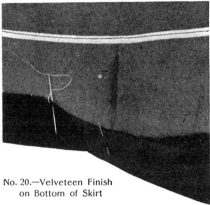

No. 20.—Velveteen Finish
on Bottom of Skirt

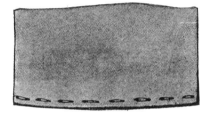

No. 21.—Correct Finish of Velveteen

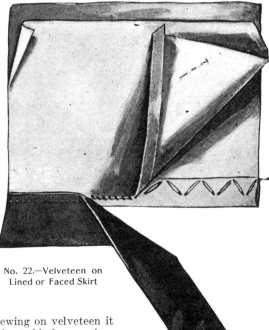

No. 22.—Velveteen on
Lined or Faced Skirt

street gowns. Costumes for evening or house wear are not of necessity completed with a binding, but have what is known as a soft finish. The usual way of applying velveteen is as follows:

After the hem or facing is finished, one edge of the velveteen is run to the lower edge of the skirt at the inside; lay the right side of the velveteen toward the skirt, beginning at the back, and allow the edge to lie on the skirt only a narrow seam's width, the rest of the width of the velveteen extending below the bottom of the skirt. No. 20 pictures the velveteen run on at the bottom of a skirt which has a hem turned up. Run this edge along with an occasional back-stitch, being careful to take the stitch into the hem or facing only and not through to the outside.

If the worker is not accustomed to sewing on velveteen it is all-important that it should be properly basted before sewing, as it is likely either to stretch or slip. If it stretches, the bottom of the skirt will be puckered, and if it slips, before the end is reached, it will be found that the velveteen is entirely too short to encircle the skirt properly; consequently, in either case the result is a very careless and unskilful piece of work.

Time is never saved in trying to do work of this kind too quickly, for it will certainly have to be ripped, and it is never agreeable to repeat a task or work with material that has been sewed and then ripped, even if the material in question is perfectly new.

After this velveteen has been properly sewed on and neatly joined, turn the skirt on the right side; allow only an eighth of an inch of velveteen to extend beyond the bottom of the skirt and baste, as seen in No. 21. Many do not allow any of the velveteen to show beyond the edge, but this is usually carelessness; they intend to have it extend beyond, but neglect to baste it or else baste carelessly, and by the time the skirt is finished nothing is seen of the velveteen from the right side. This is wrong, for the velveteen is put on to protect the bottom of the skirt and should extend a trifle beyond.

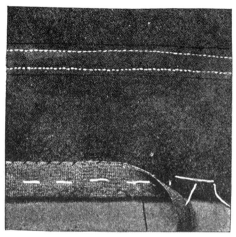

No. 23.—Braid Finish

After the last basting, the velveteen fits flat on the wrong side and is very easily finished. Turn in the top edge of the velveteen and hem it to the facing. Tailors frequently do not turn in this top edge but cat-stitch across the raw edge to hold the velveteen to the skirt. They also cat-stitch the first edge instead of running it, but this method takes more time, and the other way is quite as secure.

At No. 22 is shown the method of applying a velveteen to a lined skirt. The skirt is turned up and cat-stitched with the lining hemmed over, and the velveteen is added as described; this finish would be the same for a facing.

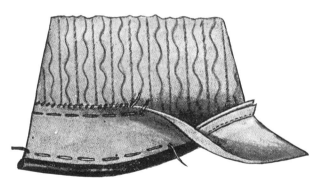

No. 24.—Cable Cord Finish

No. 25.—Inside Finish of Flare Skirt

Another method is to cut off the bottom of the skirt half an inch beyond the basting or turning-line; place the velveteen right side down on the material and stitch after it has been properly basted; turn, allow the piping to show beyond, baste, and finish by hemming on the wrong side. When braid is used instead of velveteen, it should first be shrunk by dipping it in water until it is thoroughly wet; then press it until dry, turning one edge under about one-quarter of an inch as it is pressed. Add to the bottom of the skirt by sewing at the turned-under edge to the hem or facing, then hem down the top edge. The braid may be sewed on with the same two rows of sewing, but without turning under the one edge, but the doubled edge will wear better; this can be done only with the inch-wide braid. The method is shown at No. 23.

Occasionally a cable cord binding is added to the bottom of a skirt, and it may be made of the cloth or silk from which the costume has been developed. This is a particularly useful suggestion when it is difficult to match the color of the skirt in braid or velveteen. A heavy cable cord is encased in a bias strip of the material and basted as for ordinary cording; it is then stitched to the outside of the skirt through the basting which marks the length, with the facing joined in the same seam. Turn in the remaining edge of the facing and hem as shown at No. 24. A cording may be made with one edge of the material wider than the other and slip-stitched from the right side after the skirt has been turned up; the wide end is then hemmed over like velveteen. In rebinding a skirt this is an especially desirable method, as the tendency to shortening is frustrated by the added cord.

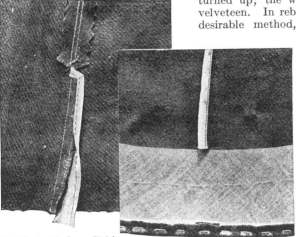

No. 26.—Inside Seam Finish for Flare Skirt

No. 27.—Crinoline Interlining in Facing

FLARE SKIRTS

The many-gored skirts that flare below the hip need special treatment in the finishing, to preserve the flare and make them hang in just the right way. This finish can be seen at No. 25. After the seams have been basted and stitched, it is advisable to try on the skirt and pin a tape around to determine the hip depth to which the flat seam shall extend. At the same time the length of the skirt should be determined by pinning it up around the bottom or by marking it with chalk. Trace the line for the bottom of the skirt with a basting thread and also mark the skirt with a thread along the edge of the tape. At this point clip both raw edges of each seam at the inside of the skirt in order to divide the flat-finished hip part from the rippled part. Make this clip or cut extend the full width of the seam edges, running in as far as the seam stitching. The seam above the clip is to be pressed open, being notched

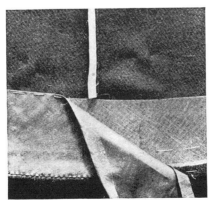

No. 28.—Facing Hemmed to Bottom of Skirt

No. 29.—Seam Stitched Across Facing to Hold Flare Effect

or nicked where necessary to make it lie flat. It may be finished with a row of machine-stitching at each side of the seam and quite close to it, or both edges of the seam may be turned the same way, a row of stitching on the outside holding them in lap-seam effect.

Mark up from the bottom edge the hem or facing depth (usually about three inches) and clip the seam in at this point; press this lower part of the seam open in order to hem or face it properly. The part of the seam between the two lengths of pressed-open seam is to be bound as seen in No. 26, using a narrow bias strip of lining material for this purpose. This part of the seam is not to be pressed to either one side or the other, but stands out straight from the inside of the skirt, and gives a fluted effect to the breadths. Interline the bottom with crinoline, turn over the edge of the skirt and the crinoline together at the tracing line that indicates the bottom of the skirt, and baste the turned-over edges as shown at No. 27. Baste a bias facing in place, then hem the lower edge to the turned-over edge of the skirt, as seen at No. 28. The upper edge may be hemmed by hand or may have one or two rows of machine-stitching to correspond with the stitching on the upper part of the seams. The skirt should now be folded at each seam and placed in the machine in the same way as when the breadths were first stitched together, and a row of stitching (shown at No. 29) made along the bound part of the seam close to the first row and extending across the facing, forming that into a small seam. If the skirt is hemmed or if the facing is of the cloth, the upper edge may be bound with a bias strip of lining, and the stitching along the top of the hem or facing made through that to avoid the extra thickness of a turned-in edge of the cloth.

SUPPORTING PLAITS INLAID AT SEAMS

Gored skirts that have a side plait or an inverted box-plait let into the seams some distance up from the bottom are sometimes troublesome through a tendency of these inlet plaits to show below the bottom edge of the skirt as there is nothing to which to attach them. This trouble may be avoided in the manner seen at No. 30. The top of each of these plaits is bound, and after the skirt is otherwise finished, a tape or a strap of lining is sewed to the top of each plait and is carried from one to the next all around the inside of the skirt; this will generally be found to be enough, but in a winter skirt of heavy cloth a short tape or strap may run diagonally from the top of each plait to the next seam and be securely sewed there to the wrong side; this also is shown in the illustration.

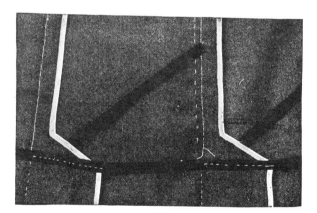

No. 30.—Supporting Inlaid Plaits

PLAITED SKIRTS AND THEIR CORRECT ADJUSTMENT

Plaited skirts are always charming and while fashion decrees that one season they will be more popular than another, it is imperative for the worker to understand their proper construction, so as to meet the difficulties presented in different designs. These include side-plaited skirts and box-plaited skirts, skirts plaited in clusters and those of single plaits with more or less space between. While all are admired when well made, it is possible, without sufficient knowledge, to make these skirts very incorrectly.

In cases where the skirts are composed of seven or nine gores the effort at proper adjustment is not so great, since alterations may be made at the seams, but in skirts where few gores are employed particular attention must be paid to the correct position of the lines, thereby insuring the symmetry of the plaits. Furthermore, the skirt must be correctly joined to the belt and the material between the plaits properly disposed, so that the plaits themselves will have a uniform appearance.

To make the skirt, first read the directions on the label carefully, examining the pattern at the same time and identifying the pieces and the notches and perforations according to the directions. Fold one end of the cloth lengthwise, exactly through the centre. Lay the pattern of the front breadth on the material with its front edge even with the fold, and pin the pattern in place.   If the material is narrow, it will be necessary to piece the lower part of this breadth at each side; but this need not be done until after the rest of the skirt is cut, as some of the pieces cut from the side gores will probably be large enough for this purpose.   Lay out all the breadths before beginning to cut, to be sure that the pattern is arranged in the correct and most economical manner.   Single width material should be laid out straight for all breadths except the front.   It may be folded *across* at half its length, or cut in two and reversed (if it has a nap), to cut double.   After all the breadths are cut, before removing the pattern, mark each perforation that indicates the plaits, also the single perforations near the bottom of the skirt w th a small chalk mark or by sticking a pin through both thicknesses of cloth, at the centre of each perforation. Remove the pattern and place a yard-stick on the cloth with its edge even with

No. 31.—Front Breadth Traced for the Plaits

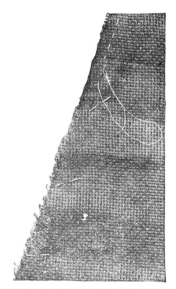

No. 32.—Basting a Bias Edge to a Straight One

each pin or chalk mark, and draw a continuous line with chalk.   Go over this line with tailors' tacks and mark each breadth in this way; the plaits outlined as described are shown at No. 31.

No. 33.—Basting the Plaits in Tucks

The long threads should be cut, the pieces separated, and the breadths joined at the seams.   In sewing a bias edge, it is essential that it be not stretched.   It is better to handle the extreme edge as little as possible; lay the piece of material straight over the one to which it is to be joined and pin the seam at the top; then straighten the breadths by smoothing both down and across with the thread of the fabric.   This will bring the bias edge into its true position, and it should then be pinned along at intervals and afterward basted in a three-eighths-inch seam.   The manner of preparing and basting this seam is shown at No. 32.

After all the seams are joined (except the back seam, which is not basted until the plaits are all laid and the skirt is ready to try on) begin at the front breadth and bring the lines of tracings at each side of the centre front together and baste a seam; this forms a large tuck.   The next two rows of tracing are then basted together to form a second tuck.   Continue in this way around each side of the skirt.   Each seam corresponds to a row of tracings and is to be basted to the line formed at the perforations on the breadth toward the front. After the plaits are basted into tucks, each one is flattened to form a box-plait, bringing the seam in the centre on the wrong side; the way of forming the plaits is shown at No. 33.

Care must be taken to get the box-plaits even, without any draw, as some of the edges come bias. As each one is flattened, it should be basted a quarter of an inch from the fold edge, as shown at No. 34, to keep the shape. This will be found a great convenience later.

The skirt is now ready to try on. Draw it up well to reach the waist all around, and pin it to the petticoat at the *hip-line*, then from the hip up, lay each box-plait in a symmetrical line. The basted seam at the centre of each box-plait can be ripped as far as the hip-line and the waist adjusted to the correct size. The bastings at the edges of the box-plaits will hold the plaits in place so that their size cannot be interfered with. They may be brought closer together to make the waist smaller or spread farther apart to make it larger.

The edges of the box-plaits should be pinned in correct position at the fitting, and when the skirt is taken off, they should be basted as pinned; the skirt can then be turned to the wrong side and the ripped seams can be readjusted. When this has been done, trace on the skirt where the edge of each plait, on which alteration has been made, comes. Then remove the bastings that hold them to the skirt, that the under seam may be stitched. The plaits are to be basted to the skirt again according to the tracings made after the fitting, and as far down as they are to be stitched. It would be advisable to rip open the back seam (it

No. 34.—The Box-Plaits Ready for Fitting

is still basted, not stitched), as the skirt can be more easily handled under the machine if it is opened out flat. Stitch the plaits down through both plait and skirt to the desired depth; then baste and stitch the back seam, apply the belt, press the plaits in place to the bottom of the skirt and try it on again to secure the correct length. Finish the hem, placket and belt in the usual way.

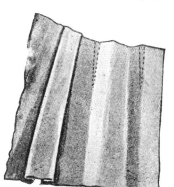

No. 35.—Arrangement of Dart under Plait

When a box-plaited skirt is correctly adjusted on the belt, it will be noted that the space between the plaits over the hips is wider than at the belt; this is necessitated by the decrease in size, and where seams are provided under the plaits the superfluous material may be fitted in. Where there is no seam, however, the fulness which occurs must be disposed invisibly under the plaits; if this fulness be not too great, the material may be held a trifle easy or, one might say, pucker or pushed toward the line of stitch-

ing. To present a thoroughly workmanlike appearance this fulness must be hidden; therefore, the plaits in this instance are very convenient for the purpose.

Notwithstanding the fact that it is possible to place all the surplus material under one plait, this should not be done, as it would throw the others out of position; moreover, there must be a uniformity of space between the plaits. Where the figure is disproportionate, that is, very large around the hips and small at the waist, the quantity of surplus material is increased. While a small amount may be held easy as directed and, after careful pressing, be unobservable, a larger quantity would be too bulky and is best treated differently, as follows:

After the plaits are laid the full length of the skirt and the latter is being fitted, side-plaits or darts are best employed for adjusting the material to a small waist. No. 35 shows the method of placing these. If a dart, it is sewed up in a position that will be well under the plait so that there will be no likelihood of its being seen. Even if folded over, the upper edges of the box-plait should not be disturbed, for this would disarrange the size and width on the outside. The material near the stitching is folded over one-eighth or one-quarter of an inch to form a dart-like tuck, and these new lines are joined or folded in such a way that they taper gradually into the line of the original plait just above the full part of the hips, as seen in the illustration. This may now be pressed flat, and the extra fold will not be objectionable. Treat in this manner where required, and keep the spaces between of equal width.

No. 36.—Side Plaits with Two Rows of Stitching

A skirt made in side plaits or kilts is represented at No. 36. The manner of preparing the skirt and marking the perforations that indicate the plaits is the same as that already described. At each line of tracing thread that represents the fold of a plait, it should be folded with the tracing thread as an edge, and the doubled goods should be basted through one-quarter of an inch back of the edge. This will hold all the plaits to the correct size no matter what alteration may be necessary in fitting. Many plaited models have one row of stitching placed just back of the folded edge, and through the two thicknesses only in the same way as the basting just described. This row of stitching answers a double purpose; it is ornamental and at the same time holds the edge of the plait in shape, and is especially desirable for wash goods or a thin woolen material that is likely to twist on a bias edge. The second row of stitching is placed a spaced distance back of the first and is taken through both plait and skirt. Stitch through to the desired depth and leave the ends of the thread two or three inches long at the lower finish of the stitching, that they may be drawn through to the wrong side and tied securely.

When a plaited skirt is made of heavy material or is lapped very much at the waist in fitting, it may be made less bulky by cutting away the surplus material after the plaits are stitched. The underlapping goods is cut away to within an inch or so of where the stitching finishes; thence it is cut across the top of the plait. The raw edges left in this way are to be bound with a bias strip of lining, that will finish across the top of each plait except where the seams that join the breadths form the inner fold of a plait, when the binding will continue down the raw edges of that seam to the bottom of the skirt. This method may be seen at No 37.

As each figure has some trifling peculiarity, a little study should

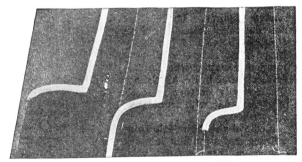

No. 37.—Inside Finish of a Kilted Skirt

be given on the pattern selected and judgment displayed as to the best means of alteration or adjustment. It must always be remembered, however, that the tucks or plaits must be evenly arranged and that the space between them must be the same, as this is quite as important as that the plaits should be folded evenly in the beginning.

When a plaited skirt is made of a washable material, the laundering is not a difficult matter if one knows the correct way. The lower part of the skirt should not be pressed out flat, but each plait as it is pressed at the stitched upper portion should be laid in position all the way to the bottom of the skirt, smoothed and arranged with the hand and pressed into position. Afterward the iron may be run under the plait to smooth the underneath part. This is the same method that is employed in pressing a similar skirt made of cloth, and it is at this time that the value of shrinking the material before cutting and of observing the "grain" is realized.

LINED SKIRTS

Lined skirts usually require some stiffening in the bottom to permit the skirt to fall in the proper folds and hold it out well from the feet. At certain times there are designs which are most desirable made with a lining throughout, and these must, perforce, have an interlining of haircloth or canvas at the lower edge. Different designs and styles require greater or less quantity, and one season may demand very stiff effects, while the following season clinging modes are *au fait*.

The method which is considered the best for making a lined skirt is the following: The lining and material are cut exactly alike, but stitched separately, then pressed and the interlining applied to the lining. Haircloth, linen canvas and crinoline are the principal materials employed for stiffening and from six to ten inches is a good depth, but the latter is more generally advised, for by the time the skirt is finished it is always somewhat less in consequence of turning up at the bottom, trimming off, and shaping to the lower edge of the skirt.

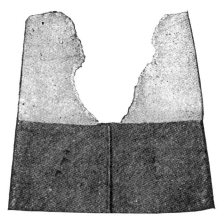

No. 38.—Haircloth Fitted to Skirt

All haircloth and linen canvas must be shrunk before putting it in the skirt and to prepare the former the projecting hairs must be cut off both sides. The shrinking may be done according to the directions given for shrinking material, or by the following method:

Place the haircloth on the press-board with a cloth underneath, lest the dye should come through, and with a large sponge, which has been dipped in water, wet thoroughly about half a yard at a time, rubbing in one direction. The iron must be very hot and the haircloth pressed until perfectly dry. When preparing the work in the beginning the haircloth may be shrunk before cutting the skirt and in this way will be ready whenever required. The haircloth is now cut across the width (from selvage to selvage) in strips ten inches deep. Fit these around the bottom of the lining skirt on the wrong side, pinning through and shaping where necessary, as pictured in No. 38, though not necessarily cutting at each seam. Join flat with small running stitches.

Remove the haircloth from the lining and strap the joinings by covering the raw edge with a strip of lining one inch wide. Do not turn the edges in, but stitch by machine as near the raw edge as possible. (No. 39.) Now baste the haircloth to the wrong side of the lining and bind the top by placing half the strip of percaline on one side and half on the other, turning over no edges whatever. Stitch this all

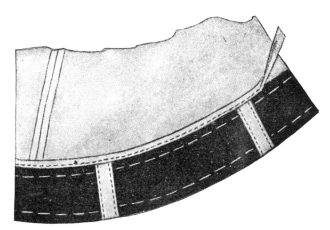

No. 39.—Fitted Haircloth Bound

around the top through both lining and haircloth--the method being shown at **No. 39**.

Linen canvas is shrunk and fitted in the same manner; however, it is not necessary to strap the top and joinings, as there are no sharp hairs to thrust through the material.

Allow the skirts to remain wrong side out and join together by placing the front gore of the lining over the front gore of the material, with the corresponding seams touching each other. Beginning at the top, run the edges of the seams together—the left-hand edge of the material to the left-hand edge of the lining—using a small basting stitch and ending just above the haircloth. Each seam of the material is tacked to its corresponding seam in the lining, until all are joined together and one skirt is the result. If care has been exercised in the beginning by cutting both material and lining precisely the same size, with seams stitched the same width, there will be no difficulty in fitting the skirts together.

Next finish the placket by separating the material from the lining on the right-hand side; place a piece of crinoline along the edge, turn the material over on the sewing line, sew the hooks on firmly, then crease the lining in the opposite direction also on the sewing line, slip it under the bills of the hooks and hem. The left-hand side is finished with a lap which is an inch and a half wide when finished. Full instructions for making plackets of various kinds will be found in this chapter under "Plackets," any of those described, which are approprate, may be substituted, if desired. Baste the belt in position and finish as previously directed.

Many prefer the old-fashioned way of basting the lining on the material and sewing all together in one seam. This is sometimes a desirable way for lining thin materials or those of open weave, when the edges of the seams would show through. With a tracing-wheel mark the necessary seams on the lining.

Many complain that, try as they will, the material always hangs loose after the skirt has been finished. The best way to avoid this is to pin the material to the table and baste the lining upon it.

Before doing this the haircloth or crinoline is basted to each piece of the lining on the wrong side; and where joined, the former is covered with a strip of percaline, also bound on the top, as directed for other lined skirts.

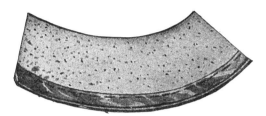

No. 40.—Finish of Band Flounce

Pin the material to the table right side down, placing the pins an inch or two apart. Pin the top of the gore first, then rub down, stretching slightly, and pin the bottom, being careful to stretch only on the straight of the goods; pin the sides down without changing the position or shape of the gore. Baste each piece of lining through the tracings to the cloth, but do not catch in the haircloth.

Those who are more accustomed to the work may place the material on top of the lining, and baste from the top, rubbing the material down while basting, so that in either case the lining will be a little full on the material. This prevents the sagging, which is so objectionable.

Before basting, the seams must be carefully pinned together through the tracing lines, then basted from the top to the bottom. Do not include the haircloth in the seams, but after the latter are stitched and pressed open the haircloth is lapped and may be caught to the seams; finish the seam edges with binding ribbon, or overcast. After measuring the length, the bottom is finished with a facing disposed in either of two ways. The skirt may be turned up and cat-stitched as explained for preparing the skirt for velveteen, and the facing hemmed top and bottom.

The second method is as follows: After being certain that the skirt is measured off the correct length trim away all the surplus material beyond the tracing, allowing simply half an inch for a seam; now place the right side of the facing against the right side of the skirt and stitch by machine through the tracing for the length. Turn the facing over and baste along the edge; turn in the opposite edge of the facing and hem down to the lining. If a velveteen be desired, it is added by hand according to the method explained.

The lining may be basted (without the interlining) to the gores, the skirt stitched and pressed and the facing cut to fit the bottom of the skirt. Cut and fit the interlining to the facing, though not quite so deep, and stitch through both near the top. Now adjust this to the skirt.

Skirts with circular and band flounces may be completed in several ways. Band flounces are unlined, and are finished with a facing of bias silk or self-material. (No. 40.) The upper edge is nicked, turned over once, and may have one, or possibly two, rows of stitching through to the skirt; or it may be sewed to the skirt to be embellished with taffeta bands or folds, or one of the fashionable trimmings. A circular flounce may be added to lengthen an upper skirt portion, or several may be applied to a full-length skirt for ornamentation.

NOVEL, ARTISTIC SEAMS

THE embellishment of seams of skirts, coats or other garments has become an important matter in the sartorial world, and these exhibit decorative features which were unheard of a few years ago.

In many instances the seams of a garment are joined in the ordinary way, with decoration applied later; but great care must be exercised to retain the symmetry of the lines. When making a garment or costume any of the seams illustrated may be chosen which are appropriate for the material and design; however, it should be remembered when making a coat and skirt suit that the same finish selected for the skirt should be carried out in the coat as well.

The first illustration pictures an ordinary seam stitched, pressed open, then stitched again with one row of ornamental stitching on one side of the seam. No. 2 shows a similar finish, but both sides of the seam are ornamented with

No. 1.—Stitching on One Side of Seam

No. 2.—Stitching Both Sides of Seam

stitching. In No. 3 the seams should necessarily be cut wider, so that after working as directed for No. 2 an additional stitching may be added on each side, half an inch from the centre or original seam.

What is known as the cord seam is shown at No. 4. The seam turnings are both pressed to one side and an ornamental stitching added on the right side, far enough from the seam to form a raised edge, simulating a cording as shown.

The welt seam appears at No. 5. This is cut with wide seam-turnings and after being stitched is pressed to one side. The ornamental stitching is placed from one-quarter to three-eighths of an inch from the seam. After stitching, however, the edge of the upper seam may be cut back to this stitching, as shown in the illustration, so that when the final pressing is given too many thicknesses are not observable.

The double-stitched welt is portrayed at No. 6. This is made precisely like No. 5, but the first row of stitching is augmented by a second, forming the cord welt. Another welt seam is illustrated at No. 7 and is known as the open welt. This is stitched in a regular seam, but instead of being pressed on this seam, the material is folded over one-half an inch beyond the stitching. The ornamental stitching is then worked one-quarter of an inch from the

No. 3.—Broad Seam Stitched

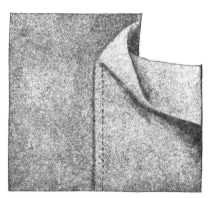

No. 4.—Cord Seam

edge, or more if desired. Furthermore, this differs from the others, inasmuch as the edge is not stitched flat but allowed to rest unrestrained, resembling a tuck. Press very flat.

The finished effect of the double-stitched slot-seam is shown at No. 8; it is easily made by joining the seams as for a plain finish. This must be done with a fine basting thread or sewing silk and the seam pressed without being stitched. An understrip of the material is cut an inch and one-quarter wide and placed directly over the centre of the seam at the back; this is stitched to the garment from the right side, three-eighths of an inch each side of the seam. The basting is then removed. The pressed edges are now free; raise them from the understrip, so as to facilitate the work and stitch each edge. A final pressing is given to the seam.

If preferred, a single-stitched slot seam may be executed by following these directions

No. 5.—Welt Seam

No. 6.—Double-Stitched Welt

with the exception of the final stitching on the edges. No. 9 pictures the reverse side of the work in the case of either the single or double stitched slot, the stitchings visible in this cut being those which secure the understrip to the forms.

For the strap seam wide turnings are allowed, and the seam is stitched and pressed. The strap, as shown at No. 10, is usually five-eighths of an inch wide when finished, and the centre is placed directly over the seam. The wide turnings underneath extend beyond the stitchings of the strap; in this way the thickness is decreased gradually. In almost all seams of this character, where it is allowable, the thickness should graduate, and where opportunity permits, as shown at No. 6 or 7, the edge of the centre material is cut away, so as not to be on a line with the other edges.

No. 7.—Open Welt

Straps *may* be made on the length of the material, from the pieces which are left in cutting the garment, but experience has

No. 8.—Slot Seam

No. 9.—Reverse Side of Slot Seam

proved that there is always a best way, and just as straps of silk should be cut bias of the material, so cloth straps work best when cut across the width or selvage of the goods.

For a strap five-eighths of an inch wide cut as many strips of cloth as will be required, each one inch and one-quarter wide. Join them and press the seams open, but when basting the straps on the seams of the coat or skirt, avoid bringing any of these joining in a prominent place; if necessary it will be better to waste a few inches and discard the piece with the seam in it.

Another method of making the strap is to fold the strip of cloth evenly through the centre, lengthwise, right side out and overhand the two raw edges together with coarse but even stitches. Flatten it out with the row of overhanding in the middle of the strap and press it well on the wrong side. Baste the strap over the seam and stitch one-eighth of an inch from each edge through both strap and garment.

An imitation strap seam is made by lapping the material as much as desired, then turning in the edge on both right and wrong side and stitching flat. This provides an equally desirable finish on both sides and is much employed in coats, and skirts which are unlined. The detail is pictured at No. 11.

A bound open-welt seam is shown at No. 12. This is made by binding the raw edge of the

No. 10.—Strap Seam

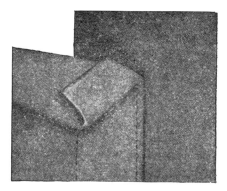

No. 11.—Imitation Strap Seam

No. 12.—Bound Open-Welt Seam

No. 13.—Raw-Edge Lapped Seam

seam with a grosgrain ribbon, which may be purchased for this purpose at a tailors' findings shop. The seam is lapped well over the opposite form and stitched as near the cording of the ribbon as possible. This seam produces no apparent thickness.

The raw-edge lapped seam is pictured at No. 13. This is intended solely for very heavy materials which will in no likelihood fray. The raw edges are lapped three-quarters of an inch, and the stitching placed directly on the edge. If the garment is lined, it is not necessary to have the second row directly on the under edge; this may be placed somewhat back, as shown in the illustration.

WEDDING AND EVENING GOWNS

T HE bridal gown may be of silk or satin, or, in fact, any of the fashionable materials which are appropriate. Chiffon or crêpe de Chine are beautifully soft and graceful, and a lace gown is charming and effective in the extreme; China silk and taffeta are also appropriate and, perhaps, less expensive. For a youthful bride, organdy and similar materials are frequently chosen.

An evening dress may be high or low in the neck, as the wearer prefers, but a wedding gown must be high in the neck with long sleeves, although elbow sleeves are permissible with long gloves. If made with a yoke of lace attached to a guimpe, it may be detached, and the dress will afterward undergo easy transition and be serviceable as a dinner or evening gown.

Taffeta or other silk should form the foundation or lining, but if organdy is chosen a lace-trimmed lawn may serve for the slip for both skirt and waist. In our book, "Weddings and Wedding Anniversaries," will be found several chapters relating to the bridal gown and a bride's trousseau, as well as full details for a properly conducted wedding and all necessary points on wedding etiquette. The price of this book is 25 cents.

Handwork is used extensively upon wedding and evening gowns and laces play an important part. The decoration may be as elaborate as one's taste and purse dictate. Sometimes yards and yards of handsome lace are used, forming a draped flounce around the bottom, or incrustations of motifs or separate medallions are preferred. Always choose the very newest effect, since it is better to be a little in advance of the prevailing mode than even a trifle behind in this regard.

The foundation or lining skirts supplied with the patterns are usually in five or seven gores, and the material of which they are made depends in a great measure upon the material selected for the gown itself. If this is chiffon, net or any extremely transparent stuff a silk lining is imperative, and a soft, lustrous Liberty satin gives a shimmering effect that no other lining can quite equal. A good lining taffeta, however, is always a reliable selection.

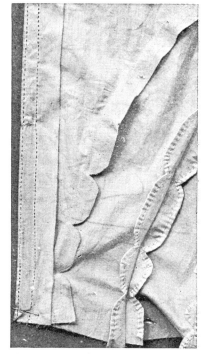

No. 1.—Notched Seam Before and After Binding

Measure the patterns and make any necessary alterations before cutting. Cut the lining by the special pattern for the lining, observing the directions on the label, and cut both waist and skirt at the same time; it is more economical. Fold the two ends of the lining together so that it will be double, and cut as previously directed, marking all perforations and indicating marks.

THE WAIST

The place of closing the waist lining, whether in the front or in the back, will generally be found to have an extra allowance for hemming under; the hem or closing line is usually indicated by a notch in the pattern at the neck and another at the bottom. Fold a line from one of these notches to the other, making the hem of equal width all the way, and with a thread of different color from the lining run a basting along the edge of the fold. This will later be turned over for the closing as shown at No. 1. Many wedding and evening gowns are now made to fasten in the back, so it is at these edges, instead of the front, that the turning under is left; otherwise the treatment is the same.

The fronts may be reinforced with an extra piece of lining, as explained in the chapter "Draped Waists," the effect being pictured at No. 2.

Baste up the lining and try it on, with the folds of the hems together or lapped, as directed in the label; be careful to pin it close and evenly at the closing edge. Make alterations, if any are needed. Stitch the seams and remove the bastings. Nick each seam (while still doubled) at the waist-line and above and below it, as many times as necessary to make the seams lie

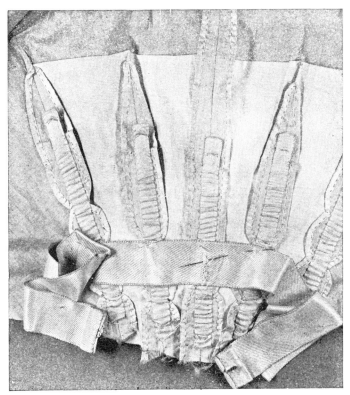

No. 2.—Reinforced Front and Manner of Attaching Inside Belt

flat when opened; trim them off even and pink them, overcast them, or, preferably, bind them with the taffeta binding ribbon which is sold for this purpose. (No. 1.) After the seams are bound press them open.

It will rarely be found necessary to make any alteration on the seam at the centre front or the darts, and under no circumstances should the seam at the centre back be changed. Place a bias strip of crinoline, two and one-half inches wide, and folded lengthwise through the centre, on the inside of the lining, with its fold at the tracing thread which marks the closing. Turn the taffeta over the crinoline at the tracing and baste; then stitch with one row of stitching an eighth of an inch back from the edge, and another row, the width of a whalebone (about three-eighths of an inch), inside of that. This is plainly seen at No. 1.

Run on the bone casing a little full, turning over the top as shown at No. 3.

The seams are now boned according to the directions given in the chapter "Draped Waists." Sew on the hooks and eyes as directed in the chapter referred to, and place the belt tape in the front; tack it to the centre seam, also to the last dart on each side. Baste an inch-wide bias strip of crinoline around the bottom of the waist on the inside; turn the edge of the waist under just a seam's width (three-eighths of an inch), cut a bias strip of lining silk one inch and one-quarter wide, turn under one edge and hem it down as a facing on the turned-under seam of the bottom of the waist; then turn under its other edge and hem it neatly to the waist.

To give the required bouffant effect at the front of the finished waist, a double ruffle of chiffon, reaching from just above the bust, if the gown is to be high neck, if not, to start from the edge of the low neck and reaching to below the waist-line, must be shirred across its top and basted through this shirring to the lining.

Two or three taffeta ruffles, pinked, are frequently placed in the same position, but not extending so low. These ruffles are best applied after the lining is placed upon the padded bust form, for the exact position can be better determined. Cut the material for the outside and drape it on the form according to the design selected.

When the skirt is worn outside of the waist the lower part of the waist drapery need not be turned under at the bottom of the waist, if for any reason this is not desirable. It may, instead, be sewed securely to the lining just below the waist-line, and the raw edge covered with a piece of seam binding laid on flat and sewed on both its edges. (No. 4.)

If an evening gown has a low neck, after placing on bertha or collar (if it has such effect) according to the directions on the label of the pattern, turn in a seam at the top of the bodice—including the top edge of the bertha, the lining and outside—baste in place, then hem on it a facing of bias silk, as the bottom of waist lining was finished, but three-quarters of an inch wide, and be careful when hemming down the lower edge to catch through the lining only. Use this facing as a casing through which to run a narrow ribbon, which is to be tied when the waist is worn, in order to hold it snug to the neck.

For a wedding gown with a lace yoke the latter should be fitted and basted in the top of the waist before the facing is applied; the finishing may be carried out in the manner directed. Line the yoke with one or more layers of chiffon to soften the effect over the skin. If preferred, a separate guimpe may be made; this is easily removed.

No. 3.—Applying Bone Casing

No. 4.—Waist Drapery Sewed to the Lining

A transparent collar should have a lining of two thicknesses of thin chiffon. The first layer of chiffon should be turned over toward the worker, a seam all around, and basted, and the second row should be turned *under* a seam at its top edge and run fast to the lace. The lace and first lining of chiffon turn over on the left end of the collar, and the second lining of chiffon turns under and is run fast to it; the hooks— very small ones—are to be sewed on this end of the collar. Cut a piece of collar bone the proper length; it should be cut one inch longer than the height of the collar in order that the woven covering may be slipped back at each end and half an inch of the bone cut off. Draw the covering over the end and turn it back and fasten it; this secures the end of the feather-bone. It is then placed at the right end of the collar a seam distant from the edge, the lace and its first lining are turned over it and the second lining is turned under and run to it. It is not necessary to place one at the left end, as when the collar is hooked the one bone will support both ends. Buttonholed loops to correspond with the hooks are worked on the outside at this end. When the waist fastens at the back, as is usual now for fancy waists, if the hooks are alternated with the eyes at the back fastening, be sure that the top hook is on the same side of the waist as the hooks of the collar—the left—so there may be no difficulty with the closing of the collar. Place a piece of collar bone each side of the centre front of the collar, and if desired one at each side, between this and the back.

Baste the seams of the sleeves, try them on, and if they are too large or too small around, make the alteration in the seam marked with the large perforations. Stitch the seams and finish as directed. Sew the sleeves in the armholes according to perforations, then overcast these seams, armhole and sleeve together, with buttonhole twist or bind with ribbon. A sleeve of elbow length may perhaps be chosen, and complete directions for making each style are given when the pattern provides for more than one.

THE SKIRT

Baste the breadths of the foundation or lining skirt according to the notches and arrange the back according to directions in the label of the pattern.

No. 5.—Adjusting Accordion-Plaiting on Skirt

Try on the lining and make any alterations it may need at the waist or hip; pin a piece of tape around at the natural waist-line and pin the placket together at the exact centre of the back. Be careful not to make the skirt too tight around the hips, otherwise, when you sit, it will wrinkle and pull up from the feet. Baste the alterations in the seams and baste the tape which is pinned around the waist. Mark the length around the bottom by turning up if it is too long; be very careful to have it long enough across the front. See this in a glass, and stand naturally. It is customary for a wedding or ceremonial gown to lie on the floor at least one inch across the front. This may be a little uncomfortable for walking, but if it can be managed it makes a much more graceful skirt. At all events, have it a little more than touch, as nothing looks more ungainly than a trained skirt which apparently "hitches up" in the front. If the outer skirt is made of transparent material the lining must be the same length, but for the wedding gown of satin or silk the lining is in short train length and the train of the gown is lined separately and faced with self-material. This facing is often further decorated with tiny frills of chiffon or silk at the lower edge.

A rather elaborate lining is desirable for a wedding gown, and this may be made by placing an accordion-plaiting around the bottom of the foundation skirt. This plaiting should be twelve to fifteen inches deep, but, if economy of material be sought, it may be made narrower. The manner of attaching this plaiting to the skirt is shown at No. 5.

The foundation skirt may be cut two or three inches shorter than the actually required length, and this length may be supplied for the purpose of fitting by adding a piece of cambric at the bottom of the skirt.

The accordion-plaiting should have a narrow hem on one edge before being sent to be plaited, and should measure at least three times the width of the foundation skirt.

After it is plaited measure the ruffle into quarters; place a colored thread as a mark at each quarter, and shirr the unhemmed edge. Measure the skirt into quarters and mark in the same way. Mark up from the correct length for the bottom of the skirt three-quarters of an inch less than the depth of the finished accordion-plaiting, and continue this mark all around the skirt with a colored thread.

No. 6.—Simple Ruche for Edge of Chiffon Accordion-Plaiting

Place the plaiting on the skirt with its right side toward the right side of the skirt, the shirred edge toward the bottom of the skirt and the edge of the plaiting even with the mark which was made around the bottom of the skirt. Baste the plaiting in this position; regulate the fulness by placing the quarter marks of the plaiting on the quarter marks of the skirt and distribute the shirring evenly all around. Stitch the seam and remove the basting, then turn over the plaiting and baste and afterward stitch it down on the right side through both plaiting and skirt. There will now be left some of the foundation skirt beneath the plaiting; the edge of this may have a narrow hem or may be pinked. A bias ruffle five and one-half inches wide should be pinked on both edges, shirred one inch from the upper edge and placed on the foundation skirt to make that the same length as the plaiting. A ruching should be cut in bias strips two inches wide, pinked on each edge, and either plaited or shirred through the centre and sewed to the hemmed edge of the accordion-plaiting.

Over the silk plaiting may be placed an accordion-plaiting of chiffon of the same depth. A narrow ruche should be placed on the edge of this plaiting also. Cut straight across the chiffon (draw a thread to keep it straight) as many strips, each two inches wide, as are required, and join with

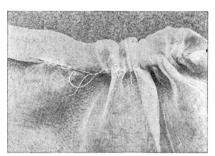

No. 7.—Puff-Ruffle

seams. Fold one edge over one-quarter of an inch, bring the other edge to the centre of the strip and fold the edge over it which has been turned under. This brings both edges to the centre, the one with a turned-under seam on top, so that no raw edge is left; it is then shirred through the centre and forms the ruche shown at No. 6. Another finish is called a puff-ruffle, and may be used in place of the deep chiffon plaiting. It is made from

No. 8.—Three-Tuck Ruche

chiffon cut across the width to measure two inches more than twice the depth of the silk plaiting; a narrow seam is turned over at one edge, the other edge is folded up to within one inch and one-half of the top, and the folded edge is laid over the raw edge, then the ruffle is shirred through; this leaves a heading and a double hemless ruffle, and is to be sewed to the foundation skirt to fall over the silk accordion-plaiting. The making of this puff-ruffle is shown at No. 7.

Still another finish is shown and is called a three-tuck ruche. The chiffon is cut seven inches wide, the strips joined and the selvages cut off; the long strip is folded lengthwise through the centre, the two raw edges are then brought up, inside, to three-quarters of an inch from the centre fold and a shirring is run one inch from this centre fold; the manner of making this ruche is shown at No. 8.

The finished ruche shows three shirred tucks of even width. This ruche is to be placed on the edge of the accordion-plaiting made of the lining in place of the silk ruche previously described, and is to take the place of the accordion-plaiting of chiffon or of the puff-ruffle. The outer skirt is prepared and fitted after the lining is fitted and made the correct length.

To make a lining of much more simple finish, mark the length of the skirt with a

No. 9.—Facing Bottom of Skirt

colored thread, then fit a bias band of crinoline three and one-half inches wide around, leaving a seam beyond the marking line; turn up the silk and crinoline and baste. Face with a bias piece of the lining cut four inches wide. (No. 9.)

Turn under the right side of the placket at the closing line and baste it. Make an underlap for the left side from a straight piece of the lining three and three-quarter inches wide and an inch longer than the length of the placket opening. This is usually ten inches, but for a very small person may be less. Sew one edge of the underlap to the left side of the placket opening with the seam on the inside, being careful not to stretch the bias, then hem the other edge of the underlap on the inside of the skirt to cover the raw edges of the seam.

No. 10.—Box-Plaited Ruche

Cut from the lining enough bias strips, each four inches wide, to measure three times around the bottom of the skirt. This may be hemmed with a very narrow hem on both edges or it may be pinked. Lay this in box-plaits and baste through the centre, forming a ruche as seen at No. 10; then baste the ruche on the skirt, keeping the edge of the ruche even with the edge of the bottom of the skirt; and stitch it fast to the skirt through the centre bastings.

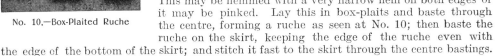

A dust ruffle, cut bias and four inches wide, should be pinked or hemmed on both edges and shirred three-quarters of an inch from the edge and sewed to the inside of the bottom of the skirt through this shirring. Tack the dust ruffle to the skirt at intervals of fourteen inches, using a French tack. This is made by taking a small stitch in the skirt and one in the ruffle, leaving, in this case, half an inch of twist between. Take a stitch again into the same place in the skirt and again into the ruffle, leaving the half-inch of twist each time. This will leave three strands of silk. Work back around all three at once with five or six buttonhole stitches, not too close together, and fasten the end off on the skirt. (No. 11.)

The method described forms the simplest finish for the bottom of an evening skirt, but if more fluffiness is desired about the feet and the quantity of material used

No. 11.—French Tack in Dust Ruffle

is no object, deep plaitings, ruchings and over-ruffles of chiffon, also ruched, may be used as prodigally as desired. If chiffon, net or other diaphanous material is selected for the skirt, a clouding of chiffon will be required to cover the silk lining. This is draped over the latter to soften the effect of the silk, that the strong contrast between the foundation and outer material may not be too pronounced. The material is now draped upon the foundation skirt according to the design selected and the directions on the label.

Cut the outside parts of the skirt and join them according to the pattern. Do not remove the tape at the waist-line of the lining skirt, but baste the drapery part over it; try on the skirt, alter the drapery at the top part if necessary, turn up the bottom at the right length, and baste. Sew up the back seam to the depth of the placket in the lining. Turn the right-hand side of the drapery placket over the already turned-under edge of the lining placket,

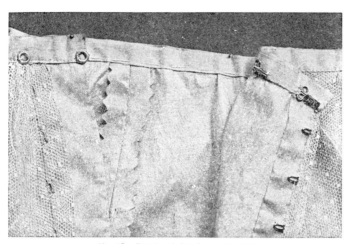

No. 12.—Finish of Placket and Belt

but only for seven inches from the waist. For the same distance, on the left side, turn under a seam and slip-stitch fast to the underlap, overlapping it on this piece just a seam's width. From these seven inches to the bottom of the placket opening hem each side neatly with a narrow hem. Cut the belt for the skirt from the lining by the pattern; turn in three-eighths of an inch at each end and on one edge of the length. Measure from one end one-half of the waist measure, place a mark here and pin to the centre front of the skirt; pin it around both sides, making both exactly the same length. The left end will have an allowance for the underlap. Baste the belt as pinned and stitch it; turn over and hem down on inside of skirt; trim away any material at the top of the skirt which may be too wide to go into the belt.

On the right-hand side of the placket sew hooks well back from the edge, one inch apart if the skirt is in habit back, one and one-half inch if there is fulness. Have hooks the entire length of the placket, sewing them on the lining only, below the seven inches, and cover the sewed-on part of the hooks with a facing cut on the straight. (No. 12.) Sew rings covered with buttonhole twist or loops worked with the twist on the left side, placing them so they will correspond with the hooks, and bring the closing together properly. Sew hooks and eyes or buttonholed rings on the belt as directed for a plain skirt. Use ordinary straight hooks for the belt and hump or patent French hooks for the placket.

If a bustle is desired, one which is both dainty and light may be made of taffeta ruffles, as shown at No. 13. A piece of lining material, silk or percaline, is cut about four inches smaller than the finished bustle is to be, a

No. 13.—A Ruffle Bustle

three and one-half-inch bias ruffle, pinked on both edges, is sewed in several rows across the foundation piece, and the whole is finished by a ruffle running around and covering the ends of these cross rows. The foundation piece has its edges pinked so that both sides of the pad show a neat finish; it should be tacked to the belt of the skirt at the left side of the centre, and one French tack at the centre of the lower edge holds it to the left side of the placket opening. A hook should be sewed to the upper right-hand corner and will catch into a covered ring sewed in a suitable position on the inside of the belt. Bustles are comparatively little worn now, but some figures, especially those having large abdominal development with a corresponding flatness in the back, will be improved by a bustle of this kind.

THE TAILOR-MADE GOWN

A T ONE time the making of a tailor-made gown was considered impossible to the home dressmaker, but now, with authoritative information at hand and greater facilities for the amateur, very creditable gowns can easily be put forth.

By observing the rules carefully and permitting no occasion to pass which may hold even one small point of information, the worker will accomplish results which will not only please but greatly surprise her.

The difficulty is not so much greater in a gown of this character than in one with a draped waist although the basting and fitting must be done very accurately, with almost innumerable pressings; while each minute detail must be given its proper consideration. Each in itself is quite simple, although all taken together, when properly executed, accomplish a perfect whole.

A tailor-made waist usually has all the seams visible on the outside, although pressed so flat that a perfectly smooth surface is the result.

Cut the material and either chalk the outlet seams or mark with tailors' tacks. Pin the forms together, beginning at the waist-line and working up, then from the waist-line down, and baste from top to bottom with small running stitches. It must be remembered that a great deal depends upon the size of the basting stitches employed; those for joining the forms together must be small running stitches, so that the waist may be snugly fitted.

Try the waist on and note that the waist-line sets well down into the curve of the figure before making any alterations. Pin the fronts together beginning at the waist-line and keep the bastings together to the neck, then pin from the waist-line down. If the fit is a little snug over the bust, a slight curve may be allowed beyond the basting, but if it is much too tight make the alterations at the outlet seams. If the armhole feels tight, snip the edge the depth of the seam (three-eighths of an inch) all around the front, and if too high under the arm, snip here also. This will increase the size of the armhole considerably and allow sufficient seam for sewing in the sleeve.

Take the waist off and rebaste, making both sides exactly alike (unless one side of the figure is different from the other), in which case both sides must be fitted. Having finished the alterations, stitch the seams just outside the bastings—this prevents the waist from being tighter and allows sufficient room for the bones and casings. Remove the bastings and press very flat.

All seams must be notched at the waist-line and again two inches above, and below if the waist is long. As the seam must lie flat, it may, perhaps, be necessary to cut another notch or two if there is a great curve.

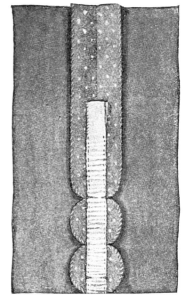

No. 1.—Bone Casing put on Full

Due consideration was given the subject of boning in the chapter "Draped Waists," but a few extra words of instruction are here given. If featherbone has been selected for this tailor-made waist it is applied to every seam and in the positions explained.

If whalebone is selected, a casing of Prussia binding is applied. Turn over the top one inch and overcast the edges of one side together, three-quarters of an inch. The remaining quarter is caught firmly to the seam with two stitches on top of each other, keeping the centre of the casing directly on the seam. Sew the casing on full, like gathers, as shown at No. 1; when half way between the waist-line and the notch above, begin to put in extra fulness until the same position below the waist-line is reached; below this the fulness is the same as at first. Sew on the other side, leaving the loop open at the top. Soak the bones in water.

When featherbone is applied the lower edge of the waist need not be finished until later, as the featherbone is easily trimmed or cut. With whalebone, however, the bottom of the waist is trimmed the correct shape and a bias strip of thin crinoline about an inch wide (this depends upon the length of the waist below the waist-line) is fitted all around the bottom over the bone casings. Turn up the edge, keeping a clean-cut line, and baste. Cat-stitch this; remove the basting and press.

Cut the corners off the bone, thus shaping a curve, and insert it through the aperture at the upper part of the casing. Push the bone through to the very bottom of the seam, then draw it back a trifle so that it will not strain the edge, and sew through the bone a quarter of an inch from the end. Tack first on one side, over and over, from centre to edge, then directly opposite in the same manner, being careful not to catch in the lining of the form.

A second tacking is made about an inch and a half above the waist-line. The bone is sprung in as much as possible—that is, it is

No. 2.—Front of Tailor-Made Waist

No. 3.—Back of Tailor-Made Waist

pushed in with great force, the fulness of the casing facilitating this—and tacked as just explained. This process requires no little strength, but is very essential if the waist be properly boned, since it produces a graceful curving around the waist. (With featherbone this springing is done by machine.) The bone is now cut off the exact length of the casing, corners are trimmed off and the bone slipped into the opening. Sometimes another tack is placed an inch and a half below the top of the bone. The aperture is now closed by overcasting the edges together.

This is a perfect method of boning. The lower tacking prevents the bone protruding through the lower edge of the waist, the second causes the spring or curving at the waist-line and also prevents the bone from thrusting through the top of the casing. In turn, the detached casing at the top prevents the bone from wearing through the material. Extra long seams require the first tacking as explained, then a second about half an inch below the waist-line, and then the springing of the bone; tacking and finishing as for the other seams.

The finished effect of the front of a basque constructed according to these directions is pictured at No. 2. If the lower edge is ornamented with machine-stitching, this is accomplished and pressed before the bones are inserted. Waists made in this manner are to be worn outside the skirt and are sometimes made with postilion backs and pointed in front.

For the invisible closing at the front insert the crinoline as directed for underneath hooks and eyes, turn over the edge on the correct basting and add the ornamental stitching at the same time as that for the lower edge. Press this, after which affix the hooks and eyes. But-tonholes and buttons may effect the closing, if desired, but for these extra width must be allowed on the fronts in cutting the waist.

A fitted canvas or haircloth may be placed over the fullest part of the bust, as explained for a coat, as this assures a good shaping to the front of the waist.

Cut the lining, which is usually silk, and join the forms as for a coat; place corresponding seams together and tack occasionally. If preferred, each lining form may be lapped and hemmed over the other. Hem down the front and around the bottom, close to the edge. At No. 3 the effect of good work, as well as the spring of the bones, is displayed in the back of this waist.

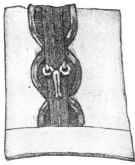

If a belt tape is used it is made a very snug fit, usually a quarter of an inch smaller than the waist measure, and is finished with either one or two hooks and eyes. Before this tape is adjusted, however, three hooks are sewed to the bones on the back seams. These hooks have the two prongs, which form rings on the ends, separated with the scissors so that they are more easily sewed to the seams without stitching through the bones. The bill of the hook just touches the waist-line, where it is fastened firmly; it is also tacked through the rings at the upper edge, as seen in No. 4.

The belt tape is slipped under the bills of the hooks with the centre to the centre-back seam of the waist. Cross-stitch with a light-colored twist, taking the needle under the bone at every stitch and fastening off firmly.

No. 4.—Hook Sewed on Seam under Belt Tape

For a standing collar linen canvas forms the best interlining. Shrink it by wetting thoroughly, then cut a double strip bias, the same shape as the collar. Stitch this double canvas back and forth on the machine as illustrated at No. 5.

The material is cut exactly like the pattern, but the seam allowance of three-eighths of an inch is cut off all sides of the canvas. Place these together and baste all around. Turn over the edge of the material without turning the canvas and baste, snipping the upper curve portion where necessary, then cat-stitch all around. This method is shown at No. 6, with the lower edge of the material ready to be turned up and cat-stitched. Adjust the collar with its

No. 5.—Stitched Canvas Collar

lower edge touching the seam line all around the neck and slip-stitch firmly; snip the neck curve that the seam may set flat against the collar and cat-stitch the neck seam of the waist to the collar. Add the hooks and eyes and face the collar with silk.

On some occasions the lapels of a waist similar to the one illustrated are formed by turning back the fronts at the top. When this is the case, the cloth and canvas collar are padding stitched together and then joined to the lapels, which have previously been covered with canvas, then padding stitched. The collar and lapel facings are adjusted as directed for coat collars in the chapter entitled "Coats and Jackets."

In the present instance, however, the entire collar and lapels are applied. These are interlined with a single layer of canvas and the seams joined and well pressed. Turn the material over the edge without turning the canvas and apply the ornamental stitching which must match the stitching on the waist. Adjust the lining so that it fits the collar exactly; turn in the edge and hem. Without catching in the lining join the collar to the neck of the waist, turn the seam up on the collar and cat-stitch. The remaining edge of the collar lining is turned in and hemmed along the former line of stitching. This should be done with great nicety—as the roll of the collar has to be preserved and the lining must be in no way full; at the same time it must not be drawn tight, else it will disturb the correct appearance of the collar on the outside.

One of the many evidences of a well-made tailor waist is the result of hard pressing. All edges should be faced with crinoline before stitching, canvas being employed for very heavy cloth. After cat-stitching the edges, remove the bastings before pressing. Press the individual parts as the work progresses and give a final pressing after the waist is finished.

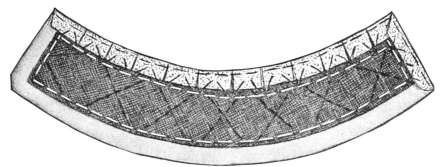

No. 6.—Material Collar and Canvas

Sleeves for a tailor-made garment are usually plain, but whether this is the case or somewhat elaborate sleeves have been selected, follow the directions on the label of the particular pattern chosen. Baste as directed in the chapter "Draped Waists," and fit carefully.

Sometimes buttons and buttonholes complete the closing at the wrist, in which case the back seam is opened and the crinoline or canvas fitted up the side to the top of the opening. After the ornamental stitching is added, the buttonholes are worked and the buttons sewed in position.

Line the sleeves as explained for coat sleeves, stitch in the armholes and hem the lining all around against the line of stitching.

The skirt should be made according to a fashionable pattern and may be unlined, if the material is a heavy cloth, since many of these follow the tailor-made effects. When light-weight cloth is chosen a silk foundation skirt is used and this is made according to the directions given in the chapter entitled "Skirts." Select an appropriate finish for the seams, also for the finish at the hem.

It is well to remember that in making a selection of material the design of the gown should, in a measure, influence both the style of material and the width. If a circular skirt or one with broad gores has been selected, a material of wide double fold should be chosen so as to avoid joinings. For a skirt with narrow gores a single width material may be cut to equal advantage.

Sometimes women complain of being advised to purchase too much material because they think it is possible to cut from less than is printed on the label of the pattern. In this regard it must be remembered that one person may cut much more economically than another. Besides, where one woman would be perfectly satisfied to piece out a width, another would refuse to do it, knowing that this is not done by those who would have first-class work. Instead, the goods must be opened to its full width, so that no joinings will be required; while this necessitates a somewhat greater quantity of material, it denotes good workmanship. There are occasions, however, when small piecings may be required at the lower edge of a gore, even in the widest goods, but this is unavoidable. Joinings should be eschewed as much as possible.

Again, it is necessary to good cutting, and fitting as well, to lay each piece of the pattern on exactly the grain of the goods designated by the line of perforations. This is essential since the entire garment may twist or wrinkle, so that it will be most imperfectly finished. This is also a means of reducing the quantity of material to be used, but it is simply an error on the part of the worker and should never be done, even to save the material, for it is most unworkmanlike.

COATS AND JACKETS

THE amateur dressmaker has many misgivings when she decides to make a coat, for, while she may be quite clever at dressmaking, coat-making is so very different that she always fears to begin. Many dressmakers, too, although they have a wider knowledge, are frequently in doubt as to how to proceed in certain stages of the work and to these the following information will be of great benefit. Coats and jackets vary in shape, but this general information will be found applicable to almost all designs.

Tight-fitted coats, closely outlining the figure, require more care and attention in the making than a fancy coat, though the latter when finished, may look much more elaborate. The plain and apparently simple coat, with its straight front and closely fitted sides and back, its stitched, lapped or strapped seams, is the severest test of the dressmaker's skill.

The first important item is to have the cloth thoroughly shrunken, and instructions for this are given in the chapter "Important Points and Aids in Dressmaking."

The cloth being ready, lay out the pattern on it to the best advantage, being careful, if there is a nap, to place the pieces so they will all run the same way of the goods. If this is not done, the pieces with the nap running in the opposite direction will shade; that is, they will look a different color. The nap should always run toward the bottom of the garment. Be sure to follow carefully the directions accompanying the pattern, which tell just how each piece must lie on the *grain* of the goods; otherwise, the completed garment will draw crooked, and no amount of fitting and refitting will ever make it straight.

When using full-width cloth—that is, fifty-two or fifty-four inches wide—if a short jacket is being made the pieces may fit in to cut economically with the cloth folded lengthwise through the centre. as it is folded when bought. For a long coat, however, it may be necessary to open the cloth to its full width. Lay it out smoothly, with the wrong side up and arrange the various pieces of the pattern on it in correct position.

Measure the length of the arm and alter the sleeve length of the pattern, when necessary, according to the directions given in the label.

Having the pattern laid out properly, outline it with tailors' chalk, remembering always that three-eighths of an inch is allowed for seams which are not marked with perforations. In almost all patterns, the seams at shoulders, under-arms, and outside edges of sleeves have perforations allowing larger seams,

No. 1.—Front Marked with Tailors' Tacks

called outlet perforations, because it is at these seams that the alterations are made in fitting. Mark the outline at these perforations, as well as at the various edges of the pattern.

When the outlines of all the pieces have been marked with chalk, cut off the length of cloth containing them and reversing the remainder of the cloth lay it out right side up and with the nap running down and lay over it the piece on which the outlines have been chalked, the right side of the latter piece facing the right side of the lower cloth and the nap of both running in the same direction. The chalk outlines, having been made on the wrong side of the cloth, will now be on top. Cut through both thicknesses. Mark with tailors' tacks (these are described and illustrated in the chapter "Practical and Ornamental Stitches") through both thicknesses of cloth, along the perforation line at all the outline seams and also the marks for pockets, notch collar turning, centre front line; in fact, at every mark that indicates a point in the construction or finishing of the garment, so that there will be no trouble later.

At No. 1 will be seen the second front portion of a coat made with a seam running to the shoulder. The tacks have been cut and the two pieces are in process of separation.

Cut from tailors' canvas, previously shrunken, the front of the coat. For a coat that is cut with the front in one piece, either loose or shaped with a dart, cut the canvas in the same shape from the front edge, across the shoulder and around the armhole to the under-arm seam. Cut it three inches deep at this seam and slope from this point to the waist-line at the dart and continuing thence in a straight line down the front to the lower edge (see No. 2). This holds the fronts firm and flat and leaves no canvas at the side hip-line, where it would break and cause the coat to wrinkle. Baste this canvas to the wrong side of the cloth, then baste all the seams of the coat, canvas and cloth together, according to the notches, and it is ready for the first fitting. When a coat is shaped with a seam running to the shoulder instead of a dart, the canvas also must be cut in two pieces and joined in a seam. Make the first piece of canvas the same size as the first piece of the cloth; on the second piece cut it diagonally from three inches below the armhole to the waist-line, making the canvas follow the same outline as when the front is cut in one piece.

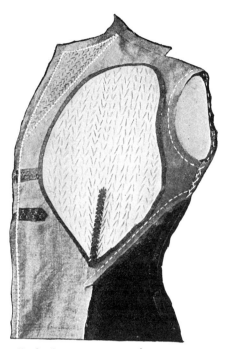

After fitting, make the necessary alterations, if any, stitch the canvas seam of the dart and the seam in the cloth separately, nick them on all curves and press them well. Stitch all the seams of the coat, and if they are to be strapped seams (a fold or strap of the cloth stitched down each seam), or if they are to be stitched with one or more rows of stitching each side of the seam, or as lapped seams, press the seams and stitch them. Other

No. 2.—Canvas and Haircloth Applied in Front of Coat

methods of ornamental stitching for seams will be found under the title. "Novel, Artistic Seams." All "top stitching," as it is called, must be done before the lining is put in.

Baste the stitched canvas pieces into the fronts of the coat again with several rows of bastings. One of the secrets of a well-tailored coat is many and careful bastings, and thorough pressing at every stage of the work.

To give the coat a round, well-shaped look over the bust, and prevent wrinkling and breaking, take a piece of haircloth, about five-eighths of a yard, shrink it and cut it to follow the shape of the front of the coat, but about two inches smaller—around the neck, shoulder and armhole—and finish it in a point about three inches above the waist-line. Do not make a seam in it at the dart seam in the coat, but cut a V-shaped piece from it to make it fit, and draw the cut edges together. Baste a strip of ordinary

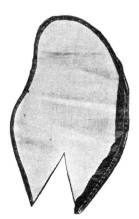

No. 3.—Haircloth Pad

lining cambric over this joining and also all around the haircloth to hold it to the canvas and to cover its raw edges. This haircloth is shown at No. 3. Attach the haircloth to the canvas by padding stitches and hem it to it at the bound edges; this is pictured at No. 2.

Where the garment is an Eton or other short jacket the canvas interlining is applied as shown at No. 4, the basting from below the armhole to the front tab indicating the outline of the canvas. The basting for the front centre is also shown indicating the amount the coat is to lap, as these markings are to be brought together when trying on; but whether single or double breasted the canvas must extend to the edge.

Baste a piece of canvas, cut to shape and about three inches wide, around the neck at the back and similar pieces around the armholes of the back and under-arm, to meet the canvas of the fronts as shown at No. 5. This stays the coat and improves the ornamental stitching.

Cut the collar by the pattern and its canvas three-eighths of an inch smaller. Mark

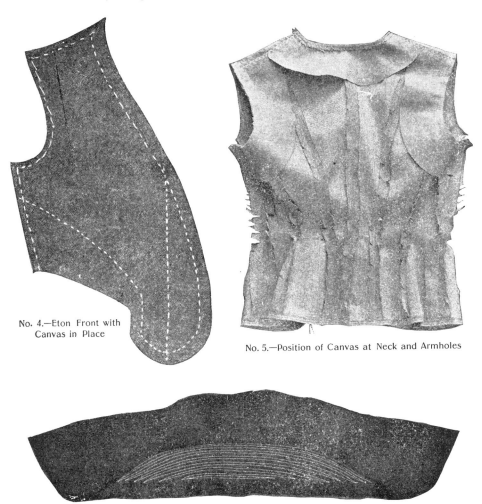

No. 4.—Eton Front with Canvas in Place

No. 5.—Position of Canvas at Neck and Armholes

No. 6.—Stitching on Standing Part of Collar

carefully the line of perforations in the collar which indicate where it is to be turned over, this will leave a crescent-shaped piece, which is the part that goes into the neck of the coat and is the "stand-up" part of the collar. This is to be stitched closely, several rows of stitching maintaining the shape of the outline. (No. 6.) The turn-over part, as well as the lapel or revers front, must be held firmly, catching the canvas and cloth together by many small padding stitches which may be about half an inch long on the canvas side and just barely catch, but not show through to the cloth. (No. 7.) In making the padding stitch on the collar and lapels hold them over the hand, the canvas uppermost, and as the stitching is done, roll and shape the section in the direction in which it is to lie. The detail for padding stitch is shown in the chapter "Practical and Ornamental Stitches."

Turn the edges of the cloth over the canvas and press; baste the collar, canvas side up, flat on the coat according to the notches in the collar and in the neck. The upper or turn-over part of the collar must lie flat, joining the turned-over lapels at the top of the fronts, to form the notched or "man's" collar.

It will be found that the pattern allows a lap of about two inches on each front edge beyond the double perforations that mark the centre of the front, which is ample for the buttonholes, when the coat is single-breasted. It may be finished with visible buttons and buttonholes, but a fly which conceals the fastenings may be used if preferred.

When the coat has advanced this far, try it on. Fold over the lapel corners at the top of the fronts and see that the collar is the correct size and fits properly. If it does not, it may be shaped by shrinking, stretching and pressing. The front edges of the coat should lie close to the figure at the bust and a well-fitted coat should hold itself in shape to the figure at this point, even when unbuttoned. If it is inclined to flare away at the front line, pin in one or two small dart-like tucks, about one-quarter of an inch at the coat's edge and running out to nothing about two inches inside the edge, far enough to shape the edge and take out the stretched appearance. Mark these tucks with chalk, remove the pins and slash in the canvas at each chalk mark. Lap the canvas the same space that the tucks were made, cut away one edge to meet the other, lay a piece of cambric over the slash and sew the cambric to hold it to shape. The cloth will now have in it the fulness that has been taken out of the canvas and must be gathered on a thread, dampened and shrunk with the iron. Narrow linen tape is sewed to the canvas toward the inside of the coat at the crease of the lapel, drawing it taut to prevent stretching. The edges of the lapel should also be taped and the front coat edges as well, drawing the tape at these edges to give good shaping and pressing smoothly.

No. 7.—Canvas and Cloth of Collar showing Padding Stitches

From the cloth, cut collar facing and facings for fronts. The front facings must be cut to the shaping of the front after the edges have been altered and taped. Lay the cloth on the fronts and over the turned lapel corners, pin it carefully in place, holding the front and lapel in their proper shape. Then cut it to the required width. It need extend only about three inches inside of the line that marks the centre of the front. Collar facing, if of cloth, must be cut on the width or cross grain of the material and must not have a seam in the centre of the back. Fit the collar facing to the canvas collar and join this facing to the front facings, matching the notches on the collar and on the front facings; press the seams open and baste to the canvas collar and to the fronts of the coat, turning in the edges of both coat and facing. This finish is for visible closing and the buttonholes are to be worked through both the outside and the cloth facing. For a fly facing, leave the facing of the right side of the front separated from the coat below the lapel, as this facing will form the fly for the invisible buttonholes. Turn the edge of the cloth under on this right side, and from the crease of the turned-over lapel to the bottom of the coat stitch on the upper or finished side of coat about a quarter of an inch from the edge as a finish, having one or more rows of stitching as desired; then face this side with a piece of the silk, satin or serge used for lining.

No. 8.—Finish of Sleeve at Wrist

This facing must be wide enough to reach past the centre front. The cloth facing for the right side must itself be faced upon its side toward the coat with a piece of the same lining and be stitched a quarter inch in from the front edge. Baste the cloth underfacing to the inside of the right side of the coat, and at the centre line stitch with one row of stitching through both coat and facing to hold them firmly together. Now continue the row of edge stitching from the place where it began at the top of the right side, around the turned-over lapels, around the collar and down the left side.

If a velvet collar facing is used instead of one of the same cloth (and this adds much to the general good effect of the coat) it should be made of a seamless bias strip of velvet; do not stitch the edges of the collar, but only the turned-over lapels, which are of cloth. The edge of the velvet is turned over the canvas collar and the **raw edge cat-stitched flat to the cloth lining** of the collar.

All pressing and shaping of the collar must be done before putting on the velvet facing. Baste up the bottom edge of the coat, unless this has been done when stitching the lapels.

If any padding is needed, a few layers of sheet wadding, decreasing in size, so it may grow thinner toward the edges, may be basted around the armhole from front shoulder to back shoulder, deepening under the arm and being made thick or thin where the figure may require it. If it is desired to make the shoulders look more square, place a triangular piece of wadding on the shoulder with the point at about the middle of the shoulder seam and the wider part at the armhole, making the wadding thick enough to give the required squareness to the shoulders.

Baste the seams of the sleeves and baste the sleeves in the armhole of the coat according to perforations and notches and give a second fitting. If the sleeves need any alteration in size around the arm, make it at the seam marked by outlet perforations, removing the sleeve from the armholes of the coat for this purpose. A bias strip of canvas three inches deep should be basted into the wrist part at the proper length and the cloth turned over and cat-stitched to the canvas. Finish the edge with one or two rows of machine-stitching to match the stitching on the edges of the coat. If stitching at cuff depth is desired it must be made before completing the outside seam. This sleeve preparation is seen at No. 8. Baste the sleeves in the armholes and stitch them.

Work the buttonholes, the top one just at the lowest corner of the turned-over lapel and sew the buttons on the left side to correspond, sewing through coat and canvas, but not through the facing. The coat is now ready for the lining.

In making a fly front, collarless coat or jacket, with a seam running to the shoulder instead of a dart, the method is a trifle different. The first front piece is entirely lined with canvas and in the second front piece the canvas reaches to the waist-line on the edge toward the front, sloping thence to a depth of about three inches at the under-arm seam. This canvas must be cut the same as the fitted cloth and is joined in a seam which should be notched and pressed open. The canvas is then basted inside the fronts of the jacket with the seam edges of the canvas toward those of the cloth. Tailors' canvas of soft quality should be used in the fronts, but for the canvasing at the neck and arm-holes of the back portions French canvas is used, cut to the shape and basted in place. The left front and the neck edges are now turned over the canvas and basted. The right front is faced with a narrow strip of silk and one or two rows of machine-

No. 9.—Inside View of Fly-Front Coat

sitching are made along these edges. A piece of haircloth, cut and bound as directed for No. 3, is fitted into each front to hold the coat into a well-rounded shape over the bust. The fly piece is next fitted to the right side of the front and the row of stitching to hold it to the coat is made at the centre line. The buttonholes are then worked in it at even spaces and from the *cloth* side. All of these are shown at No. 9.

If any padding is necessary at shoulders or under-arms it should now be tacked in place, after which the coat is ready for the lining, though if interlining is to be used to give greater warmth it should be put in before the front facing is applied. Cotton flannel is frequently used for the interlining, though a soft all-wool material, that comes especially for the purpose, is preferable, as it gives greater warmth in proportion to its weight than the cotton. The interlining is not cut in pieces like the silk lining and the outside, but is fitted across the back in one piece from one under-arm seam to the other and should terminate three or four inches above the waist. Slash it in places, if necessary, to make it fit, and tack the slashed edges together. Fit pieces into the fronts in the same way; do not make regular seams, but slash it along the outline of the seam in front, lap one edge over the other, cutting away superfluous material, and baste the edges together one over the other, avoiding all possible thickness.

Turn up the lower edge of the coat all round. The front of this coat is pictured at No. 9 and is now ready for the lining.

LINING A COAT OR JACKET

Silk or satin is unquestionably the only satisfactory lining for a coat. One of the several silk substitutes may be used for lining a gown, but only the absolute necessity for economy should permit its use as coat lining. Skinner's satin is probably the best wearing, all-round material for coat lining, though silk serge and taffeta also are used. White satin of a good, firm quality is the most attractive, but satin matching the shade of the cloth is more serviceable. The lining is the final stage of coat-making; the outside must be entirely finished, the pockets in and all the ornamental stitching in place before beginning the lining.

Cut the lining from the same pattern as the cloth, allowing for any alterations

No. 10.—Plaited Wadding for Top of Sleeve

No. 11.—Fitting the Lining in the Front

which have been made in fitting and cutting the lining of the fronts to extend to the front facings only, and cut the back pieces each one-half an inch wider than the pattern to allow for a small plait in the · tre back; leave good seams, as the lining must be quite easy. If it is tight it will draw the outside of the coat and cause wrinkles. Stitch the seam down the centre back, then baste a small plait just at this seam to avoid any possibility of tightness. Having the two back pieces of the lining basted in the coat, there is a raw edge at their two outer edges; catch these raw edges flat with a loose basting to the inside of the seams of the coat over which they lie. Now take the next piece of the lining and baste it through the centre to the corresponding piece of the coat, then turn under the edge toward the back and baste it down like a hem over the raw edge of the back pie e, notching the edges of both seams at the waist-line and immediately above and below, so they will fit the curves of the coat. Continue this method with each piece of the lining and turn in at the bottom, allowing about an inch of the cloth to show. After all the edges are turned under and basted over the preceding pieces and over the raw edges of the facings in front and around over the edges of the collar at the neck, they are to be neatly felled down; be careful not to catch through the cloth to the outside.

The lining of the sleeves is cut like the outside and the seams are stitched and pressed. The lining is hemmed down at the hand part and on the small opening allowed in the pattern (if there be one) at the back of the sleeve; it is then carefully drawn up in place and basted through the cloth of the sleeve all around about five inches from the top. Now take a piece of wadding, fifteen inches long and two inches wide, round one side of it, and plait up the straight side in three-quarter-inch plaits. (No. 10.) Baste this into the top of the armhole to hold out the top of the sleeve, then draw up the sleeve lining, turn in the raw edge and hem it down on the coat lining all around the armhole, first basting it in place, covering all previous stitches.

A slightly different method of lining is as follows:

After the jacket has been fitted, if any alterations are necessary make the same alterations on the pattern, as the patterns of the back and of the sleeve portions are used to cut the lining.

Fit a piece of silk into the front in the manner shown at No. 11. Make the selvage parallel with the row of stitching at the centre front that holds the fly piece to the front, turn this selvage under and pin it along evenly. Fit the silk straight across at the fullest part of the bust and lay a graduated plait from this point to the shoulder seam. Fit the silk into the lower part of the jacket by pinning it

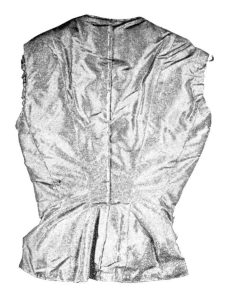

No. 12.—Lining Basted in Jacket

No. 13.—Sleeve Lining Basted at Armhole

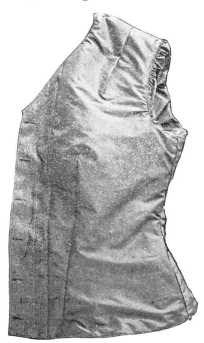

No. 14.—Finished Lining

to form a dart and fitting out carefully to the under-arm seam. Turn the silk over and sew this dart in a seam and cut away the superfluous material. Tack this dart seam loosely to the canvas or the interlining. Baste the front in place and tack the edges to the cloth seams at the under-arm and shoulders. Turn under the lower edge and baste to the jacket.

This way of lining the front should be attempted by an experienced person only, otherwise it will be safer to cut the linings for the fronts the same as the pattern.

Cut the lining for the backs, using the corrected pattern, and allowing one-half inch beyond the pattern at both sides of the centre-back seam. Stitch the pieces of the lining of the backs and under-arms together. Lay a plait one-half inch wide down the length of the back seam and baste it to hold it in place. Pin the back pieces of the lining to the coat and fit the next seam of the lining directly over the corresponding seam of the cloth and baste the raw edges of both seams lightly together.   If the coat is interlined, tack the seams of the silk lining to the interlining.   Be sure the seam of the silk lies directly over the seam in the cloth, and make the basting stitches somewhat loose.   Turn under the edges of the back lining at the under-arm and shoulder seams and baste them over the edges of the fronts of the lining.   Turn under the back lining at the neck and the lower edges and baste to the cloth.   The lining will now be all basted in position as seen at No. 12.   Gather the tops of the sleeves and baste and stitch them into the armholes.   Turn under the edge of the sleeve lining and gather it along the fold.   Draw the gathered edge of the sleeve lining over the raw edges of the armhole and baste in position as shown at No 13.   Hem or fell all the basted edges of the silk into place so as to cover the machine-stitching.   The finished lining is shown at No. 14.

COAT POCKETS

Some coats and jackets are not supplied with pockets but are completely finished without them. When pockets are desired they are generally inserted during the construction of the garment, and before the lining is inserted.

For a loose front coat a pocket is usually inserted between the coat and lining at one of the front edges. It should be made of the lining like an ordinary pocket one would put in the seam of a skirt and placed in an opening which should have been left for that purpose when the lining was hemmed down against the facing at the front. This opening should begin about four inches below the waist-line and may be

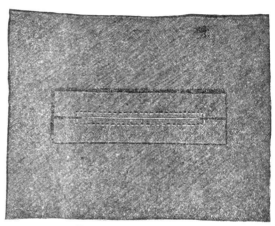

No. 15.—Pocket Slash Stitched

No. 16.—Finished Slash Basted Together

placed on whichever side is more convenient for the intended wearer.

An inserted pocket requires great care to be made nicely, but if the directions are followed accurately, step by step, a great deal of the difficulty will be obviated. There are always, however, structural matters to be considered, as the various designs are constructed on different lines.

For the slash pockets the opening is faced and the pocket inserted, the same method being pursued whether the slash is perpendicular or horizontal.

Mark for the slash in the correct position and place over this, on the right side of the coat, a strip of material for a facing. Beneath this on the wrong side arrange a larger piece of stay linen and baste both in position.   Now make two rows of stitching one-quarter of an inch apart, along both sides of the mark for the slash or opening, as shown at No. 15.   Cut through between these lines, continuing the cutting of the facing to the ends.   Turn this facing

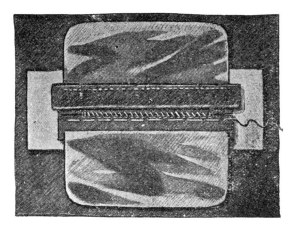

No. 17.—Pocket Showing Facings

in through the opening and baste, allowing only a slight edge of the facing to show, resembling a cording. This is known as a "welt edge." The opening is now basted together (No. 16), and these bastings are not removed until the garment is finished, as they serve to preserve the correct shape of the pocket. Press this well.

The pocket is cut of lining, the lower portion, as shown at No. 17, being joined to the welt facing. The upper portion is faced with a strip of the material.

Turn the coat on the right side and stitch just back of the welt, as pictured at No. 16. This stitching also includes the portion of the pocket which has been faced with material and previously basted to position. Join the two sections of the pocket by stitching all around the edge, as indicated at No. 18.

For a perpendicular slash, the finish is exactly as explained, but the pocket is long and of an entirely different shape; nevertheless it is inserted in the same manner as the pocket illustrated. Bar-tacks finish the ends of the slash in each case, and a final pressing is given. No. 16 shows the finished effect on the right side before the bastings are removed.

No. 19 represents an in-and-out pocket-lap, which may be applied or

No. 18.—Reverse Side with Pocket Stitched Around Edge

No. 19.—In-and-Out Lap Completed

not as desired. It is cut, lined with silk and stitched, then inserted in the opening far enough to catch its upper edge to position when the welt stitching is worked, the pocket being included at the same time in the sewing. The upper row of stitching is subsequently added.

What is designated a patch pocket is, as its name implies, applied like a patch on the outside of the jacket according to the perforations in the pattern. This, however, is a very simple matter, as is the finishing of other pockets of a similar character, which may very easily be adjusted by the worker who has mastered the foregoing instructions.

Practical and Ornamental Stitches

TAILORS' tacks are used by tailors and dressmakers when basting two sides of a garment so as to have them both exactly alike. Instead of basting both sides separately, this method is used where practicable, requiring much less time. It is generally employed after cutting, when the material has been marked with chalk on one side, and the seams and other indicating marks of the forms are desired exactly alike on both. As the stitches pass through both thicknesses it is hardly possible for the lines to deviate. It is accomplished as follows:

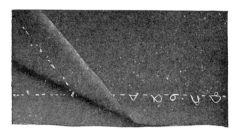

No. 1.—Tailors' Tacks

With a double thread of basting cotton baste through the two thicknesses of cloth with one long stitch and two short stitches, leaving the long stitch loose enough to form a loop under which the finger may be placed, and repeat all around through the chalk mark. Cut every long stitch, then take hold of the two edges of the cloth and gently separate the two pieces so the stitches which hold them together can be plainly seen. Separate the cloth about a quarter of an inch and cut the stitches as they show between; this will leave a few threads in each piece of cloth, which will represent the sewing line, and both sides will be marked exactly alike. The method of making the tailors' tacks is shown at No. 1, with the material turned up displaying the cut stitches. In making these tacks on long straight lines to mark tucks or plaits in skirts, for instance, the loose stitch may be made an inch and a half or longer, and need not be left in a loop; its length will supply the necessary thread for pulling through between the two pieces of cloth; but for coats, or any smaller markings that follow a shape or a curve, the tack stitches should be short.

In coat-making, a stitch known as *padding stitch* is used on the lapels and collar, because the canvas and cloth must be held firmly together. This is effected by many small stitches, which may be about half an inch long on the canvas side and just barely catch, but not show through on the right side of the cloth. The method of working these is clearly shown at No. 2. The canvas is held uppermost and both cloth and

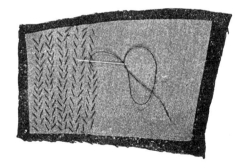

No. 2.—Padding Stitch

canvas are held over the first finger of the left hand, curving the lapel or collar in the direction in which it is to lie. The stitch should be started at the line of the fold of the lapel or collar and worked thence in successive rows to the edge.

In *tying threads after tucks are stitched*, always leave both upper and lower thread in an end about two inches long. These threads are to be drawn through to the wrong side at the point where each tuck finishes, and tied in two or three knots; the ends beyond the knots are then cut off. This is illustrated at No 3. If this is done the stitches then cannot rip open.

Many occasions will arise when it will be found necessary to tie the threads at the end of a line of stitching as well as at the end of tucks and this method will be found useful. In fact, wherever the sewing line is not finished by turning over in a hem or otherwise securing the ends, this precaution of tying the threads should be observed, for it will prevent the unsightly look of a ripped seam or a tuck of incorrect length.

THE TAILORED BUTTONHOLE

A garment that is perfect in every other respect may be greatly injured in appearance by badly cut and poorly worked buttonholes. The latter condition of buttonholes is often due to their having been poorly cut; it is, therefore, absolutely necessary to exercise the greatest care in cutting them. One of the most noticeable faults seen in buttonholes is that resulting from cutting the holes so that there is a break in the slash, which produces an uneven or "jagged" edge. This is frequently caused by the use of dull scissors, or from the habit of some dressmakers of cutting a buttonhole with two or more clips or movements of the scissors. And again it is due to the slipping of fabrics which are very thick, soft or elastic, like the heavy cloths used for coats and jackets. To prevent as far as possible this very common accident, all thick fabrics should be firmly basted together at each side of the line for each buttonhole before the latter is cut. Buttonholes should always be properly spaced and marked before being cut. The desired closeness of the buttons should be decided upon, and then the points for the top and bottom buttonholes should be marked; after this the edge between the two points should be divided by measurement into the number of spaces required by the desired closeness of the buttons. These spaces should always be alike.

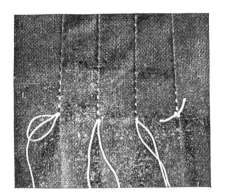

No. 3.—Tying Threads

If a buttonhole scissors having a gage is to be used, the length of the buttonhole need not be marked—it will be sufficient to mark the point for the front end only.

Different kinds of buttonholes are employed for different garments, several of these being described and illustrated in the chapter "Hand Sewing Stitches." For garments of heavy cloth and for many bodices the round-end or eyelet buttonhole, shown at No. 4, is the best and most satisfactory in all respects, as it provides a resting place for the shank of the button or the stitches holding the button.

In cutting this buttonhole great care must be taken to see that the under side as well as the upper side is cut exactly in the centre of the round hole. If a punch is not obtainable, the end may be clipped out with the scissors after the ordinary buttonhole has been cut.

In the lower figure of No. 4 is shown a tailored buttonhole cut, with the end snipped in one-eighth of an inch on each side. The second figure shows these cut across and the triangular piece removed.

No. 4.—Tailored
Buttonhole

After cutting, the buttonhole should be stayed or barred around; this may be done with several threads of twist so that the worked edge of the buttonhole will be firm and distinct. Tailors follow the plan of using cord formed of several strands of the buttonhole twist, or linen thread twisted together, or a gimp cord. An end of this cord or thread is secured at the back end of the buttonhole between the fabrics, and then the other end is fastened to the knee or to some convenient place and kept taut by a slight strain upon the work as it is held in the hands. The cord is kept straight and just back of the edge of the buttonhole by this strain, and the stitches are worked over it by the usual movements; and after each stitch is drawn down the loose twist should be picked up firmly by the thumb and forefinger quite near the stitch, and two or three circular, twisting movements should be made so that the loop formed will settle securely and neatly into its proper position. Be careful to complete each stitch with uniform movements. The buttonhole in process of working is the upper figure in the illustration.

Finish the buttonhole with a "bar-tack" made by passing the needle up and down through the goods until two or three threads cross the end of the buttonhole quite close to the stitches; then the needle is brought up through the fabric at one side of these threads and put down through it at the other side until they are entirely covered with these cross-stitches and the stay looks like a fine cord or bar; this makes a firm stay for any buttonhole.

In working a round-end or eyelet buttonhole, as illustrated, when the eyelet is reached the work should be adjusted a trifle so that the twirling movement of the working thread may be made in a slightly different direction, thus forming a corner at the beginning of the eyelet; and these movements should be reversed at the opposite side to produce

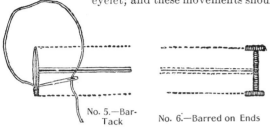

No. 5.—Bar-Tack   No. 6.—Barred on Ends

a similar corner at the end of the eyelet. The back end of an eyelet buttonhole may be "tacked" or "bar-tacked"; and after the buttonholes are worked, their straight edges should be closely basted together by an over-and-over stitch, made by pushing the needle up and down over the edges just back of the stitches. Then they should be pressed through a dampened cloth (as should all buttonholes when the goods will permit), and before they are dry a stiletto or some similar ivory or metallic implement should be pushed vigorously up through each eyelet until that opening becomes perfectly round and the stitches around its edges are regular and distinct. Then when the bastings are removed, the buttonholes will be symmetrical in appearance.

SEWING BUTTONS ON COATS AND OTHER GARMENTS

In preparing garments made of heavy fabrics, such as cloakings., etc, for the buttons, places for them should be marked as soon as practicable, and after the canvas facing is adjusted under the edge, a small extra section of it should be set under the lines marked for the buttons, for a stay. In ordinary garments, a stay-tape for the buttons is placed between the outside fabric and the lining. Buttons that have wire shanks should be carefully sewed through the outside fabric, the canvas facing and the stay, but not through

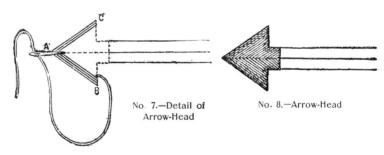

No. 7.—Detail of Arrow-Head   No. 8.—Arrow-Head

the facing of the fabric itself; and in setting such buttons for sewing, place them so that the wire shank will run parallel with the buttonhole, and not across it.

Buttons that have no shanks, but are to be sewed on through holes in them or through goods left on their undersides for that purpose, should not be drawn down tightly, but left quite loose; and after a sufficient number of threads have been passed through the button, the threads should be wound a number of times around these threads between the button and fabric to make a thread shank; for, if such a button is very closely sewed to a garment, it will not have room to rest easily in the buttonhole and will thus crowd the latter out of shape and make the spacing seem imperfect. The loose sewing and the winding really increase the durability of the work, since the sawing sort of strain that results from too tightly sewing on a button is thus prevented. When beginning to sew on a button, place the knot in the thread upon the outside of the fabric under the button, or between the outside and facing. A pin may be placed over the button, as described in the chapter "Hand Sewing Stitches," when there are holes in it, but in any event, the stitches must be taken only through the cloth and interlining or stay-tape, not through the material facing.

ORNAMENTAL TACKS AND ARROW-HEADS

A very neat finish in the way of fancy tacks, etc., may be given to tailor-made garments at the ends of the seams, tucks and plaits, and at the corners of collars, pockets and pocket laps. The simplest staying tack, known as the bar-tack, is shown partly made at No. 5. It is much used at the ends of pocket openings, etc. The detail of this tack is as follows: First decide on the length of the tack, marking the line with chalk; then pass the needle up from underneath at one end of the line, down through at the opposite end, up again at the starting point, and down again at the opposite end; and make as many of these long stitches as desired. Not less than two stitches should be made, but as many more may be made as the worker may elect—the greater the number, the thicker and heavier will be the tack. Then, without breaking the thread, bring the needle up at one end, just to one side of the upper and under long stitches, and pass it down at a point exactly opposite on the other side of the long stitches, to form a short stitch that will be square across the long stitches on top. Cover the entire length of the long stitches with such short stitches, being careful to bring the needle up at the same side of the long stitches every time, so that the *under* part of the long stitches will be crossed as well as the *upper* part, taking the stitches very close, and pressing the long stitches together with the needle so as to produce as narrow an effect as possible.

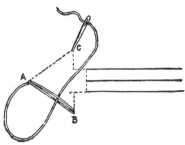

No. 9.—Detail of Crossed Arrow-Head

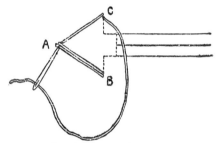

No. 10.—Second Movement

In garments that are finished with machine-stitching, bar-tacks at the ends of pocket openings usually extend from a second row of stitching above the opening to a second row below the opening, and are sometimes crossed at the ends with short bar-tacks, as illustrated at No. 6, working the over-and-over stitches of the latter in the opposite direction.

Tacks that are commonly called arrow-heads are seen in a variety of shapes and stitches, and are made at the tops or bottoms of plaits and laps, and at the ends of seams and pocket openings, etc. One of the simplest of these tacks is illustrated in detail at No. 7. To make this style of tack, mark an outline of the tack with chalk or a pencil. Bring the needle up through at point A and pass it down at point B; then up inside and very close to point B, and down on the centre line close to point A; up at point A, exactly where the needle was first passed through and down at point C; up inside and close to point C, and down on the centre line exactly at the second stitch extending from B to A. Fill in the entire outline in this way, always making two stitches on one side and then two on the other, and being careful to keep all the stitches even on the centre line. At No. 7 the work is shown with three stitches on one side and two on the other, and the needle correctly placed for the fourth stitch on line BA. The finished arrow-head is seen at No. 8.

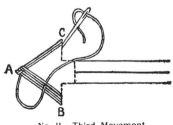

No. 11.—Third Movement

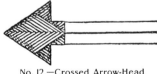

No. 12.—Crossed Arrow-Head

A more artistic and durable arrow-head is depicted completed at No. 12, and in detail at Nos. 9, 10 and 11. Mark the outline with chalk or a pencil. Bring the needle up at point A.

and pass it down at point B; then up inside and very close to point B, down on the line AC close to point A, and up at point A outside and very close to the first stitch made. Then pass the needle under the second stitch and down at point C, as illustrated at No. 9. Bring the needle up inside and close to point C and then pass it down near point A outside and very close to the first stitch made, as shown at No. 10. Next bring the needle up outside and very close to the first stitch running from A to C, and quite close to the second stitch in line AB; and then pass it down near B. Bring the needle up again on line BC inside and close to the third stitch in line AB; and pass it down outside the first stitch on line AC. Then bring the needle up outside and very close to the first stitch on the line AB, pass it under the fourth stitch in line AB, and down on line CB close to the second stitch on line AC, as illustrated at No. 11. Now bring the needle up on line CB close to the third stitch on line AC, and pass it down outside the first stitch on line AB close to the third stitch on line AC. Proceed in this manner to fill in the outline, always making two stitches parallel with line AB, then two stitches parallel with line AC, and being careful to pass the third, fifth, seventh, etc., stitches, running parallel with line AC, respectively under the second, fourth, sixth, eighth, etc., stitches, running parallel with line AB, as illustrated at Nos. 9 and 11.

No. 13.—Plain Crow Foot

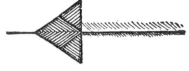
No. 14.—Crossed Triangle

Other fanciful figures are displayed at Nos. 13 and 14. They are worked exactly as described for the crossed arrow-head shown at No. 12, and will be found quite simple.

Probably the most ornamental of the fancy tacks ordinarily used at the ends of pocket openings and seams is the crow tack or crow foot, as it is sometimes called. It is illustrated completed at No. 17, and in detail at Nos. 15 and 16. Outline the tack with chalk or a pencil. The dotted outline seen at No. 15 shows the correct outline for the tack. Bring the needle up at point A, and pass it down at B, and up again at B outside and close to the stitch in line AB, then down at C, up at C outside and close to the stitch in line BC, and down at A just outside the stitch in line

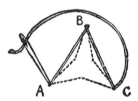
No. 15.—Detail of Crow Foot

AB, as illustrated at No. 15. Now bring the needle up on dotted line AC outside the stitch on line AC close to A; and pass it down on dotted line BC outside the stitch on line BC close to B; up on dotted line AB outside both stitches on line AB close to B; down on dotted line CA outside the stitch on line CA close to C; up on dotted line BC outside both stitches on line BC; and down on dotted line AB outside both stitches on line AB,

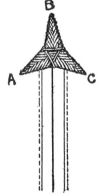
No. 16.—Second Movement

as illustrated at No. 16. Fill in the entire outline in this way, until the completed foot looks like No. 17. It will be noticed in making this tack that all the stitches are taken on the dotted lines and always outside the made stitches, thus compressing the first laid stitches so as to curve the sides of the tack like the outline.

For working these ornamental tacks and arrow-heads coarse buttonhole twist or twisted embroidery silk is usually employed, and this is generally the same color as the material. The work is done on the same order as embroidery, keeping the stitches very close together without overlapping,

No. 17.—Crow Foot

so that a smooth, even surface is the result. The selection of any particular figure is at the option of the worker; all are very dainty and add greatly to the finish of the gown, particularly when the figures are well executed. In fact, they should not be worked on the gown at all until one has attained proficiency through executing the selected figure several times on a sample of cloth.

Bias Bands and Folds—Turning Corners

BIAS bands, facings, ruffles and folds are so much used in dressmaking that it is desirable to know the best and quickest way to cut them accurately. A piece of silk, muslin or whatever the material to be used, should be placed flat on a table, and from the lower left-hand corner mark on the left selvage, four inches up; and on the lower edge make a mark at four inches from the starting point toward the right side. This marks off the left-hand lower corner of the material. Place a ruler or yardstick across from one mark to the other and draw a line with chalk if on dark goods, or with pencil if on light. From this line mark the desired width for the bias strips and by the marks so made draw another line with the stick, and continue till the requisite number are marked off. This way of marking for the strips is shown in No. 1. Cut through the marks and join the strips together. Accuracy is very important in this as in every other detail.

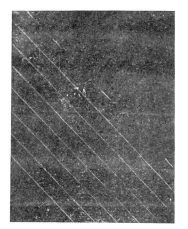

No. 1.—Marking Bias Strips

Bias strips can be cut from pieces if not too small; in joining the strips do not attempt to join directly across the bias, but trim each end off on the straight, or with the grain of the material and make a diagonal joining as shown at No. 2.

Narrow milliners' folds of silk or satin are much used for trimming cloth and other dresses, and are sometimes applied, like braid, in rows or in fanciful designs; the method of making is shown at No 3. The folds should be not more than three-eighths of an inch in width when they are finished.

No. 2.—Diagonal Joining for a Bias Strip

Bias folds are used for many purposes, frequently instead of tucks, and have much the same effect when made of the same material as the skirt. In this case the top fold is usually a finished or milliners' fold, made with a small heading, and may be machine stitched if desired.

As there are various styles and widths of folds it is necessary to study the label on the pattern selected, and follow the directions carefully. If, however, no folds are provided in the pattern the worker will have to use judgment in selecting any of the folds here presented. For the lower folds. the bias strips are cut twice the width desired for the fin-

No. 3.—Narrow Stitched Milliners' Fold

ished fold, allowing also for a narrow turn-in at each edge. Fold each through the centre lengthwise, bringing the two raw edges together; turn these raw edges in a narrow seam toward the inside of the fold and run them along close to the edge. (No. 4.) Be careful to keep the two sides folded evenly that the finished fold may not twist. The upper fold, being a milliners' fold, is made by turning the top edge

No. 4.—A Plain Fold

of the bias strip over half an inch. The lower edge is then turned over a seam and is brought up to within an eighth or a quarter of an inch (this is decided by the size of the fold that is being made) of the top edge. (No. 5.) A row of stitching may be placed on the turned-up edge, and the fold slip-stitched to the garment under this row of stitching, or the turned-up edge may be slip-stitched to the fold below it. The completed fold may be slip-stitched to the garment with no stitching visible. In making the folds of very thin material the work will be much easier if the folds are made over a strip of moderately stiff paper, which may be slipped out as the work progresses.

A cord is sometimes introduced into the upper edge of the milliners' fold, though the manner of making is just the same. If the material, after the raw edges are turned over and basted or pressed, is laid on a table and pinned along a short distance ahead of the basting, the edges will be less likely to twist. After the folds are made, they should be carefully pressed.

No. 5.—Broad Milliners' Fold

Crêpe may be lightly pressed with a rather cool iron. Folds made of crêpe should be cut, if possible, straight across the goods, as this will show the crinkles running diagonally. If they are cut bias the crinkles will run straight, and the effect is not so good; so, unless many curves and close turns are to be made, necessitating a bias, it is better to cut them straight.

When making cloth straps, to decorate the seams of coats or skirts, these straps may be made on the length of the material, from the pieces which are left in cutting the garment, but experience has proven that there is always a best way, and, just as straps of silk should be cut bias of the material, so cloth straps work best when cut across the width of the goods.

For a strap five-eighths of an inch wide, cut as many strips of cloth as will be required, each one inch and one-quarter wide. Join them and press the seams open, but when basting the straps on the seams of the coat, avoid bringing any of these joinings in a prominent place; if necessary, it will be better to waste a few inches and discard the piece with the seam in it.

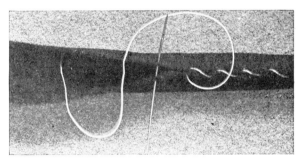

No. 6.—Making Strap for Seam

Fold the strip of cloth evenly through the centre, lengthwise, right side out and overhand the two raw edges together with coarse but even stitches. (No. 6.) Flatten it out with the row of overhanding in the middle of the strap and press it well on the wrong side. Baste the strap over the seam and stitch near each edge through both strap and coat.

TURNING CORNERS

No. 7.-Marking Off for Corner

To be able to turn corners correctly is a very important thing and the several methods here explained will be found of great assistance when lining or turning the corners of coat-skirts, collar and cuff corners, and also the linings of pocket-laps, etc., it is quite an important feature, as the work must be neatly done.

The method of turning in the edges of the outside (and its interlining, if it has one) and felling in the lining is the one ordinarily adopted, and is a very good one. By the "bagged" method a careless worker may do less effective work than by the felling process, for she may cut the corners too closely and thus cause them to fray, or she may get the parts slightly twisted; but a careful worker will not fail to appreciate its advantages after one trial of its details and an examination of the results.

By the "bagged" lining method the work may be done on the sewing machine and with a much neater result than by the other process. Even with curved edges (No. 11) the completed work will be perfectly flat and smooth, and all the corners will be properly formed without the ruinous process of "picking" them out with a pin or some other sharp instrument.

To insert a "bagged" lining and turn the corners properly, proceed as follows: If the seam joining the outside to the lining is to be one-quarter of an inch in from the finished edge, cut the outside fabric half an inch larger along the edges to be finished than you want the section to be when finished (one-quarter inch for the seam and another quarter of an inch for the distance the seam is to be from the edge); then cut the lining of the same shape as the outside,

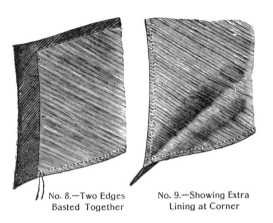

No. 8.—Two Edges Basted Together

No. 9.—Showing Extra Lining at Corner

but half an inch smaller along the edges only that are to be finished, which will make the lining when cut just the size the section will be when the lining is added. (If the seam is to be farther away from or nearer to the edge than one-quarter of an inch, follow this rule: Make the outside as much larger along the edges to be finished as the distance the seam is to be from the edge when completed, plus one-quarter of an inch for a seam, and make the lining twice the distance the seam is to be from the edge smaller than the outside along these edges.) Now lay the lining upon the outside fabric, with the right sides of the parts together, so that the edges of the lining to be finished will be from the corresponding edges of the outside fabric twice the distance that the seam is to be from the completed edges; and then mark each as seen in No. 7, using a card for squaring the points or marks so that the corresponding points in the lining and outside section will be exactly at right angles with the edges. When the edges have both round and hollow curves, marks must be made just where the curve changes its direction in each edge.

Having carefully marked the points, bring the two corresponding edges of the lining and outside together placing the corresponding marks in each, as you would notches in a pattern, exactly opposite each other; and pin or baste them securely (see No. 8). In sections where the edges are rounding part of the way and hollowing at another part, fulness will exist between the marks both in the lining and the outside, the lining being full where the edges are hollowing, and the outside where they are rounding. This fulness must be basted in smoothly. Now, on the machine, stitch the basted edges to within a quarter of an inch of the next edge of the lining; then pin and baste the adjoining edges according to the marks, and fold the fulness which will come at the corner exactly diagonally through the centre, and turn it back under the end of the seam just made, as seen at No. 9, so that you can begin the next seam exactly where the first one ended in the lining portion without sewing in the fulness. Having sewed this seam, pin, baste and sew the remaining corresponding edges according to their marks.

Now carefully smooth out the section so that the inturn will be of the width desired all round the seamed edges, taking especial care to have the corner fold so that the point will be in an exact line with the corner of the seam. Then cut the point open (see No. 10) from the outer edges to within a few threads of the corner made by the inturn, giving the goods at the end of

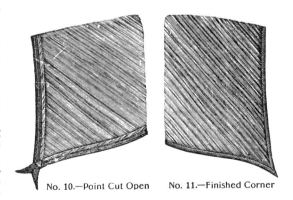

No. 10.—Point Cut Open

No. 11.—Finished Corner

the cut a gentle stretch in order to make the point perfectly flat. Then open the point, and press it down with the nail. These tiny folds may be stitched together by sticking back and forth through the folds or by catching them together with an over-and-over stitch, done with very fine thread or twist, being careful not to stick deeper than half-way down the folds. Cut off the extensions, turn the section right side out (No. 11) and press it smooth.

AN EMPIRE TEA-GOWN

WHILE a wrapper or tea-gown does not require the perfection of fit of a dress and is much less difficult to make, there is in some of them a tendency toward elaboration and dress effect that calls for careful treatment as the work advances.

Generally, the waist only is lined, and the first step is to cut this lining from silk or percaline, marking on it all the perforations and notches that are found in the pattern. Baste the lining and fit it, make alterations if any are necessary, then stitch all the seams except the shoulders, notch or bind them and press them open. The seams of a gown of this description are usually not boned. With a colored thread, mark on the lining the outline of the yoke if there be any, or other necessary marks, and the perforations that indicate where the front seams of the skirt are to be placed when it is joined to the waist. As the lower waist portion in the model illustrated is somewhat looser than the lining to allow for a slight bloused effect, the front edges of the lining should be faced with a piece of the gown material. The lining with this facing applied and the colored tracing thread outlining the yoke line is seen at No. 1.

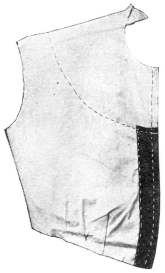

No. 1.—Waist Lining showing Facing and Yoke Outline

The fronts of the lining are to be under-faced when hems are not allowed in the pattern. Turn under three-eighths of an inch at each front edge and baste it. Cut the material for the outer waist portions, observing all the notches and perforations, and place a colored tracing thread down the centre of the back. Turn under the allowed hems of the outside front portions according to the notches, stitch them or, preferably, hem them by hand. Gather the upper edges of the back and front portions, according to the indicating notches and again three-eighths of an inch below. Baste the outer back portion to the lining, making the first row of gathers come even with the yoke outline. Make the traced centre back of the outer portion come directly over the seam in the centre of the lining.

Baste around the armhole and along the under-arm seam. Baste the fronts to the lining along the traced yoke outline and around the armhole. Place the fold edge of the hems of the outer portions even with the fold edge of the lining fronts. Turn the fronts under at the under-arm seam and baste them over the back portions, following the line of the seam in the lining.

No. 2.—Outer Front Portion Basted to the Lining

Slip-stitch the front to the back along this fold edge. Make two rows of gathers in the lower edge of the front and back portions between the notches and baste them to the lower edge of the lining. The front in this state of preparation is shown at No. 2.

If the yoke is made of lace or other transparent material it will be necessary to line it with silk. Cut both silk and lace by the yoke pattern and baste the lace to the silk. Turn under the lower edge of both a seam (three-eighths of an inch), baste the yoke back to the lining back, bringing the folded edge even with the first row of gathers in the outer waist portion. Baste the front yokes in place, rip the basted shoulder seams and include the seams of the yokes and outer waist portions with the lining and baste the seams again. Stitch them, finish the edges as are the other waist seams—overhanded, notched or bound—and press them. Turn the front edges of the yoke over the turned-under edges of the lining fronts. Sew hooks on the right front and eyes on the left. Make one hook and eye come at the double row of gathers at the yoke line and another in the same position at the lower edge of the waist and arrange the other hooks and eyes at even distances between.

No. 3.—Application of Under-lap on Front

An underlap will be necessary, and this should be made of the material of the outer waist to reach from the lower edge to the yoke and of the yoke material (or that under the lace) from the yoke to the neck. Join these two strips to make one continuous length and press the seam open. Baste this underlap to the left front over the eyes already applied. Seam a length of the lining material to the outer edge of the underlap, turn it over toward the inside of the waist and baste the underlap and its lining together near this fold edge. Sew both securely to the waist lining at their inner edges. Cut a narrow strip of lining, about an inch and one-quarter wide, turn under both edges and hem them to the lining to cover where the underlap is sewed. The inside view of the left front with the eyes, the underlap and the facing in process of application is seen at No. 3. A facing should be hemmed down to cover the sewing of the hooks on the right front. Spring hooks or small hump hooks should be sewed to the under side of the hem of the outer front portion on the right, and loops should be worked with buttonhole twist in the same color at the edge of the left side; these may be two and one-half or three inches apart.

To avoid an opening down the centre front, the skirt of this gown opens at the seam joining the front breadth to the first side breadth at the left. This seam is basted in the usual way, matching the notches near the top, but is left unstitched for ten or twelve inches—a comfortable placket length—at the top. The other seams are stitched, notched and pressed open. The centre of the front breadth should be marked with a colored tracing thread. To make the underlap for the skirt opening, a straight piece three and three-quarter inches wide, of the same material, is sewed to the front edge of the side breadth, the seam toward the inside of the skirt; it is folded over and its other long edge is turned under and hemmed down to cover the seam just made. The seam on the left side of the front breadth is turned under and a piece of the same material is faced to

No. 4.—Placket Opening and Underlap on Skirt

it. The top of the skirt is gathered in two rows one-half inch apart, although a number of rows may be added giving a shallow yoke effect. The placket opening in the skirt is shown at No. 4.

Greater strength will be given to the joining of the skirt and waist if a cord is introduced as seen at No. 5. In order that it might show plainly in the illustration a contrasting color was used to cover the cord, but the gown material should be used. A bias strip is cut, and a rather fine, soft cotton cord is laid in the centre, the strip is doubled and a line of stitches is run along by hand to hold the cord in place. This is basted to the lower edge of the waist, the raw edges downward and the cord just above the lower row of gathers. Leave an end of the covered cord beyond the right front and long enough to reach to the placket opening at the left side. The cord should begin at this point on the left side, and the lower edge of the waist front between the front and the place of the placket opening should be bound with a piece of the gown material as shown in No. 5. This also shows the effect of the yoke and blouse.

No. 5.—Cord Introduced in Seam Joining Waist and Skirt

The joining of the skirt to the waist should be done by sewing the two together in a seam from the inside of the garment. Place the centre front of the skirt at the edge of the right front of the waist, the first side seams at the marks on the waist between the first and second darts and distribute the remainder of the fulness around the waist, throwing the most of it to the centre back. Baste the portion of the front breadth that extends from the centre front to the placket opening to the end of cord that was left beyond the right front. Try on the gown to see if the skirt fulness is properly arranged, make alterations if necessary and baste again.

Cut a bias strip of lining an inch and one-quarter wide, baste this (against the waist lining) to the seam joining skirt and waist, which now includes the skirt, the cord, the outer waist and lining and the bias strip which is to serve as a facing to cover the raw edges of the seam. The seam is not to be opened, but is to turn down toward the skirt, and the free edge of the bias strip is to be turned under and hemmed to the second row of gathers in the top of the skirt. The piece of material binding the lower edge of the waist between the centre front and the placket opening is to be turned over and hemmed to the lining on the inside. This inside finish is shown at No. 6. Hooks are placed at the top of the front breadth and down the placket opening, with corresponding eyes on the lower edge of the left front of the waist and on the underlap.

The sleeves are made according to the directions on the label of the pattern. If a bolero jacket is added, it is made quite separate from the waist portion, joining it only at the under-arm part of the armholes. If the bolero is of lace it must have an under-lining of silk like the yoke.

If a collar is used it should be made of the same material as the yoke, interlined with crinoline, or if a transparent collar is preferred, the interlining should be omitted and the collar supported with collar-bone. Turn

No. 6.—Inside View of Waist and Skirt Joining

the collar under a seam all around and slip-stitch it to the edge of the waist. The collar lining is turned under in the same way and hemmed to the top and ends of the collar and to the inside of the neck of the waist covering the seam. If the collar is to be transparent make the lining of chiffon. The collar is left loose on the left side from the point of closing of the waist to the centre back and the unattached portion of the neck of the waist is bound. The bottom of the skirt may be finished with a simple hem, or with two or three folds, like tucks.

DESIRABLE GARMENTS FOR MATERNITY WEAR

A NUMBER of garments for maternity wear have been especially designed so they may be adjusted comfortably to the changing figure and yet have the trim appearance of a fitted gown. The principal difficulty has been the lining, as when that was once made and fitted there was no way. of gradually enlarging it. This has been overcome by lacing the front and darts; and other necessary changes may be made by moving a few hooks and tapes.

The physical imperfections of many children are due to the manner in which, through pride or ignorance, the mother has clothed herself. Her clothing should be so adapted to her changing figure that no undue pressure will rest upon any part of her body. If corsets are worn they must be very loosely adjusted and have rubber lacings at the back and over the abdomen. The outer garments should be so arranged that they may be gradually enlarged by means of the closings. Dresses and negligées may be made of attractive materials, preferably of soft wool or silk, and plain, solid colors are better than figured effects. They may be given a pretty touch by the addition of lace, embroidery and ribbon, so that one need not at any time appear unattractively gowned. For afternoon or more dressy occasions, a sun-plaited skirt made of crêpe de Chine, or one of the numerous weaves of veilings will be suitable and should be shirred at the waist

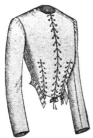

No. 1.—Lacing in Darts and Front

into a belt of soft taffeta several inches larger than the waist measure and a ribbon run through this to draw it to the right size.

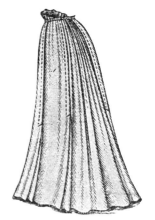

The waist lining should be basted and fitted in the usual way, making it a neat fit but not too tight. Turn back the hem at the front of the lining and stitch it with the usual two rows of stitching, but make the first one three-eighths of an inch, and the second three-quarters of an inch from the edge. Work eyelets near the edge the entire length of the front on both sides, as shown at No. 1, and run a very soft and pliable bone in the casing formed by the two rows of stitching.

Another way is to place the bone near the edge, as in the ordinary lining, and sew eyes, but not the hooks, in the usual manner and lace through these. It would be well to sew a fly or underlap underneath each front. Make each about two inches wide and sew hooks and eyes on the front edges that they may form a protection under the lacings. Lace with a round elastic cord such as is used for corset lacing. Rip the darts open and mark the seams with a basting thread; then make that thread the edge of a tuck, one-quarter inch deep, running not quite to the top of the dart. Work eyelets or sew eyes just back of the tucks at each edge of the dart seams, then slip a round bone into each tuck.

No. 2.—Extension at Top of Skirt

The unsightly shortening in the front, which makes the ordinary skirt undesirable even when the belt is enlarged, is provided against in the pattern by an extension at the top as seen at No. 2. The cross-line perforations indicate where a ribbon is to be sewed on, through which should be run a ribbon or tape to come through a small buttonholed opening cut in the centre front. When fitting the skirt, observe whether this casing mark is at the proper height by pinning a piece of tape around where the belt would naturally come. The part of the skirt which extends above the casing should have its raw edge overcast or bound; if the skirt should become too short across the front and sides, the casing may be moved up toward the top to lengthen it. Petticoats and drawers should be finished with a casing at the top with draw-strings.

MAKING AND FINISHING UNDERWEAR

LTHOUGH there is a particular daintiness and charm about hand-made underwear, much fine and beautiful work may be done on the machine, and the saving of time is so great that this method is usually given the preference when a number of pieces are to be made. A few of the smaller pieces, a corset-cover or a simple chemise, may be readily accomplished by hand, but the amount of work necessary to make night-dresses and petticoats inclines one toward the machine method. Care should be exercised to have the tension draw evenly on both the upper and the lower threads. Many sewers prefer the single-thread machine because the chain-stitch has greater elasticity than the two straight threads of the lock-stitch machine; this quality, as well as the very great ease in running the single-thread machine, makes it a favorite for the making of underwear. Whichever machine is used, however, a careful regard for pressure, tension and size of the stitch is the principal requirement. One should not expect to get good results by using the same size needle and the same tension on nainsook that have been used in stitching heavy cloth or linen. No. 80 cotton is the best for white work except on very sheer and fine material, when No. 100 or No. 120 may be used for tucks and hems and all outside stitching. Every make of machine has a table of the sizes of needles that should be used with certain number threads, and it is wise to follow these directions. Remember that a looser tension is required in sewing with cotton than when silk is used.

No. 1.—Facing on Drawers

The hemming and tucking attachments are great time savers, but most neat sewers gather ruffles, puffs, etc., by hand and "stroke" them rather than use the shirring attachment.

No raw edges of material are left at the seams in this class of work; every seam is either a French seam or is felled. The French seam is used at what may be called the "regular seams" —those joining the breadths of the garment or the front and back portions together, as in night-dresses, chemises, corset-covers and drawers—but when the seam is for the purpose of adding width to a breadth, as is sometimes necessary in cutting drawers or any garment for which the material provided is not quite wide enough for a breadth of the pattern, a felled seam is made. The usual three-eighths of an inch seam is stitched; then one seam edge is trimmed away close to the stitching and the other seam edge is turned under and hemmed over the cut-away edge, making a perfectly flat joining, with the single disadvantage that one row of stitching shows on the right side of the completed breadth; in many cases this is no objection. The hemming over the seam edge may be more quickly done, and the necessity of folding it over by hand is avoided if the narrowest hemmer among the machine attachments is used. Both the felled and French seam are illustrated and explained in the chapter "Hand Sewing Stitches."

In making a pair of drawers, the French seam is used to join the edges of each leg portion and also to join these portions together in the seam that runs from the front belt to the back. When open drawers are made this seam is not joined, but each portion is faced along this edge with a bias strip of the same material. Stitch the bias facing (which should be about an inch and one-quarter wide) to each leg portion from the waist at the front around past the joining seam, easing the facing on at the curve, and continuing it up the back edge to the waist. Turn in the free edge of the facing and hem it to the inside of the garment. The manner of applying the facing is shown at No. 1.

With dress skirts that fit snugly about the hips, the fit of the undergarments is quite an important matter, and for this reason underskirts and drawers are frequently made with yokes. In buying the pattern the same rule should be followed as when ordering an outside skirt. The table of relative waist and hip measurements is given in the chapter "The Correct Method of Altering Patterns," and this should always be consulted in selecting a pattern. Hip measures are printed on the labels of outer-skirt patterns only, but the same proportions are observed in cutting the patterns of undergarments, and the table should always be consulted; if the waist and hip measures are disproportionate to those in the table, order the pattern the · hip measurement of which is nearest, and alter the pattern at the waist-line. The yoke patterns are

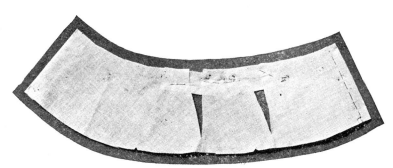

No. 2.—A Circular Yoke Fitted to a Large Waist

cut in one piece, so there are no darts that may be changed. Before cutting the garment, cut the yoke from ordinary lining cambric, mark the centre front with a colored thread and fit it; if the waist is too small slash the yoke down from the waist where necessary and pin a piece of cambric at each slash to hold it to the correct size, as shown at No. 2; use this fitted yoke as a pattern from which to cut. Do not alter any of the notches in the lower part of the yoke, as the changes at the waist-line do not affect the construction of the rest of the garment. If the waist measure is smaller than that of the pattern, pin little darts into the cambric yoke to make it fit. This process will repay the slight trouble involved by giving a smooth and comfortably fitted garment. Two yokes should be cut from the fitted pattern for each pair of drawers.

The top of the drawers is gathered according to the directions on the·label of the pattern, the right side being lapped across the left at the front, and the gathers are stroked. The centre front of both the yoke pieces is marked with a colored thread, and the lower edge of one yoke is basted in a seam to the gathered top of the drawers, matching the notches in both and making the

No. 3.—Yoke Sewed to Drawers

seam toward the outside; the garment may then be tried on to see if the distribution of the gathers is correct or if the drawers portion may need raising a little into the yoke at either front or back to secure a better fit. After any needed alterations are made the seam is stitched; the second yoke is then placed even with the one joined to the drawers, but toward its wrong side—that is, the inner side of the garment—and a seam is stitched around the top or waist edge that will hold the two yokes together. The one on the inside (that has not been seamed to the drawers) is then turned over toward the outside, covering the seam just made at its top, its lower edge is turned under a seam's width and is basted and afterward stitched down from the outside, to cover the seam joining the top of the drawers to the first yoke. This process may be readily understood by examining No. 3. If tucks are desired as trimming on the drawers, sufficient length to make them must be allowed in cutting. In thin material one-eighth-inch tucks in clusters of three or five are effective, either with or without an insertion of lace or embroidery between the clusters. The tucks should be made before the drawers are seamed together, but the hem at the edge should be turned up afterward.

A gathered ruffle of either the plain material or of embroiderd edging makes a good finish, and this should be inset in the hem, which is cut through its folded edge for this purpose. Each of the two edges of the material thus separated is turned under a quarter of an inch for a seam, the two turnings facing each other, and the gathered and stroked ruffle is basted to the lower turned edge, and the upper is basted over the seam and stitched to it, as seen at No. 4. If no hem is allowed, the gathered edge of the ruffle is basted in a seam to the lower

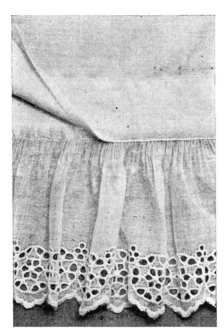

edge of the drawers, the seam toward the inside, and a strip of material about an inch and one-half wide, for a facing, is basted over the ruffle, in the same seam, which is then stitched and the facing is turned over; its free edge is turned under a seam and it is stitched to the drawers. This method is sometimes called a false hem. A gathered ruffle should always be divided, before gathering, into halves or quarters, or even eighths if it is a long one. Each division should be marked with a colored thread, and the portion of the garment to which it is to be joined should be divided and marked in the same way. When the ruffle is to be applied it should be pinned at each mark to the corresponding mark in the garment and the fulness distributed evenly.

Insertion, whether of lace or embroidery, should be basted in position with a row of basting stitches on each edge; the material underneath should then be cut through at the centre of the insertion, the raw edge so formed is turned back at each side, creased to hold it flat and one row of stitching through the bastings on the outside

No. 4.—Embroidered Ruffle Set in Hem

will secure the insertion and the turned-back edge of the material. Th's method will leave a raw edge of the material on the wrong side and, if a better finish is desired, the basted edge of the insertion should be stitched before the under material is cut. After stitching, cut the material through under the centre of the insertion, and trim it away to leave only enough to make a tiny hem turned back from each row of stitching. This hem is then

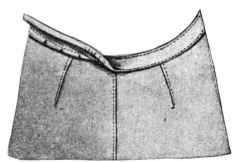

No. 5.—Facing at Top of Drawers

stitched either by first turning it under by hand or by using the small hemmer as described for the felled seam. If preferred, it may be inserted in the beginning by a French seam.

Drawers are sometimes fitted with darts instead of a yoke, and in this case the darts are closed with French seams or may be felled, and the plaits that are laid in the back to hold the fulness in place are stitched down a short distance on each fold edge. The waist edge of the drawers is then finished with a bias facing. No. 5 pictures the upper portion of a pair of drawers showing the first row of stitching. Clip the seam at the curves, turn over the facing and stitch at the top and bottom, as shown at the right-hand side of the illustration. In finishing the back, the facing may be added on the straight of the goods. The drawing-strings are put in, one on each side and fastened firmly. If a belt is preferred at the back, the upper edge of the drawers may be gathered and the belt finished with a buttonhole and button, thereby fitting exactly the figure for which they are intended. If one does not want to make the waist a certain size, the plaits need not be made in the back of the drawers, but after the darts have been made the entire top can be faced and a tape run between the facing and the outside; the waist can then be drawn to any desired size.   The tape does not run all around the waist, but should start from the second dart on each side and be securely tacked there.

An attractive combination garment comprises a corset-cover and an under-petticoat. In cutting a garment of this description, where the position of the tucks is indicated by perforations, if a rather coarse needle or pin is stuck through both thicknesses of the material, at each perforation, while the pattern is on the cloth, both sides may be accurately and quickly marked at the same time, as the hole the large needle leaves will correspond to the perforation in the pattern. The tucks may be creased by hand, or the tucker attachment may be set to correspond with the spaces indicated in the pattern. Always leave ends about two inches long on both upper and lower thread. These ends should be drawn through to the wrong side and tied; the tucks then cannot rip open. After the tucks are stitched in the corset-cover the seams should be basted in both corset-cover and skirt and they should be tried on.

No. 6.—Underlap and Facing Stitched to Slashed Opening in Skirt

Be careful in cutting the slash in the left side of the front breadth to make it exactly the length directed, otherwise the strip provided in the pattern for a facing and underlap of the placket opening will not fit. This piece should be applied to the front breadth before the skirt is joined to the corset-cover. The long, straight edge is sewed, according to the directions in the label, to both sides of the slashed opening in the front breadth with the seam toward the inside of the skirt. Make the seam as narrow as possible and run it almost to a point at the lower end of the placket opening, as shown at No. 6. The free edge of the wide part of the applied piece is turned under a seam, and the wide part is folded along its length to allow the turned-under edge to reach the stitching of the seam first made and to cover that seam. The narrow end of the strip is turned under a seam at its free edge and is folded under at the seam first made; this forms a facing to the one side, while the under piece extends to form an underlap, as shown at No. 7. Both of these edges are to be stitched in place; the end of the underlap side is turned under and basted and then stitched across, and the neat and secure closing seen at No. 8 is accomplished.

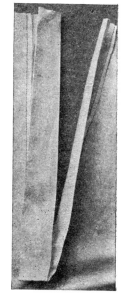

No. 7.—Underlap and Facing Folded to Position

No. 8.—Placket Opening Finished

The darts and seams of the skirt are stitched, also the under-arm and shoulder seams and the front hems of the corset-cover. The neck and armholes of the corset-cover may be narrowly hemmed or faced, and lace may be stitched or overhanded to the edge, or a lace beading, through which ribbon may be run, can be sewed to the faced edge, and the lace edging sewed to the beading. The lower edge of the corset-cover and the top of the skirt should be joined together in a seam, which should also include a narrow bias strip of the material, basted next to the skirt. After the seam is stitched the bias strip is turned under a seam and is basted and then stitched to the corset-cover. If embroidered beading is preferred it may be stitched over this facing, observing that the facing shall not be wider when finished than the beading. Or, if preferred, the material may be cut away back of the beading (in which case the facing strip should have been omitted in joining the corset-cover and the skirt) and the inside finished in the way described for insetting insertion. These methods are also described in the chapter "Hand Sewing Stitches."

A novel idea in corset-covers is shown at No. 9. The body part is made of flouncing in the usual way, but an extension piece in yoke shape is added at the top and gives a much more finished appearance. This yoke may be omitted if desired, but the usual objection to corset-covers of this description has been that they are so low cut that they do not afford sufficient protection. Embroidered flouncing thirteen inches wide was used for this garment. It differs from the usual corset-cover of this description in being drawn into a belt or beading that is the proper waist measure. The lower edge of the flouncing is shaped that it may slope from the back to a dip length to form a blouse in the front and is then gathered into the waist size at the centre back and the centre fronts. To avoid an extra thickness of material at the waist the lower edge is not faced but is turned over a seam on the right side of the material and gathered along the edge of the fold; another row of gathers is made above this one, the space to measure a little less than the width of the beading.

Notches in the pattern show where the gathers should be placed in the front and back, and the places where these notches occur

No. 9.—A Dainty Corset-Cover

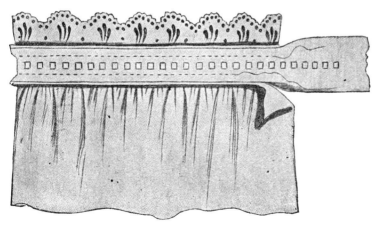

No. 10.—Method of Inserting Beading

should be marked with a colored thread so they may be plainly seen when basting on the belt. The beading should be turned under at each side, leaving space to allow a row of machine-stitching to be run in the plain portion of it and it should then be basted on both edges flat over the gathered lower portion of the corset-cover. The hem and the underlap on the front should have been finished before this.

The yoke portion is cut from all-over tucking that can be bought ready made and in various materials. It is joined at the shoulders by French seams and at the neck is turned over a seam toward the right side in the same manner as the lower edge of the flouncing. This is not shirred, but lace beading is sewed flat over it and conceals the raw edge. The lower edge is hemmed over, also toward the right side and is afterward hemmed with fine stitches to the inside of the upper edge of the embroidery. The embroidery may be left under the arm to turn over to form a sort of cap protection, or it may be cut away in curve shape, and the armhole edged with narrow lace slightly fulled on.

The front may be closed by buttons and buttonholes, and sometimes buttonholes are worked on both sides and a set of studs used as fastenings. Either of these plans is satisfactory in the plain portion, but when the embroidered part is reached buttonholes are very difficult to make, so loops of fine cord sewed along the right side on the under side of the hem and fastening over round pearl buttons, sewed in corresponding positions on the left

No. 11.—Finished Effect of Beading

side, prove satisfactory. The cord is not cut between these loops but is carried from one to the next, as may be seen in the illustration. This is a favorite method of closing lace or embroidered shirt-waists, but for a waist the loops and buttons must be placed very close together and care taken that the loops are not too loose but just the right size to fit over the button.

When embroidered beading is employed for a belt, as on a child's dress, material is usually placed behind the beading for strength, as there is great strain at this point. When the beading is placed between a gathered portion of a garment and the embroidered edging, as for the top of a corset-cover or between the yoke and lower portion of a waist, the beading is joined to the garment in a French seam. If the opposite side is an edging, gather this and stitch in the same manner to the beading; first a seam on the right, then again on the wrong side, being careful that the seams are the exact width of those of the opposite side as seen in No. 10.

Observe carefully that the margin is the same width on both sides of the embroidery before proceeding; if these differ, trim one side like the other so that the same margin will be displayed beyond the beading when the work is finished. The correct effect is pictured at No. 11.

In finishing the upper edge of a petticoat skirt the back gores may be folded to form an inverted box-plait and a skirt belt added, or the edge may be

No. 12.—Tape Drawn Up in Top of Skirt

faced. A very good method of finishing the top of a petticoat is to dispense with the placket entirely. Instead, the entire upper edge is finished with a facing, which is preferably bias at the front and sides, but cut on the straight across the back gores. Stitch to the skirt with the seam on the wrong side, turn over and stitch directly on the edge; the remaining edge is turned in and stitched down flat. At the back, where the fulness should commence, cut a slit in the facing at each side, and work these like buttonholes, as shown at No. 12. Insert a tape or drawing string through one buttonhole and draw it over a short distance beyond that on the opposite side; tack it here firmly. A second tape is put through the buttonhole near the last tacking and brought out on the opposite side; tack it here firmly, just beyond the buttonhole.

THE BATH-ROBE

THE finishing of a bath or lounging robe is quite a simple matter. A suitable pattern is selected; the material chosen usually being eider-down flannel. If the model has double-breasted closing at the front, the perforations marking the centre front are traced with colored thread on both front portions and these tracings are brought one over the other in fitting the garment. The seams are joined according to the notches and the garment is tried on. If no alterations are necessary, the seams are stitched. The under-arm and shoulder seams are finished on the inside in a flat fell. The seam edge of the back portion is trimmed to within one-quarter of an inch of the stitching and the seam of the front portion has its edge turned under and is hemmed down to the back, covering the raw edge of the trimmed seam. The stitches are taken in the foundation only of the flannel and do not show on the right side.

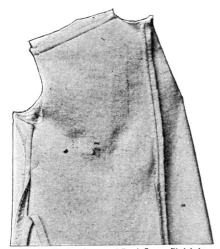

No. 1.—Under-Arm and Back Seam Finish in Bath-Robe

If there is a seam down the centre back it may be bound on each edge with seam binding, but a simpler finish is to open the seam, turn under each edge and hem it to the flannel. The finish of the under-arm and the back seams is shown at No. 1. The shoulder seam is felled like the under-arm seam. The seam of the sleeve may be bound, felled, or hemmed down on each side like the back seam.

A deep band bordering the neck and extending down the front in stole effect is the usual finish, and if made of another material or color harmonizing with the robe is very attractive. White cashmere or light-weight broadcloth would look well on eider-down flannel. This must be shaped on the robe after it is fitted and the shoulder seams are stitched. The garment should be laid out as flat as possible on a table, and a width of cambric long enough to reach from the bottom of the robe to the centre-back seam is pinned in place along the front edge and around one-half of the neck. It is then cut away even with the neck line. The band is made wide enough to reach from the front edge to the colored tracing that marks the centre front, and this same width is continued around the neck by measuring from the neck edge and cutting the cambric to the desired width. This pattern may be cut in paper instead of cambric if care is exercised in pinning and shaping the paper on the robe. If economy of material is desired, the front band and the neck-band need not be cut in one but may be joined at the front in a mitred seam. After the band is cut from the material it is joined in a seam at the centre back and is basted to the outside of the robe. The neck and front edges are left raw-edge, but the other side is turned under and hemmed or stitched to the robe. An underfacing the same shape is cut from lining. The front and neck edges are turned under a seam, and the underfacing is hemmed to the inner side, preserving the shaping of the neck.

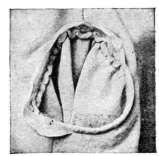

No. 2.—Binding the Armhole

The sleeves are gathered as directed and basted into the armhole. A bias strip of lining has one edge basted to the seam, which is then stitched. The bias strip is turned over and hemmed to the sleeve forming a binding to the seam as shown at No. 2.

It is always advisable to place a second row of gathers just below the first, as this holds the fulness well in place, particularly when the sleeve is full.

CHILDREN'S CLOTHES

THE one-piece dresses for girls and boys are on the Russian-blouse order, in that they hang from the shoulder with waist and skirt in one. Bloused knickerbockers are often worn underneath in lieu of petticoats; the construction of these is the same whether they are made of cloth or linen. The two methods illustrated are suitable for a little girl, or a boy who has not yet been graduated into knickers.

The first dress is a box-plaited model closing in the front. At No. 1 is seen one side of the front with the plaits prepared. When the garment is being cut all the perforations must be plainly marked. The front edge is to be turned under at the large perforations to form a hem, but this hem is not stitched separately; it has its edge caught in the stitching of the first plait or tuck, as can be seen in the illustration. The perforations indicating the sewing-line of the box-plait are brought together and stitched to form a wide plait, which is then shaped into a box-plait by bringing its centre line over the row of stitching and flattening it. It should be pressed and may be stitched at each side three-eighths of an inch from the fold edge, the stitching answering the double purpose of being ornamental and of holding the box-plait in shape. A crow foot may be worked at the end of each row of stitching, as seen at No. 2, or others described in "Practical and Ornamental Stitches" may be used.

No. 1.—Hem, Tuck and Plait in Front

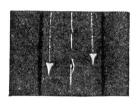

No. 2.—Stitching on Box-Plait Finished with Crow Foot

The back is cut with the straight edge (which has a double perforation) on a fold of the material, and if this is single-width goods it is probable that it may be necessary to piece it at each side, concealing the seam under the box-plait. Bring the lines of perforations together and stitch the box-plaits as for the fronts, then lap the line that marks the single row of perforations between the box-plait and the centre of the back till its edge is even with the centre back and baste it there, but do not stitch it in a tuck as the front was stitched. Measure the width of the front tuck and at the same space from the centre back make a row of stitching flat through the folded plait and the back portion underneath it. This will make the back correspond with the front, but the plaits at the centre, being lapped much deeper than the

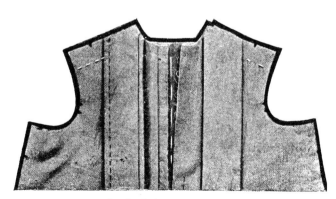

No. 3.—Plaits Laid in Back

front tucks, will give the necessary fulness in the skirt part below the stitching. The edges of the box-plaits should be stitched to correspond with the front. The back with one side in state of preparation is shown at No. 3.

The sleeve is finished with three little box-plaits laid in the wrist portion. No. 4 shows how to prepare them. Bring the fold edges at each side of each continuous line of thread over even and baste the plait so formed; stitch through both plait and sleeve. After the plaits are stitched, stitch the seam of the sleeve and underface the wrist. Lay the box-plait in the top of the sleeve, and gather the sleeve from each edge of the box-plait to the notches but do not gather across the box-plait.

A similar dress closes in the back, and the front is finished at the top with a yoke. No. 5 shows the sim-

No. 4.—Box-Plaiting at Wrist

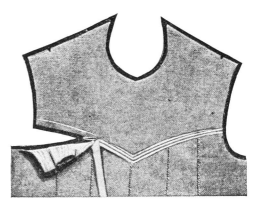

No. 5.—Attaching Yoke to Front

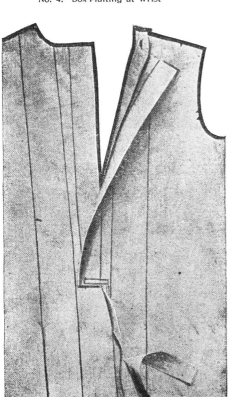

No. 6.—Hemmed Closing at the Back

plest way of attaching the yoke to the lower part. Cut the front, marking all the perforations carefully, and join the pieces necessary to complete the width where they may best be concealed. Form the plaits, stitch them and press them open, and stitch their fold edges if they are to have that finish. Cut the yoke and turn the lower edge under a seam, slashing the edge, where necessary, to make it lie flat. Baste the yoke to the top of the plaited portion and to the wrong side baste a piece of tape, seam-binding or a bias strip of the material with its edges turned under. Place two rows of stitching across the yoke, stitching from the outside. These will catch through the tape that is basted underneath and which covers the raw edges of the seam, making a neat finish on the inside. This finish is desirable for a summer dress as it avoids lining the yoke, but if a lining is used it is cut like the yoke; and the top of the dress portions is enclosed between the turned-under edges of the yoke and its lining.

The way of arranging the hems and finishing the back is shown at No. 6. Explicit directions referring to the finish most desirable for each pattern will be found on the label accompanying it. The excess material in the skirt part of the dress below the lapped hems may be cut away and the raw edges of the seam bound with a strip of lining; or the extra material (after being cut across at the finish of the hem) may be turned over to form a binding, cutting away only about an inch of it, as shown in No. 6. The hems may be stitched and lapped, the right over the left, the fold edge of the right side reaching almost to the sewing-line of the first box-plait on the left side. Turn under about one-quarter of an inch at the finish of the hems and stitch across with two rows of stitching to make the closing secure and neat. Close with buttons and buttonholes.

Lapped, instead of plain seams may be made down the sides. In this case both edges of the seam are turned to one side and a row of stitching is made, from the outside, about one-quarter of an inch from the seam, the stitching going through the three thicknesses—the outside and the two seam edges on the inside. When lapped seams are made, the hem and any other outside stitching should have two rows instead of one, with the same spacing as that at the seams.

WASH DRESSES

In making up wash frocks and those for Summer wear the garment is cut and fitted, after which the lace insertions are added; these are laid on in the proper position and basted. If

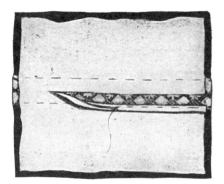

No. 7.—Method of Applying Lace Insertion

No. 8.—Finished Effect of Tucking and Insertion

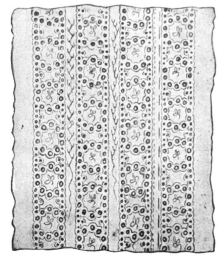

No. 9.—Strips of Embroidery Joined

the insertion is narrow, the material is cut through the centre, as seen at No. 7; but if the insertion is wide, the material is cut away from underneath, allowing simply a seam on each side. The edge of this is turned in and then turned again on the line of the basting, as for a hem. The insertions are now sewed down from the right side, catching through the material which has been turned over. This will also be seen at No. 7. If the material frays badly this method will have to be followed, but if it is firmly woven it may simply be folded over at the edge of the insertion and not again for a hem.

Some of the very expensive wash dresses are made mostly by hand, but as these are out of the reach of the majority, one daintily made by machine will answer all practical purposes. If a yoke, collar or other portion is to be made of tucks and insertion, the clusters of tucks may be made and a space the width of the insertion left between. Baste the lace in position, cut the material from the back and turn under the edge (No. 7), as no raw edges must show on dainty work of this kind. The finish is shown at No. 8.

Although numberless designs in all-over lace and embroidery are shown, one is frequently at a loss to procure a design which is entirely to one's taste. If a satisfactory pattern can be purchased in a narrow insertion, this can be diverted very dexterously into a charming and dainty yoke in the following manner:

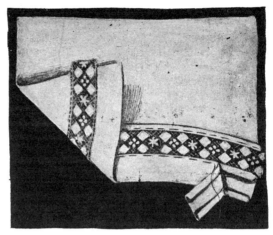

Cut the yoke pattern in heavy paper and crease the centre. Place a width of insertion directly down the centre of the pattern and a second next this, allowing the margin to show between. Turn in the edge of the margin on both upper and under sides for a finish and baste together. Note if the embroidery has an up and down and place all the sprays in the same direction, cutting the insertion after each strip is fitted.

When the pattern has been covered remove the yoke and work a brier or feather stitch on the margin between each strip, as illustrated at No. 9. The first margin shows a single feather stitch and the second a double feather stitch, while the third simply depicts the margin turned over and basted.

No. 10.—Insertion Above Hem

For an insertion that is added above a hem, similar to that seen at No. 10, the method is a trifle different. The insertion is basted on in the proper position and the upper edge treated in the manner shown at No. 7. If the outline below this is straight, a hem is turned up and the raw edge turned in before the hem is stitched. If the outline is curved or in points, or if lace is to be added, a facing serves for the finish. The lace is gathered and basted to the lower edge and

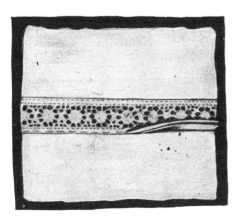

No. 11.—Hamburg Embroidery Inserted

No. 12.—Finished Effect of Insertion

a facing of a sufficient depth to meet the insertion basted on and all stitched in a seam together; otherwise the facing is added plain to the edge (No. 10), then turned up and the remaining edge turned in and basted to position, just touching the insertion and covering all raw edges. Extreme care must be observed in fitting the facing at curves and points.

Insertions of Hamburg or other embroideries, when inserted in piqué and like materials, are treated somewhat differently from the lace, as they have not a finished edge but a margin for sewing on. Mark the width of the insertion on the piqué either by creasing or basting and cut, allowing a seam on each side of the basting. Sew the insertion to the piqué on this line with none of the margin showing, and stitch by machine; crease the seam over on the piqué, turn the edge of the margin—but not the material—as seen at No. 11, and stitch an even line.

This row of stitching is not objectionable, as will be seen in the finished effect developed in piqué and shown at No. 12. Often two rows of stitching are visible, the extra one being at the edge of the insertion. If preferred, no stitching at all need be visible if the work is joined according to the method known as a French seam.

A simple way of making imitation hemstitching on the machine is shown at Nos. 13 and 14. Fold up the hem, and one-quarter of an inch above where the hem would be sewed cut it off from the rest of the skirt. Fold enough blotting-paper or soft paper of any sort to make almost one-eighth of an inch thickness; place the cut edge of the skirt and the edge of the piece just cut off together, as if to sew a seam; slip the blotting-paper between the two, loosen the tension of the machine and stitch an ordinary quarter-inch seam through the two edges of material and the paper between, as seen at No. 13. When the seam is stitched all the way around, cut the paper close to the stitching and pull it out. The stitches between the two edges of the material will then look like No. 14. The edge toward the hem is folded back, the hem edge is folded over it, and a row of fine machine-stitching close to the edge holds the hem. Another row or a row of feather stitching should be made to hold back the edge of the skirt part.

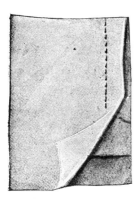

No. 13.—Seam Edges with Blotting-Paper Between

Frequently berthas and scalloped edges are desired unlined or without facing, and the method illustrated at No. 15 makes a pretty finish. To accomplish this add the gathered edging to the bottom of the flounce or bertha in an ordinary seam on the right side. Turn this seam up on the material and cover with a feather-stitched braid, stitching on at both edges. Unlike No. 19, this feather stitching is made by machine and can be purchased in a number of different designs. Many occasions arise when it will be found a most desirable finish. Frequently when one is at a loss to know just how to accomplish a correct finish, this little braid will be found to answer all requirements.

EMBROIDERED AND HEMSTITCHED FROCKS

An admirable feature in the making of embroidered and hemstitched frocks for infants and children, is the arrangement of the material at the under-arm, whereby it may be cut with a straight lower edge, or with a bias seam under the arm and a shaped lower edge. The straight lower edge is occasioned by straight breadths front and back with the material under the arm disposed in inverted fulness. The same patterns are so arranged that they may be cut with the bias seam under the arm if desired, the latter requiring a curved lower edge. This feature will be found in some of the infants' dresses, as well as in many of the children's and girls' sizes; it has been provided in all the newest patterns where it is considered to be of particular advantage, the idea being peculiar to Butterick patterns alone. Application for patents is now pending in the Patent Office at Washington.

When the straight lower edge is desired, the fulness at each under-arm is laid in an inverted box-plait, according to the directions on the label of the pattern; this throws ample fulness into the skirt and is known as inverted fulness. This effect is desirable for different styles, as, for

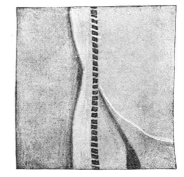

No. 14.—Hemstitching by Machine

instance, where a yoke is preferred, an excessive amount of fulness is avoided across the front and back, since to provide the requisite width at the bottom of the skirt the fulness must be divided on the front and back alone, thus leaving a plain portion at the under-arm. Instead of this unequal division, the inverted fulness at this point distributes the material more evenly around the entire skirt and permits the latter to hang evenly at all times, similar to a gathered skirt.

Although designs with this inverted fulness may be selected to develop almost all materials used for children's clothes, it is especially desirable for a dress which is to be made of embroidered flouncing, or with a hemstitched hem or drawn-work. When using embroidered flouncing, the lower portion may be made without cutting into, or destroying the design of the embroidery, simply allowing the full depth of the needlework and margin; or, if this is longer than the pattern, cutting the length as directed on the label. Join the seam up the back to a point sufficient for the placket.

When a dress is to be hemstitched at the bottom, this feature is equally desirable, because, whether the material is double or single width, the straight breadths are joined together and, with the inverted fulness, produce the straight lower edge which is necessary in this case as

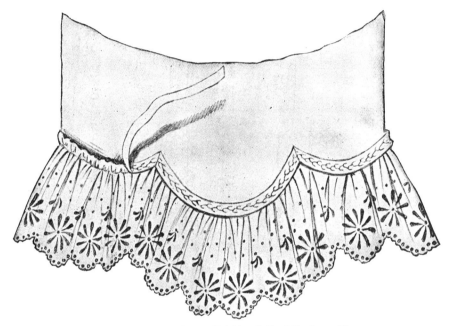

No. 15.—Embroidered Edging Finishing Unlined Bertha or Flounce

well. Without this straight lower edge, hemstitching or designs of drawn-work which are so popular in children's dresses, could not be properly executed since the full length of the straight threads could not be drawn; besides these, the worker will find many other occasions when this feature will be most desirable.

On the other hand, should a shaped under-arm be preferred in the patterns of same design (as for an infants' robe or other dress), a slightly fitted or shaped effect may be produced under the arm by cutting away the material beyond the line of perforations which are provided from the armhole to the lower edge, and joining as in an ordinary seam. This lower edge is shaped by cutting the pattern away at the line of perforations near the bottom, and may be finished with a hem, a ruffle, or trimmed as otherwise desired.

Judgment may be used in cutting away the material and only the surplus from the armhole to the waist cut away, leaving the inverted fulness intact from the waist-line down, so as not to reduce the fulness in the skirt. In the same way a design of Empire style may have the material cut away only from the armhole to the depth desired. Variations may be made at the point of inverted fulness by the clever woman, to carry out the design of her needlework or for other reasons which present themselves to her. Much individuality as well as preference is permitted the worker, and several dresses of quite different character may be made from the one pattern by exercising the liberty permitted in the shaping, and effecting different modes of trimming, whether these be lace and embroidery or simply hand-work for ornamentation.

INFANTS' WEAR

It would seem that there is not much opportunity for change in the making of infants' garments and, while this is more or less true, there are improvements tried from time to time, more especially with a view to making the process of dressing an infant a less tedious operation and to insure greater comfort to the child in the wearing of the garments. As buttons and buttonholes are not desirable, except on the dresses and slips and other outer garments, it is

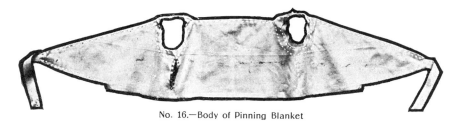

No. 16.—Body of Pinning Blanket

usual to pin the petticoat bodies; but another plan is seen at No. 16, by which the body may be tied in place with wide tapes; this kind of body may be used on either the pinning blankets or the petticoats.

Patterns of infants' sets are issued which include a dress, a slip or nightgown, a wrapper, a skirt and a pinning blanket; the latter garment was used for the illustration. The body should be cut from fine cambric and, though the edges may be bound or faced, it will be found generally more satisfactory to make the body double. For this purpose twice the quantity of cambric the pattern calls for should be provided, and two body portions should be cut by the pattern. Join the shoulder seams of each portion and press them open, then lay the two body portions evenly together, the shoulder seams of both toward the outside, and stitch a seam around the outer edge, except at the points at each end and the space between the notches that indicate the part to be left open, to insert the upper edge of the skirt or pinning blanket.

After being stitched, the two body parts are turned to bring the seams inside, the edges

No. 17.—Petticoat Joined to Ordinary Body

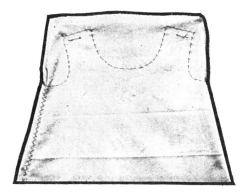

No. 18.—Petticoat that Fastens on the Shoulder

at the pointed ends are turned in and the end of a piece of three-quarter-inch wide tape is slipped in each opening; the edge is then basted, as seen in the illustration, and stitched. Baste around the armhole about one inch from the edge to keep the two portions evenly together, nick the raw edges and turn one in a seam's width and baste it, then turn the other edge in and baste it to the first. Stitch by machine or overhand the two folded edges together to finish the armhole. Baste about an inch each side of the perforations that indicate the opening to be made at the left side. Cut through the perforations and bind the opening with soft ribbon or silk tape. The edges of the blanket should be bound, and the upper edge gathered and basted into the opening left in the lower part of the body or band, where a row of machine-stitching will hold it in place.

A petticoat body of the usual style that is to be lapped in the back and pinned with safety pins, is seen at No. 17. It is, of course, a matter of choice which shall be used. This body is not made double but is hemmed at the back edges and faced at the neck and armholes after

No. 19.—Petticoat on Double Waist Band

the shoulders and under-arms are joined in French seams. The top of the petticoat is gathered and basted in a seam to the lower edge of the body. A bias strip of the cambric is placed next to the petticoat in the same seam, which is then stitched, and the facing piece is turned over and hemmed to the body. The seams in the skirt should be French seams, and the placket opening may be finished with an ordinary narrow hem on each edge, in which case the skirt should be sewed to the body to reach three-eighths of an inch inside of the fold edge of the hem, and the hem only will lap in fastening.

Still another petticoat model hangs from the shoulders and has no separate body and no placket opening, the closing being effected on one or both shoulders by tying with ribbons or by buttons and buttonholes. The neck and armholes of this kind of petticoat are usually bound with ribbon or tape, though a scolloped edge, worked with white embroidery silk, makes the little garment much prettier. If it is to be embroidered, do not cut out the neck and armholes, but mark the outline of the pattern with a colored thread as shown at No. 18. The design

can then be stamped along the outline and cut out after the embroidery is done. The shoulder seams are not joined but the embroidery extends across. The seams under the arm should be joined before the embroidery is begun, in an ordinary seam, pinked or notched, the seam pressed open, and a row of brier or coral stitching worked, ornamenting the outside and holding the pressed seam open on the inside, or the seam may be felled. The bottom of the petticoat may be embroidered in scollops, or a hem may be turned up and finished on the outside with the same stitch used on the side seams.

For the second size the petticoats are made a trifle different from that shown at No. 17, inasmuch as they are made on double-shaped waist-bands exactly the same as those worn by older

No. 20.—Front of Slip

children. These waists are cut from two layers of muslin; place these together and stitch all the edges except the shoulders and lower one. Clip the seams at curves, turn the waist inside out and crease all the edges sharply. These may be again stitched on the outside to strengthen the edges and hold the seams in position. This double waist is shown at No. 19.

The lower edge of the skirt may be finished with tucks, insertions and edgings, according to preference. The upper edge is gathered with fine stitches and joined to the waist after the placket has been hemmed with a very narrow hem on the left side and one three-quarters of an inch on the right side.   Lap the wide hem over the narrow and tack firmly at the bottom of the placket with two rows of machine-stitching, preferably running slanting.

The centre of the skirt is pinned to the centre of the underside of the waist, the gathers distributed evenly, and both basted together, then stitched.   Turn this seam up on the band,

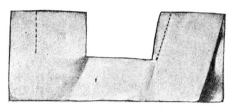

No. 21.—Hem, Cut Across to Make Placket Finish

No. 22.—Placket Finish

turn in the remaining edge and s t i t c h through the gathers, covering all previous s t i t c h i n g . This m e t h o d i s shown at No. 19.   The shoulders are stitched in a fell seam, although a French seam may be used, if preferred; and the closing is completed with buttons and buttonholes.   Unless the back hems are cut wide it is advisable to put a stay-tape between the layers under the buttons.   No. 20 shows a slip, which is always desirable. This is made of fine sheer Persian lawn.   Fine nainsook is equally popular for infants' wear, and some little slips are seen made of fine white dimity.   The slip is invariably made very plain and loose.   In the garment shown the neck is finished with a bias band, through which is run a narrow tape or wash ribbon by which it is drawn up to the required size when worn.   The sleeves are hemmed at the wrist and narrow lace is overhanded to make a little frill around neck and sleeves.   All the seams should be felled or made French seams.

The back is cut down through the centre to the indicating perforation, and each side of this opening is finished with a half-inch hem.   Infants' garments usually lap from left to right, and in order to allow space for this it is necessary to cut across the turned-under part of the hem on the left side of the placket opening, as shown at No. 21.   This cut piece is then laid in one or two small plaits and sewed to the underfold of the hem of the right side; this right side hem is then lapped directly over the hem of the left side, and a row of fine back-stitching w i l l hold the two hems and little plaits together.   The hem of

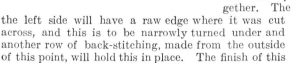

No. 23.—Inside Finish of Slip

Nos. 24 and 25.—Hand-Run Tucks and Fancy Stitches

the left side will have a raw edge where it was cut across, and this is to be narrowly turned under and another row of back-stitching, made from the outside of this point, will hold this in place.   The finish of this placket is shown at No. 22.

Small lace or pearl buttons are sewed on the left side and corresponding buttonholes are worked on the right side.   The bias neck-band is cut across, through the outside only, just in front of the hem on the left side of the back opening, and this cut is buttonholed around and one end of the ribbon is drawn through it that it may just meet the other end that falls from the opening in the end of the neck-band at the right side.   This, as well as the inside finish of the garment and the finished placket opening, is shown in the slip at No. 23.

The dress is made in practically the same way as the slip, with the variation of a yoke. Nos. 24 and 25 give suggestions for decorating yokes, ruffles and the bottom of dresses with hand-work, the number of tucks in each cluster and the fancy stitching being varied to suit.

The yoke of the dress is generally made of tucking combined with lace or embroidery, and a bias seam at the centre of the yoke, making the tucks join diagonally, is a variation from the usual way. To do this the front and back portions of the yoke pattern are joined at the shoulder seam, and each side of the yoke, from front to back, is in only one piece. No. 26 shows the way the pattern should be laid on material, previously tucked, in order to make the bias front seam. A piece of French lawn measuring a trifle more (on the length of the material) than the yoke measures from back to front should be hemmed on one edge and as many clusters of tucks, evenly spaced, made as are required by the outline of the yoke. Two of these pieces are required, the hems and tucks reversed that they may match on the opposite sides. The front seam should be joined with hemstitch-beading, and for this the seam on the yoke may be turned back and the beading overhanded to the turned edge; or, the seam may be trimmed away to leave only one-eighth of an inch, then rolled and the beading whipped on. The dress is gathered between the notches and basted, then stitched to the yoke in a seam turned toward the outside of the garment; this seam is pressed to one side and a narrow band of the dress material, turned in at both

No. 26.—To Cut a Yoke with a Bias Seam in Front

sides, is basted over the joining, concealing the seam. (No. 27.) A narrow frill usually finishes the yoke, and this should be gathered and stroked and basted to the seam joining the skirt and yoke before the band is applied. The band should be finished with a row of stitching at each edge. The back is attached to the yoke in the same way, the placket being first made as already described.

Little shoes and slippers, made of washable material, are a change from the inevitable knitted sock. The slipper shown in No. 28 is made of fig-

No. 27.—Yoke Joined to Skirt

ured piqué and is lined with flannel. Allowance is made on the pattern for seams, but a prettier way is to bind the edges with the narrow bias bands that can be bought ready cut and folded. This does away with the seam inside the finished shoe or slipper. In this case the seam allowance must be trimmed off both sole and upper part. The piqué or other material selected is cut from the slipper pattern according to the directions contained in the label. The sole is cut from two thicknesses of silesia or other stout lining material. A lining for both upper and sole is then cut from flannel.

No. 28.—Piqué Slipper

The outside material and the flannel lining are seamed separately at the back and the seams are pressed open; the lining and the outside are basted together evenly. The upper and lower edges of the slipper are then bound with the bias binding. The upper part and sole are overhanded together on the wrong side and the shoe is turned right side out. The ankle straps are lined with cambric. Work the buttonhole in the right-hand strap of one slipper and in the left-hand strap of the other. Little rosettes of lace or of baby ribbon may furnish the decoration, or the toe may be daintily embroidered in tiny flowers.

BOYS' SUITS

WHILE the making of a boys' suit is not at all a difficult matter, there are a few details of finish, more especially the pockets, that explanation may simplify. The pocket should be in place in each section of the garment before the portions are joined. If the directions are followed, the rest of the finishing will be found an easy matter.

After the cloth is shrunk and pressed, lay the entire pattern out at the same time, disposing it to the best advantage, according to the directions on the label. Trace with tailors' chalk the seams along the perforations that mark the sewing line of the outlet seams. Mark these seams with tailors' tacks through the two thicknesses of cloth, with one long and two short stitches, as described in the chapter "Practical and Ornamental Stitches"; cut the stitches and separate the pieces. Two fly pieces should be cut from the cloth and three from lining material. A strip of lining will be needed to face the top of the trousers, and the inside band in which the buttonholes are to be worked should be cut from strong drilling.

Mark the position of all the pockets as indicated by the perforations. The pocket in the right side of the back of the trousers and in the left side of the front of the jacket are welt-pockets without overlapping pieces.

THE TROUSERS

After the darts in the back portions of the trousers are stitched and pressed open, a thread of colored cotton should be run along the mark for the welt-pockets, so that it will show through both sides of the material. A piece of the cloth two inches wide and one inch longer than the pocket mark should be basted with its right side facing the right side of the material and in such position that the pocket mark will run directly through its centre and leave half an inch of the cloth beyond the mark at each end.

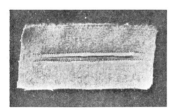
No. 1.—Preparing the Pocket Opening

No. 2.—Facing Drawn through Pocket

From the wrong side make another basting mark through the one already made in order that it may show through the applied piece on the outside. A piece of canvas the same size as the piece of cloth is basted, in just the same position, to the wrong side of the material. From the right side two rows of stitching, each one-eighth of an inch distant from the pocket mark, are made through cloth and canvas. This distance may vary according to the material used. If it is loose-woven canvas, mohair or woollen crash, the seam must be made a little farther away from the pocket mark, but the neat finish of the pocket depends on its being as narrow a seam as possible. Finish the two rows of stitching exactly even and tie the ends of the thread firmly; do not stitch across at the ends; cut through carefully exactly on the pocket mark; use a small pair of sharp scissors or a knife, and cut exactly the length of the mark. If a wider seam has been made, it will be necessary to make a diagonal cut from not quite the end of the mark to the end of the row of stitching, leaving a little pointed piece of the material across each end; when the seam is narrow, however, this is not necessary. These rows of stitching and the cut pocket opening are shown at No. 1. The piece of cloth is now pushed through the pocket opening and basted around from the outside, letting the loose piece of cloth form a welt or cord beyond the stitched edge of the seam, but no more than an eighth of an inch, that the opening may have a corded and not a bound appearance. At the

122

ends the cloth piece can be drawn entirely through the opening and basted flat on the wrong side as shown at No. 2, being careful that it is smooth and even all along both sides.

It will be found more satisfactory to press the pocket opening thoroughly before stitching it from the outside, and it should be held in position by drawing the two cord edges together with loose overhand stitches. The outside stitching should be placed as close to the seam as possible. The pocket may be stitched in at the same time if the pocket opening is on a straight line.

Cut from stout lining material two pieces for each pocket, leaving one piece an inch longer than the other. Lay the two pieces of the pocket together in such position that they will hang straight when the garment is worn; if in the jacket, make them hang parallel with the front edge of the jacket and mark the top edges on the exact line of the pocket opening. The longer piece should be faced at its top edge with a piece of the cloth two inches deep, and stitched at its lower edge to the pocket.

It is advisable to round the lower corners of the pockets and both portions should be trimmed off alike. Lay the shorter pocket piece on the inside of the garment, the lower edge of the pocket toward the upper part of the garment, and the straight edge of the pocket extending one-half inch below the pocket opening and on a line with it. Baste the piece securely in place and then place the row of finish stitching on the outside. This row holds both the welt edge and the lower pocket portion in place. The lower pocket portion is now turned down, its rounded end toward the bottom of the garment and the upper or longer pocket portion is laid over it, their lower or rounded edges even, and both toward the bottom of the garment and with the facing on the longer portion toward the cloth of the garment; baste this portion firmly in place and stitch through from the outside close to the seam as on the lower edge. The two pocket portions are shown in No. 3. The edges of the pocket

No. 3.—Pocket Portions Stitched in Place

portions should then be turned over a seam all around and stitched close to the edge fold, the raw edges toward the inside of the pocket. Sew only the pocket portions; do not catch through the cloth. A buttonholed bar, as described in the chapter "Practical and Ornamental Stitches," stays the ends of the pockets. Sometimes this pocket opening is shaped in a curved line, and when this is the case it will be better to apply the stitching to hold the welts first, then cut the tops of the pocket pieces in corresponding shape and hem them in place by hand. A stay-piece of soft canvas should run from each end of the pocket to the waist-band.

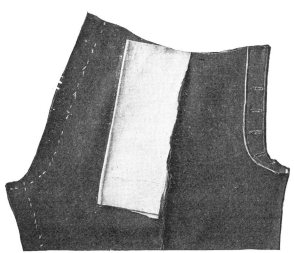

No. 4.—Inside View of Fly and Pocket

The fly portions should be sewed to the fronts next. This is illustrated at No. 4. Baste one of the pieces of lining material, cut by the fly-piece pattern on the outside of the front edge of the left front portion, with the notches even. Stitch a narrow seam from the top to the notch and turn the facing over to the wrong side, allowing the cloth edge to extend a trifle that the lining may not show at the edge; baste this firmly in place. Take the cloth fly piece that will fit directly under this faced left front when the wrong side of the cloth of the front portion and the wrong side of the fly piece face each other and face it with a fly piece of lining, making the seam on the curved side and extending it to the notch; stitch the seam and turn it and baste the facing in place. The buttonholes may be worked in this fly piece now or after it is stitched in place; they are worked from the cloth side, the first one to come just below the waist-band. A row of stitching one-quarter inch back of the buttonholes and through both outside and fly piece holds it in place against the facing of the left front portion. The raw edges at the inside should be overcast. The other cloth fly piece is faced with lining, but the seam is sewed at the outer or rounded side. The curved side of the cloth only is sewed in a seam to the curved edge of the right front portion. This seam is pressed open. The facing of lining has its curved edge notched and turned under a seam, and is basted over this pressed-open cloth seam, and a row of stitching màde on the front portion close to the seam holds the facing in place.

No. 5.—Front Showing Lap and Pockets

There should also be a row of stitching on the free edge of this extension fly piece to hold it and its facing securely together. Small trousers buttons are sewed on to correspond with the buttonholes in the fly.

The side pockets are next to be sewed in place, and the method is shown in No. 5. A piece of cloth an inch and one-half wide should be basted to the front portions by a narrow seam, and extend half an inch above and one inch below each of the perforations in the pattern that indicate the size of the pocket opening; these points should have been carefully marked with a thread when the seams were marked. The pockets are cut from silesia or other strong lining material. One piece eight and one-half inches wide and eight inches deep is required for each pocket, in the seven-year-old size. In the larger or smaller sizes, the size of the pockets will vary accordingly. Seam one side of the silesia pocket piece to the front portion over this

small facing piece so that one seam will hold both, and stitch as far as the mark for the pocket opening. The raw edge of the cloth facing should be turned under and stitched to the inside of the pocket. The back edge of the lining pocket should have one edge folded over a seam and the fold edge thus made should be basted even with the seam mark to the under or wrong side of the back portion of the trousers. A row of stitching, extending from the waist to the bottom of the pocket opening will hold this in place, and the edge of the extension piece on the back portion of the trousers forms the facing for the other side of the pocket. It should be turned under at its edge and stitched to the inside of the pocket. Tie the ends of all stitching securely.

No. 6.—Outside Effect of Fly and Pocket

The outside seam of the leg, below the pocket, may now be seamed, then both edges of the seam are turned toward the front and a row of stitching is placed on the outside one-eighth of an inch from the edge, giving a lap or welt seam finish. The seam should be closed all the way down if the legs are to be finished over an elastic in knickerbocker style, or the allowed hem on the front portion may be turned under and have buttonholes worked in it, and the underlap on the back portion may be underfaced and have buttons sewed on it. The seam from the top of the pocket to the waist should also be stitched in a seam. Bring the finished pocket edge of the front portion over even with the seam mark on the back portion and baste firmly in position, the pocket turned toward the front as shown at No. 6.

This description is for trousers that close at the front with a fly; for smaller boys the small facing is attached to the right side of the front according to the notches, and the front seam is closed from the upper notch to the waist. The extension piece on the back portion of the trousers is not slipped inside the pocket, but the back edge of the pocket is faced with a piece of cloth both inside and outside for the space of the pocket opening, and a back and front waistband are used. An illustration of this pocket is shown at No. 7. The fronts lap over the back portions to bring the double perforations, indicated in the label, together, and the extension piece on the back portion is underfaced to form an underlap.

The pocket portion attached to the front piece is arranged in the same way as in the fly-front finish. The inside of these trousers is pictured at No. 8.

A row of stitching close to the edge makes a firm finish for the pocket opening on the front portion, and a second row is usually placed a quarter of an inch inside of the first, while a bar

No. 7.—Side Pocket Stitched to Front Piece of Trousers

No. 8.—Front and Back Portions of Trousers with Side Pocket

of several threads of silk, overcast or buttonholed, caught through the cloth and both sides of the pocket, runs from one row of stitching to the other at the upper and lower finish of the pocket opening. The edges of the lining pocket are turned in a seam toward the inside and stitched together close to the folded edge; one or both corners of the pocket may be rounded.

The inside seam of each leg is now to be stitched and the seams pressed open; the two leg portions should then be joined by a seam down the back, extending from the waist to the notch in the lower edge of the fly piece, including the seams of the fly pieces below the notches in the seam with the trousers portions. This seam should be pressed open and covered with a tape or a bias strip of lining basted flat on the open seam and stitched from the outside with a row of stitching each side to form a stay. The end is turned under and neatly hemmed down at the end of the fly stitching. A strong stay stitch or overcast bar should be worked on the outside at the finish of the fly opening.

The top of the trousers should be turned over a seam toward the wrong side and a facing hemmed to it. The band should be made and the buttonholes worked in it according to the perforations. It is basted in place, and one row of stitching made from the outside holds the lower edge of the band and the facing. A strong tack thread should catch the band and the outside portion together between the buttonholes. The fly piece should be caught to the facing of the left front in the same way. The buttonholes in both fly and waistband should be worked with twist or stout thread and made strong at the ends.

A RUSSIAN BLOUSE JACKET

THE making of a Russian blouse jacket is quite a simple matter.   Mark the pocket with tailors' tacks, face the pocket opening and insert the pocket as explained for Nos. 1, 2 and 3. Join the seams and finish on the outside with a row of machine-stitching at each side of the seam.   The seams, however, should be bound first, and this may be accomplished by stitching a bias strip of farmer satin on the edge; turn it over to be held in place by the top stitching; other methods of binding, as explained in the chapter "Important Points and Aids in Dressmaking," may be adopted if desired.   Should a finish be preferred which will require no binding, the seam edges may be cut wider and arranged for lap seams, as explained in the chapte· "Novel, Artistic Seams," or any of the other finishes described in this chapter may, if desired, be chosen.   Fold over the front edges according to the perforations, also the hem on the bottom and finish with two or three rows of stitching.

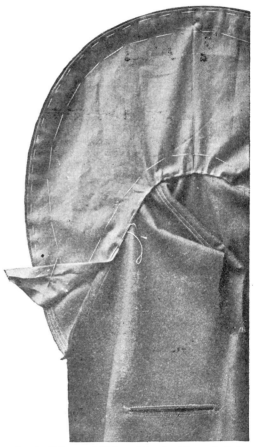

The deep collar on the jacket or blouse should be lined with a piece of lining material of the same shade.   The collar should be turned under a seam at its edge, and one or more rows of stitching or braid placed around it; the lining, also turned under a seam, is hemmed to the underside of the collar and covers the wrong side of the stitching.   The neck portion of the collar is joined to the neck, according to the notches, with the seam toward the outside of the jacket or blouse.   The collar lining is then turned under at its neck edge and hemmed to the neck of the blouse, concealing the seam; this method is shown at No. 9.

Bind the seams of the sleeves in the same manner as the seams of the jacket were bound, and face the wrist, finishing with a cuff or not, according to the directions on the label of the particular pattern.   Baste the sleeves in the armhole, and if the position is correct, stitch them in by machine, and bind the raw edges.   Russian blouse jackets of this character are rarely made up with linings.

Buttons and buttonholes effect the closing whether the jacket is single or double breasted and a belt either of the material or leather (preferably patent leather) is slipped

No. 9.—Collar and Lining of Russian Blouse Jacket

through loops of the material which are fastened at each under-arm seam.   When a cloth belt is used it should be stitched around to correspond with the stitching on the collar and the front and lower edge of the jacket.

There are many variations of the Russian blouse jacket, but the methods of finishing vary so little from the model just explained that the worker will have no trouble whatever in accomplishing a correct finish.   The buttonholes should be carefully worked, and for these the eyelet buttonhole is preferred.   Directions for working this, as well as the correct manner of sewing on the buttons, will be found in the chapter entitled "Practical and Ornamental Stitches."

A NORFOLK JACKET

In making a Norfolk suit the method is very similar to the Russian blouse. Cut the material carefully as directed for the previous suit, observing and marking perforations for seams, pocket opening, etc. Take up the darts in the back of the trousers and insert the pocket, finishing the trousers according to the general directions just given.

The jacket illustrated was made with a seam running to the shoulder in both the front and back portions; the simulated box-plait is afterward applied directly over these seams and covering them.

Join the first and second front pieces, if the front is not in one piece, and press the seams open. Leave open the space between the notches that indicate a pocket opening in the seam in the left front. A small pocket is set

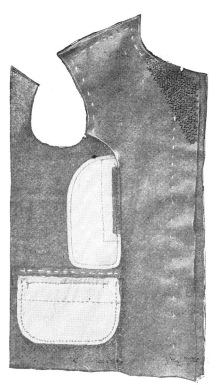

No. 10.—Jacket Front with Canvas and Pockets

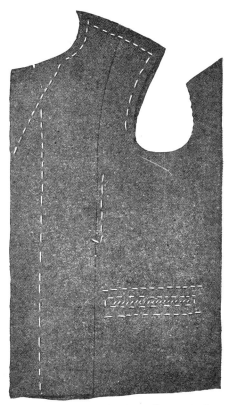

No. 11.—Outside of Jacket Front Showing Pockets

in here by sewing a piece of drilling in a seam to each side of the opening, the seam toward the inside. Push the drilling pocket through the opening and stitch it around. Insert a pocket in each side of the jacket in the manner already described for the trousers back. Face the fronts with canvas from the shoulder as seen in No. 10. Join the back of the jacket to the side and front pieces and press the seams open. The upper corner of the front that is to turn over as a continuation of the collar is to have the canvas and cloth held together with "padding stitch." This is described in the chapter "Practical and Ornamental Stitches." At No. 11 is shown an outside view of the front with the canvas and pockets in place.

The collar is cut from cloth, and a canvas interlining is cut a seam smaller all around. The perforations that mark the turning line of the collar should be traced, and several rows of machine-stitching fill in the space. The remainder of the collar is to be filled with padding stitch as shown at No. 12.

Cut canvas interlining for the box-plaits three-quarters of an inch narrower at each side than the plait. Turn over this three-quarters of an inch, baste it, then stitch three-eighths

No. 12.—Collar with Machine and Padding Stitches

No. 13.—Box-Plait Ready to Apply to Jacket

of an inch from each edge. It is better to stitch the plaits separately and slip-stitch them to the jacket. The plait is shown at No. 13. Interline the belt with canvas, and hem a lining to the turned-over cloth.

The cloth edges of the collar are turned over the canvas all around and cat-stitched to it. The collar is then hemmed by hand to the outside of the jacket, the end of the collar and the turned-over corner at the top of the jacket fronts forming a notch-collar. The canvas should be trimmed away a seam from this corner and down the front of the jacket. Cut a facing for the collar and a front facing like the front, extending back an inch beyond the turned-over corner at the top. Lay the front facing face down on the outside of the jacket fronts and stitch a seam around the corner and down the front of the jacket; turn over and baste near the edge. Baste the collar facing to the collar, turn under the edges and slip-stitch to the collar, and to the front facing where it joins it at the top. Stitch one or two rows around the edge of the collar and down the fronts ; turn up the bottom of the jacket.

Cut the back lining like the cloth back, but allow a half-inch plait down the centre of the lining. Cut the lining of the front and side pieces in one, laying a dart-like plait from the shoulders, running out to nothing about five inches down. Many valuable points will be gained by reading the chapter "Coats and Jackets," as much of this information is applicable to the making of boys' coats and jackets, particularly in regard to the collar, facings and the inserting of the lining.

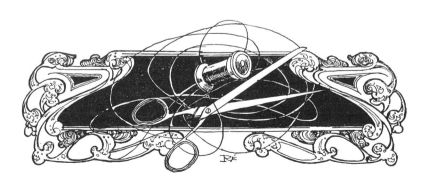

A CATALOG OF SELECTED
DOVER BOOKS
IN ALL FIELDS OF INTEREST

A CATALOG OF SELECTED DOVER
BOOKS IN ALL FIELDS OF INTEREST

CONCERNING THE SPIRITUAL IN ART, Wassily Kandinsky. Pioneering work by father of abstract art. Thoughts on color theory, nature of art. Analysis of earlier masters. 12 illustrations. 80pp. of text. 5⅜ x 8½.   23411-8

ANIMALS: 1,419 Copyright-Free Illustrations of Mammals, Birds, Fish, Insects, etc., Jim Harter (ed.). Clear wood engravings present, in extremely lifelike poses, over 1,000 species of animals. One of the most extensive pictorial sourcebooks of its kind. Captions. Index. 284pp. 9 x 12.   23766-4

CELTIC ART: The Methods of Construction, George Bain. Simple geometric techniques for making Celtic interlacements, spirals, Kells-type initials, animals, humans, etc. Over 500 illustrations. 160pp. 9 x 12. (Available in U.S. only.)   22923-8

AN ATLAS OF ANATOMY FOR ARTISTS, Fritz Schider. Most thorough reference work on art anatomy in the world. Hundreds of illustrations, including selections from works by Vesalius, Leonardo, Goya, Ingres, Michelangelo, others. 593 illustrations. 192pp. 7⅛ x 10¼.   20241-0

CELTIC HAND STROKE-BY-STROKE (Irish Half-Uncial from "The Book of Kells"): An Arthur Baker Calligraphy Manual, Arthur Baker. Complete guide to creating each letter of the alphabet in distinctive Celtic manner. Covers hand position, strokes, pens, inks, paper, more. Illustrated. 48pp. 8¼ x 11.   24336-2

EASY ORIGAMI, John Montroll. Charming collection of 32 projects (hat, cup, pelican, piano, swan, many more) specially designed for the novice origami hobbyist. Clearly illustrated easy-to-follow instructions insure that even beginning papercrafters will achieve successful results. 48pp. 8¼ x 11.   27298-2

THE COMPLETE BOOK OF BIRDHOUSE CONSTRUCTION FOR WOODWORKERS, Scott D. Campbell. Detailed instructions, illustrations, tables. Also data on bird habitat and instinct patterns. Bibliography. 3 tables. 63 illustrations in 15 figures. 48pp. 5¼ x 8½.   24407-5

BLOOMINGDALE'S ILLUSTRATED 1886 CATALOG: Fashions, Dry Goods and Housewares, Bloomingdale Brothers. Famed merchants' extremely rare catalog depicting about 1,700 products: clothing, housewares, firearms, dry goods, jewelry, more. Invaluable for dating, identifying vintage items. Also, copyright-free graphics for artists, designers. Co-published with Henry Ford Museum & Greenfield Village. 160pp. 8¼ x 11.   25780-0

HISTORIC COSTUME IN PICTURES, Braun & Schneider. Over 1,450 costumed figures in clearly detailed engravings–from dawn of civilization to end of 19th century. Captions. Many folk costumes. 256pp. 8⅜ x 11¾.   23150-X

ANATOMY: A Complete Guide for Artists, Joseph Sheppard. A master of figure drawing shows artists how to render human anatomy convincingly. Over 460 illustrations. 224pp. 8⅜ x 11¼. 27279-6

MEDIEVAL CALLIGRAPHY: Its History and Technique, Marc Drogin. Spirited history, comprehensive instruction manual covers 13 styles (ca. 4th century through 15th). Excellent photographs; directions for duplicating medieval techniques with modern tools. 224pp. 8⅜ x 11¼. 26142-5

DRIED FLOWERS: How to Prepare Them, Sarah Whitlock and Martha Rankin. Complete instructions on how to use silica gel, meal and borax, perlite aggregate, sand and borax, glycerine and water to create attractive permanent flower arrangements. 12 illustrations. 32pp. 5⅜ x 8½. 21802-3

EASY-TO-MAKE BIRD FEEDERS FOR WOODWORKERS, Scott D. Campbell. Detailed, simple-to-use guide for designing, constructing, caring for and using feeders. Text, illustrations for 12 classic and contemporary designs. 96pp. 5⅜ x 8½. 25847-5

SCOTTISH WONDER TALES FROM MYTH AND LEGEND, Donald A. Mackenzie. 16 lively tales tell of giants rumbling down mountainsides, of a magic wand that turns stone pillars into warriors, of gods and goddesses, evil hags, powerful forces and more. 240pp. 5⅜ x 8½. 29677-6

THE HISTORY OF UNDERCLOTHES, C. Willett Cunnington and Phyllis Cunnington. Fascinating, well-documented survey covering six centuries of English undergarments, enhanced with over 100 illustrations: 12th-century laced-up bodice, footed long drawers (1795), 19th-century bustles, 19th-century corsets for men, Victorian "bust improvers," much more. 272pp. 5⅜ x 8¼. 27124-2

ARTS AND CRAFTS FURNITURE: The Complete Brooks Catalog of 1912, Brooks Manufacturing Co. Photos and detailed descriptions of more than 150 now very collectible furniture designs from the Arts and Crafts movement depict davenports, settees, buffets, desks, tables, chairs, bedsteads, dressers and more, all built of solid, quarter-sawed oak. Invaluable for students and enthusiasts of antiques, Americana and the decorative arts. 80pp. 6½ x 9¼. 27471-3

WILBUR AND ORVILLE: A Biography of the Wright Brothers, Fred Howard. Definitive, crisply written study tells the full story of the brothers' lives and work. A vividly written biography, unparalleled in scope and color, that also captures the spirit of an extraordinary era. 560pp. 6⅛ x 9¼. 40297-5

THE ARTS OF THE SAILOR: Knotting, Splicing and Ropework, Hervey Garrett Smith. Indispensable shipboard reference covers tools, basic knots and useful hitches; handsewing and canvas work, more. Over 100 illustrations. Delightful reading for sea lovers. 256pp. 5⅜ x 8½. 26440-8

FRANK LLOYD WRIGHT'S FALLINGWATER: The House and Its History, Second, Revised Edition, Donald Hoffmann. A total revision—both in text and illustrations—of the standard document on Fallingwater, the boldest, most personal architectural statement of Wright's mature years, updated with valuable new material from the recently opened Frank Lloyd Wright Archives. "Fascinating"—*The New York Times*. 116 illustrations. 128pp. 9¼ x 10¾. 27430-6

PHOTOGRAPHIC SKETCHBOOK OF THE CIVIL WAR, Alexander Gardner. 100 photos taken on field during the Civil War. Famous shots of Manassas Harper's Ferry, Lincoln, Richmond, slave pens, etc. 244pp. 10⅝ x 8¼. 22731-6

FIVE ACRES AND INDEPENDENCE, Maurice G. Kains. Great back-to-the-land classic explains basics of self-sufficient farming. The one book to get. 95 illustrations. 397pp. 5⅜ x 8½. 20974-1

SONGS OF EASTERN BIRDS, Dr. Donald J. Borror. Songs and calls of 60 species most common to eastern U.S.: warblers, woodpeckers, flycatchers, thrushes, larks, many more in high-quality recording. Cassette and manual 99912-2

A MODERN HERBAL, Margaret Grieve. Much the fullest, most exact, most useful compilation of herbal material. Gigantic alphabetical encyclopedia, from aconite to zedoary, gives botanical information, medical properties, folklore, economic uses, much else. Indispensable to serious reader. 161 illustrations. 888pp. 6½ x 9¼. 2-vol. set. (Available in U.S. only.) Vol. I: 22798-7
Vol. II: 22799-5

HIDDEN TREASURE MAZE BOOK, Dave Phillips. Solve 34 challenging mazes accompanied by heroic tales of adventure. Evil dragons, people-eating plants, blood-thirsty giants, many more dangerous adversaries lurk at every twist and turn. 34 mazes, stories, solutions. 48pp. 8¼ x 11. 24566-7

LETTERS OF W. A. MOZART, Wolfgang A. Mozart. Remarkable letters show bawdy wit, humor, imagination, musical insights, contemporary musical world; includes some letters from Leopold Mozart. 276pp. 5⅜ x 8½. 22859-2

BASIC PRINCIPLES OF CLASSICAL BALLET, Agrippina Vaganova. Great Russian theoretician, teacher explains methods for teaching classical ballet. 118 illustrations. 175pp. 5⅜ x 8½. 22036-2

THE JUMPING FROG, Mark Twain. Revenge edition. The original story of The Celebrated Jumping Frog of Calaveras County, a hapless French translation, and Twain's hilarious "retranslation" from the French. 12 illustrations. 66pp. 5⅜ x 8½. 22686-7

BEST REMEMBERED POEMS, Martin Gardner (ed.). The 126 poems in this superb collection of 19th- and 20th-century British and American verse range from Shelley's "To a Skylark" to the impassioned "Renascence" of Edna St. Vincent Millay and to Edward Lear's whimsical "The Owl and the Pussycat." 224pp. 5⅜ x 8½. 27165-X

COMPLETE SONNETS, William Shakespeare. Over 150 exquisite poems deal with love, friendship, the tyranny of time, beauty's evanescence, death and other themes in language of remarkable power, precision and beauty. Glossary of archaic terms. 80pp. 5$\frac{3}{16}$ x 8¼. 26686-9

THE BATTLES THAT CHANGED HISTORY, Fletcher Pratt. Eminent historian profiles 16 crucial conflicts, ancient to modern, that changed the course of civilization. 352pp. 5⅜ x 8½. 41129-X

THE WIT AND HUMOR OF OSCAR WILDE, Alvin Redman (ed.). More than 1,000 ripostes, paradoxes, wisecracks: Work is the curse of the drinking classes; I can resist everything except temptation; etc. 258pp. 5⅜ x 8½. 20602-5

SHAKESPEARE LEXICON AND QUOTATION DICTIONARY, Alexander Schmidt. Full definitions, locations, shades of meaning in every word in plays and poems. More than 50,000 exact quotations. 1,485pp. 6½ x 9¼. 2-vol. set.
Vol. 1: 22726-X
Vol. 2: 22727-8

SELECTED POEMS, Emily Dickinson. Over 100 best-known, best-loved poems by one of America's foremost poets, reprinted from authoritative early editions. No comparable edition at this price. Index of first lines. 64pp. 5³⁄₁₆ x 8¼. 26466-1

THE INSIDIOUS DR. FU-MANCHU, Sax Rohmer. The first of the popular mystery series introduces a pair of English detectives to their archnemesis, the diabolical Dr. Fu-Manchu. Flavorful atmosphere, fast-paced action, and colorful characters enliven this classic of the genre. 208pp. 5³⁄₁₆ x 8¼. 29898-1

THE MALLEUS MALEFICARUM OF KRAMER AND SPRENGER, translated by Montague Summers. Full text of most important witchhunter's "bible," used by both Catholics and Protestants. 278pp. 6⅝ x 10. 22802-9

SPANISH STORIES/CUENTOS ESPAÑOLES: A Dual-Language Book, Angel Flores (ed.). Unique format offers 13 great stories in Spanish by Cervantes, Borges, others. Faithful English translations on facing pages. 352pp. 5⅜ x 8½. 25399-6

GARDEN CITY, LONG ISLAND, IN EARLY PHOTOGRAPHS, 1869–1919, Mildred H. Smith. Handsome treasury of 118 vintage pictures, accompanied by carefully researched captions, document the Garden City Hotel fire (1899), the Vanderbilt Cup Race (1908), the first airmail flight departing from the Nassau Boulevard Aerodrome (1911), and much more. 96pp. 8⅞ x 11¾. 40669-5

OLD QUEENS, N.Y., IN EARLY PHOTOGRAPHS, Vincent F. Seyfried and William Asadorian. Over 160 rare photographs of Maspeth, Jamaica, Jackson Heights, and other areas. Vintage views of DeWitt Clinton mansion, 1939 World's Fair and more. Captions. 192pp. 8⅞ x 11. 26358-4

CAPTURED BY THE INDIANS: 15 Firsthand Accounts, 1750-1870, Frederick Drimmer. Astounding true historical accounts of grisly torture, bloody conflicts, relentless pursuits, miraculous escapes and more, by people who lived to tell the tale. 384pp. 5⅜ x 8½. 24901-8

THE WORLD'S GREAT SPEECHES (Fourth Enlarged Edition), Lewis Copeland, Lawrence W. Lamm, and Stephen J. McKenna. Nearly 300 speeches provide public speakers with a wealth of updated quotes and inspiration–from Pericles' funeral oration and William Jennings Bryan's "Cross of Gold Speech" to Malcolm X's powerful words on the Black Revolution and Earl of Spenser's tribute to his sister, Diana, Princess of Wales. 944pp. 5⅜ x 8⅜. 40903-1

THE BOOK OF THE SWORD, Sir Richard F. Burton. Great Victorian scholar/adventurer's eloquent, erudite history of the "queen of weapons"–from prehistory to early Roman Empire. Evolution and development of early swords, variations (sabre, broadsword, cutlass, scimitar, etc.), much more. 336pp. 6⅛ x 9¼. 25434-8

AUTOBIOGRAPHY: The Story of My Experiments with Truth, Mohandas K. Gandhi. Boyhood, legal studies, purification, the growth of the Satyagraha (nonviolent protest) movement. Critical, inspiring work of the man responsible for the freedom of India. 480pp. 5⅜ x 8½. (Available in U.S. only.) 24593-4

CELTIC MYTHS AND LEGENDS, T. W. Rolleston. Masterful retelling of Irish and Welsh stories and tales. Cuchulain, King Arthur, Deirdre, the Grail, many more. First paperback edition. 58 full-page illustrations. 512pp. 5⅜ x 8½. 26507-2

THE PRINCIPLES OF PSYCHOLOGY, William James. Famous long course complete, unabridged. Stream of thought, time perception, memory, experimental methods; great work decades ahead of its time. 94 figures. 1,391pp. 5⅜ x 8½. 2-vol. set.
Vol. I: 20381-6 Vol. II: 20382-4

THE WORLD AS WILL AND REPRESENTATION, Arthur Schopenhauer. Definitive English translation of Schopenhauer's life work, correcting more than 1,000 errors, omissions in earlier translations. Translated by E. F. J. Payne. Total of 1,269pp. 5⅜ x 8½. 2-vol. set. Vol. 1: 21761-2 Vol. 2: 21762-0

MAGIC AND MYSTERY IN TIBET, Madame Alexandra David-Neel. Experiences among lamas, magicians, sages, sorcerers, Bonpa wizards. A true psychic discovery. 32 illustrations. 321pp. 5⅜ x 8½. (Available in U.S. only.) 22682-4

THE EGYPTIAN BOOK OF THE DEAD, E. A. Wallis Budge. Complete reproduction of Ani's papyrus, finest ever found. Full hieroglyphic text, interlinear transliteration, word-for-word translation, smooth translation. 533pp. 6½ x 9¼. 21866-X

MATHEMATICS FOR THE NONMATHEMATICIAN, Morris Kline. Detailed, college-level treatment of mathematics in cultural and historical context, with numerous exercises. Recommended Reading Lists. Tables. Numerous figures. 641pp. 5⅜ x 8½. 24823-2

PROBABILISTIC METHODS IN THE THEORY OF STRUCTURES, Isaac Elishakoff. Well-written introduction covers the elements of the theory of probability from two or more random variables, the reliability of such multivariable structures, the theory of random function, Monte Carlo methods of treating problems incapable of exact solution, and more. Examples. 502pp. 5⅜ x 8½. 40691-1

THE RIME OF THE ANCIENT MARINER, Gustave Doré, S. T. Coleridge. Doré's finest work; 34 plates capture moods, subtleties of poem. Flawless full-size reproductions printed on facing pages with authoritative text of poem. "Beautiful. Simply beautiful."–*Publisher's Weekly.* 77pp. 9¼ x 12. 22305-1

NORTH AMERICAN INDIAN DESIGNS FOR ARTISTS AND CRAFTSPEOPLE, Eva Wilson. Over 360 authentic copyright-free designs adapted from Navajo blankets, Hopi pottery, Sioux buffalo hides, more. Geometrics, symbolic figures, plant and animal motifs, etc. 128pp. 8⅜ x 11. (Not for sale in the United Kingdom.) 25341-4

SCULPTURE: Principles and Practice, Louis Slobodkin. Step-by-step approach to clay, plaster, metals, stone; classical and modern. 253 drawings, photos. 255pp. 8⅛ x 11. 22960-2

THE INFLUENCE OF SEA POWER UPON HISTORY, 1660–1783, A. T. Mahan. Influential classic of naval history and tactics still used as text in war colleges. First paperback edition. 4 maps. 24 battle plans. 640pp. 5⅜ x 8½. 25509-3

THE STORY OF THE TITANIC AS TOLD BY ITS SURVIVORS, Jack Winocour (ed.). What it was really like. Panic, despair, shocking inefficiency, and a little heroism. More thrilling than any fictional account. 26 illustrations. 320pp. 5⅜ x 8½. 20610-6

FAIRY AND FOLK TALES OF THE IRISH PEASANTRY, William Butler Yeats (ed.). Treasury of 64 tales from the twilight world of Celtic myth and legend: "The Soul Cages," "The Kildare Pooka," "King O'Toole and his Goose," many more. Introduction and Notes by W. B. Yeats. 352pp. 5⅜ x 8½. 26941-8

BUDDHIST MAHAYANA TEXTS, E. B. Cowell and others (eds.). Superb, accurate translations of basic documents in Mahayana Buddhism, highly important in history of religions. The Buddha-karita of Asvaghosha, Larger Sukhavativyuha, more. 448pp. 5⅜ x 8½. 25552-2

ONE TWO THREE . . . INFINITY: Facts and Speculations of Science, George Gamow. Great physicist's fascinating, readable overview of contemporary science: number theory, relativity, fourth dimension, entropy, genes, atomic structure, much more. 128 illustrations. Index. 352pp. 5⅜ x 8½. 25664-2

EXPERIMENTATION AND MEASUREMENT, W. J. Youden. Introductory manual explains laws of measurement in simple terms and offers tips for achieving accuracy and minimizing errors. Mathematics of measurement, use of instruments, experimenting with machines. 1994 edition. Foreword. Preface. Introduction. Epilogue. Selected Readings. Glossary. Index. Tables and figures. 128pp. 5⅜ x 8½. 40451-X

DALÍ ON MODERN ART: The Cuckolds of Antiquated Modern Art, Salvador Dalí. Influential painter skewers modern art and its practitioners. Outrageous evaluations of Picasso, Cézanne, Turner, more. 15 renderings of paintings discussed. 44 calligraphic decorations by Dalí. 96pp. 5⅜ x 8½. (Available in U.S. only.) 29220-7

ANTIQUE PLAYING CARDS: A Pictorial History, Henry René D'Allemagne. Over 900 elaborate, decorative images from rare playing cards (14th–20th centuries): Bacchus, death, dancing dogs, hunting scenes, royal coats of arms, players cheating, much more. 96pp. 9¼ x 12¼. 29265-7

MAKING FURNITURE MASTERPIECES: 30 Projects with Measured Drawings, Franklin H. Gottshall. Step-by-step instructions, illustrations for constructing handsome, useful pieces, among them a Sheraton desk, Chippendale chair, Spanish desk, Queen Anne table and a William and Mary dressing mirror. 224pp. 8⅛ x 11¼. 29338-6

THE FOSSIL BOOK: A Record of Prehistoric Life, Patricia V. Rich et al. Profusely illustrated definitive guide covers everything from single-celled organisms and dinosaurs to birds and mammals and the interplay between climate and man. Over 1,500 illustrations. 760pp. 7½ x 10⅛. 29371-8

Paperbound unless otherwise indicated. Available at your book dealer, online at **www.doverpublications.com**, or by writing to Dept. GI, Dover Publications, Inc., 31 East 2nd Street, Mineola, NY 11501. For current price information or for free catalogues (please indicate field of interest), write to Dover Publications or log on to **www.doverpublications.com** and see every Dover book in print. Dover publishes more than 500 books each year on science, elementary and advanced mathematics, biology, music, art, literary history, social sciences, and other areas.